A Gambler's Instinct

A Gambler's Instinct
The Story of
Broadway Producer
Cheryl Crawford

Milly S. Barranger

Southern Illinois University Press
Carbondale and Edwardsville

13   12   11   10   4   3   2   1

Library of Congress Cataloging-in-Publication Data
Barranger, Milly S.
  A gambler's instinct : the story of Broadway producer
Cheryl Crawford / Milly S. Barranger.
    p. cm. — (Theater in the Americas series)
  Includes bibliographical references and index.
  ISBN-13: 978-0-8093-2958-8 (alk. paper)
  ISBN-10: 0-8093-2958-1 (alk. paper)
  ISBN-13: 978-0-8093-8570-6 (e-book)
  ISBN-10: 0-8093-8570-8 (e-book)
  1. Crawford, Cheryl, 1902–1986. 2. Theatrical produc-
ers and directors–United States—Biography. I. Title.
  PN2287.C665B37 2010
  792.02'32092—dc22
  [B]   2009043159

To Liz Woodman

CONTENTS

Illustrations follow page 102

PREFACE

When I began work on this biography, I asked friends and acquaintances what they remembered about Cheryl Crawford. I expected the answers to touch upon her producing skills, her taut personality, her lesbian lifestyle, her exceptional dreams. To a person, each began with her accidental death as though the *unexpected* defined her progress for sixty years through one of the toughest careers in American commerce—that of an independent producer in the commercial theater.

The accident that proved fatal took place on West Forty-fourth Street in Manhattan. At eighty-four, Cheryl Crawford, thinking about understudy auditions for a new Southern play, walked slowly up the stone stairs of her beloved New Dramatists. Accidents happen, but this one was without precedent in its location. Cheryl Crawford had survived failed idealistic enterprises and Broadway flops, but these seven steps would be the costliest journey of her remarkable life.

Neither student nor producer expected the abrupt encounter nor the cruelty of the staircase. A student rushing from class burst through the windowless entranceway just as the elderly woman reached for the outer doorknob. The swinging door knocked her backwards and she fell onto the sidewalk below. Cheryl Crawford never fully recovered from the fall and died of complications one October day in New York City, where she had worked for over sixty years.

Cheryl Crawford lived at the center of the American commercial theater as an independent producer and as a stubborn advocate of a studio system to assist professional actors explore and learn apart from the demands of the commercial theater. Her name is permanently linked with the Group Theatre and the Actors Studio, and with Broadway musicals and major plays of Tennessee Williams. She grew up in Akron, Ohio, attended Smith College, and arrived in New York City determined to open doors to a profession that she little understood then, but would master over the next sixty years.

Crawford wrote an autobiography called *One Naked Individual: My Fifty Years in the Theatre* in 1977, in which she says that hers is the story of a Broadway producer's life and that her private life has been mentioned only in passing. "The theatre has been my life," she declared. This remark sets aside her lesbianism, which she wore undisguised in her tailored clothing, her hair style, her masculine tone of voice, and her circle of women friends. Crawford's life story presents a conundrum to contemporary biographers interested in issues of gender and sexuality. She downplayed her private existence in favor of the producer's life wherein she records her successes and failures in a profession where, even today, few women have emerged as independent producers.

Cheryl Crawford's accomplishments are well-documented. Harold Clurman wrote about their mutual efforts with the Group Theatre, Theresa Helburn with the Theatre Guild, Elia Kazan with the Group Theatre and the Actors Studio, Margaret Webster with the American Repertory Theatre, and there are records of the over one hundred musicals and new plays by Kurt Weill, Alan Jay Lerner, Frederick Loewe, Paul Green, Tennessee Williams, Ketti Frings, James Baldwin, June Havoc, Edward Chodorov, Marc Connolly, Elinor Jones, Romulus Linney, James Kirkland, Harvey Schmidt, and Tom Jones found in the *New York Times, Variety, Theatre World*, and elsewhere. Despite the glare of public scrutiny, the private life of Cheryl Crawford was closely guarded. Unlike Eva Le Gallienne and Margaret Webster, her associates with the American Repertory Theatre, Crawford was a taciturn individual who did not indulge in personal correspondence that revealed her innermost feelings about her companions and coworkers. Her papers, found in extensive archives in the University of Houston Libraries in Texas and the New York Public Library for the Performing Arts at Lincoln Center, contain business letters written to playwrights, actors, managers, and theater owners. There are no private notebooks, no daily journals, and few personal letters. Nowhere is there a single note written to close friends and her partner of many years, cookbook author and restaurateur Ruth Norman. Most likely, these personal items were lost in a mysterious fire that destroyed her Connecticut home in Norwalk in the late sixties.

The theater was, indeed, Cheryl Crawford's life, but it was the woman of poker-playing instincts and gaming skills, the individual of courage and fortitude, the legendary risk-taker and penny-pincher who mastered the art (and gamesmanship) of producing on Broadway at mid-century.

It is this face beneath the "stern, rock-like expression" of her public persona that is the heart of the matter in this search for the legendary individual known as Cheryl Crawford. Whatever we discover about the circumstances of Crawford's life, it was lived in the rhythms of the commercial theater with its openings and closings, successes and failures, euphoric highs and painful disappointments. The through-line of her life from college days forward reveals the gambler at heart, taking risks with her own and other people's money, placing bets on musical books, their composers, and artists. She once said, famously, that picking a winner on Broadway was much the same as at the race-track—the odds were stacked against you, regardless of the horse's pedigree and rider.

Despite the many straight plays she produced, her legendary track-record was built show-by-show on musicals: *Porgy and Bess, One Touch of Venus, Brigadoon, Love Life, Regina,* and *Paint Your Wagon.*

What she does not dwell upon in her autobiography is her greatest gamble. For forty years, she bet the odds that a woman could prove successful in the male-dominated establishment of the American commercial theater. That success brought her mixed blessings: anxieties, disappointments, loneliness, but chiefly dreams of the next production, the next winning playwright, the next critical success. There were always other irons in the fire, other bets to be placed, other dreams to be realized in an evanescent profession where hopes and dreams vanish behind the closing curtain.

Why, then, have the screen memories of friends and acquaintances recalled, firstly, the accident that ended her life? The answer lies in the likelihood that her accidental progress up the steps of New Dramatists contains the attributes of her life: loyalty, independence, persistence, risk, confidence, trust, and betrayal. In the end, Cheryl Crawford at eighty-four was a frail legend slowly climbing the stairs to a playwrights' haven while teasing another *dream* of a new Southern playwright leading, under her guidance, to renewed success and notoriety.

ACKNOWLEDGMENTS

I have been assisted in this search for the legendary woman with the stern expression, bright blue eyes, and laconic wit by coworkers, friends, and acquaintances and by the libraries and research centers that have colluded in the preservation of her papers.

I am singularly grateful to the following for sharing memories and insights into the life and career of Cheryl Crawford. The actors, directors, designers, writers, editors, composers, lyricists, managers, friends, and admirers who talked with me are Laurence W. Avery, Paul Bogart, Robert Bray, Martha Coigney, Tandy Cronyn, Margaret Croyden, Sandra Deer, Lenore DeKoven, Ray Dooley, Scott Edmiston, Mitchell Erickson, Jesse Feiler, Gerald Freedman, Tammy Grimes, George Grizzard, Aileen Hale, Jeffrey Hayden, Norma Hill, Foster Hirsch,W. Kenneth Holditch, Anne Jackson, Elinor Jones, Tom Jones, Robert Kalfin, Willa Kim, Mark Lamos, Romulus Linney, Marshall Mason, Ruth Mayleas, Linda Wagner Martin, Stephanie Pace, Carrie F. Robbins, Vera Mowry Roberts, Horace W. Robinson, Lynne Rogers, Eva Marie Saint, Robert A. Schanke, Harvey Schmidt, John Shank, Gina Shields, Mira J. Spektor, Kent Stephens, Dolores Sutton, Eli Wallach, John Weidman, Berenice Weiler, Peter Wexler, Don B. Wilmeth, and Glenn Young.

Moreover, I have benefited from the autobiographies and personal histories written by Harold Clurman, Janet Flanner, Theresa Helburn, Norris Houghton, Elia Kazan, James Kirkwood, Lawrence Langner, Arthur Laurents, Eva Le Gallienne, Robert Lewis, Mary Martin, Alan Schneider, Eli Wallach, Margaret Webster, Tennessee Williams, and Audrey Wood and Max Wilk. The collections of letters and notebooks containing the correspondence of Paul Green edited by Laurence W. Avery, the letters of Tennessee Williams edited by Albert J. Devlin and Nancy M. Tischler, and the notebooks of Tennessee Williams edited by Margaret Bradham Thornton are invaluable sources of first-hand material on interactions between Cheryl Crawford and playwrights central to key stages of her career.

I am grateful to those biographers, scholars, and critics who have written about people and subjects related to the American theater and Cheryl Crawford's work with the Theatre Guild, the Group Theatre, the Actors Studio, and Broadway. They are, notably, Cindy Heller Adams,

Robert Bowman, Jared Brown, Virginia Spencer Carr, Helen Krich Chinoy, Harold Clurman, David Garfield, William Goldman, Mel Gussow, Bill J. Harbin, Foster Hirsch, Kimball King, Ken Mandelbaum, Kim Marra, Ethan Mordden, Davi Napoleon, Esther Newton, Margot Peters, Jay Plum, Robert A. Schanke, Richard Schickel, Helen Sheehy, Wendy Smith, Donald Spoto, Sherill Tippins, Margaret Webster, John Wilson, and Stacy Wolf.

My special thanks to literary executors, archivists, and research libraries and centers. Eloise Armen, literary executor for the estate of Eva Le Gallienne, and the late Diana Raymond, longtime literary executor for the estate of Margaret Webster and current executor Peter Raymond, have been generous friends who have given access to materials and letters relative to the American Repertory Theatre. Other materials have been made available from the New York Public Library for the Performing Arts by Tom Lisanti, permissions librarian, Jeremy MeGraw, photographic librarian, and Alan Pally, program series producer; Dave Stein, archivist, for the Weill-Lenya Research Center, housed in the Kurt Weill Foundation for Music, New York, made available the collection of letters that pertained to the composer's professional activities with Cheryl Crawford and the Group Theatre and transcripts of oral history interviews with composers and artists; Regan Fletcher of the Shubert Archives, New York, provided assistance with photographic research; Robert S. Dalton and Thomas J. Nixon, reference librarians, helped with sources at Davis Library, the University of North Carolina, Chapel Hill; Walter C. West, curator of manuscripts, guided me through the Paul Green archive in the Southern Historical Collection, Wilson Library, at the University of North Carolina, Chapel Hill; Alexandra Lightfoot, executor director, and Marsha Warren, literary executor, of the Paul Green Foundation, Chapel Hill, approved requests for this project; Anne Naughton of the Office of the Registrar, Smith College, Northampton, Massachusetts, provided information on Crawford's matriculation and degrees, and Deborah A. Richards, archive specialist for the Smith College archives assisted with materials on Crawford's years at Smith and on the honorary doctorate awarded in 1962; Bridget Pieschal of the Southern Women's Institute at the Mississippi University for Women, Columbus, and the Mississippi Humanities Council supported my talk on Cheryl Crawford and Tennessee Williams.

The most extensive collection of Cheryl Crawford's papers is found in Special Collections at the University of Houston Libraries, Texas. In 1978, Crawford gave 3,335 items to the University of Houston, ranging from correspondence to sheet music and sound recordings. I am most grateful to Sidney Berger, former head of Theatre at the University of Houston for the history of Crawford's gift; and to Patricia Bozeman, head of Special Collections, and Julie Grob, archivist for the Cheryl Crawford Collection, at the University of Houston Libraries for providing access to the valuable archive.

I want to thank LeAnn Fields for her suggestion that Cheryl Crawford was a neglected subject in the American theater and Robert A. Schanke, editor of the Theater in the Americas series for the Southern Illinois University Press, Carbondale, for his encouragement in the writing of the Cheryl Crawford story.

Once again, I want to thank Liz Woodman for her friendship and guidance through the convoluted "business" of the American theater.

Part One

Lighting the Fire, 1902–1936

1

THREE BROTHERS AND A SISTER

How does a girl from a nice, normal Midwestern family become a Broadway producer? I'm still wondering.

—Cheryl Crawford

Every evening she went to bed in a comfortable two-story house on a pleasant Akron street lined with maples and elms. Her mother tucked her in and then moved along the hallway to look in on the younger children—Alden, Newell, and later Robert, born when Cheryl was thirteen. She dreamed of being a missionary and soothing the unconverted in far-off jungles by singing her favorite Congregationalist hymn, "The Little Brown Church in the Vale." Sometimes she was dancing the tango with Irene and Vernon Castle, or standing guard with her great grandfather in Ford's Theatre the night President Lincoln was shot. These childhood dreams took place in a church-going Midwestern home in Ohio inhabited by her mother, father, her maternal grandmother, and her younger brothers.

Cheryl Aileen Crawford was born in Akron on September 24, 1902. A friend suggested "Cheryl" to her mother, who thought it was a lovely name. Her parents were well-off, college-educated, and church-going. Her father, Robert Kingsley Crawford (called "King" for his height of six feet, blue eyes, and handsome features) was in the real estate business. After attending Allegheny College in Meadville, Pennsylvania, where his brother was the president, and then Northwestern University in Evanston, Illinois, he settled in Akron and developed Crawford Real Estate. He sold property in the same booming-voiced evangelical style he developed for church services as Sunday school superintendent of the local First Congregational Church. His daughter said that he was "faintly rich."[1]

The Crawfords were Scots. Cheryl's paternal grandfather relocated to County Fermanagh, Ireland, and over time joined other pioneers in Willow Center, Illinois. In Downers Grove, a suburb of Chicago, Cheryl's paternal grandmother became a power in the Woman's Christian Temperance Union and in Methodist church circles.

Her Akron-born mother figures less vividly in her daughter's memories. A graduate of Buchtel College in Akron, the former Luella Elizabeth Parker (called "Lou") wore a size three shoe which earned her a large collection of half-priced sample shoes. The Parker forebears were from Ashburnham, Massachusetts, and had lived in New England before the Revolutionary War. Members of the Parker family migrated to Virginia and then to Kentucky. Cheryl's great grandfather served with the Northern army during the Civil War and was disowned by his Virginia relatives. After the war, he moved to Ohio, and his son, Alden Parker, married Cheryl's beloved grandmother (Lavinia Lynn Parker) who came from Kentucky.

The three pillars of Cheryl's girlhood were family, church, and school.

In later years, she mused, "How does a girl from a nice, normal Midwestern family become a Broadway producer?"[2] Despite her eighty-four years, she never arrived at a satisfactory answer.

Cheryl Crawford was a child of normal misadventures. On the sly, she smoked her father's cigars, tasted his sherry, and concealed bread crusts because her mother told her if she ate the crusts her hair would be curly. She read *Mademoiselle de Maupin* about an adventuress who has affairs with men and woman and stuffed the forbidden novel under her mattress. She also drew black marks over her red conduct marks for misbehavior at school. She was a prodigious reader, an excellent student, but conduct was her schoolgirl cross to bear. One of her father's punishments for her infractions was to demand that she memorize the names of all the books of the Old Testament. She could still recite them fifty years later and considered the memory exercise a reward, not a punishment.

The threads of her theatrical beginnings can be found in her passion for inventive storytelling, for voracious reading of children's classics and the novels of Sir Walter Scott and Charles Dickens, and for the poetry of Elizabeth Barrett and Robert Browning. Poetry became one of the cornerstones of her life. During her lifetime, she collected seven or eight hundred books of poetry, many in first editions.

As the neighborhood children gathered night after night on the porch of the Crawford house, they challenged Cheryl to concoct fables from such lists as "a prince, a tin can, a pony, a rotten apple, and their math teacher." Accepting the challenge, she would fashion a narrative using all of the disconnected things, animals, and people. Entertaining her listeners challenged her to be "inventive," a useful tool in later years as she worked with the imperfections of new plays that often lacked coherent narratives.

Nevertheless, her maternal grandmother of ample figure and personality to match left a deep impression on her oldest grandchild. Lavinia Parker lived with the Crawfords and was referred to by her ward as an "unpaid babysitter." She was the family historian and storyteller and rocked young Cheryl to sleep with Civil War ballads, popular songs, and tall tales about her great grandfather who had been a scout under Lew Wallace, the author of *Ben Hur*.[3] Among other legends was the story of her great grandfather standing guard duty at Ford's Theatre the night Lincoln was shot and riding with the posse that searched for John Wilkes Booth.

Her grandmother's oft-repeated story was of proudly shaking the hand of President Lincoln when he passed through the Kentucky town where she grew up. Whenever she washed her granddaughter's hands, she would say, "Now you can shake the hand that shook the hand of Lincoln."[4] When Cheryl told the Lincoln hand-shaking story to friends in later years, she held out her hand and repeated the well-worn coda.

Lavinia Parker also tantalized her granddaughter by insisting that a distant ancestor from the Carolinas had been a Cherokee Indian. Cheryl declared herself greatly influenced by this ancestral claim of Native American blood and cultivated a stern, rocklike expression that served her well in later poker games and theatrical negotiations. She claimed to have flummoxed theatrical agents into believing that she would not pay what they asked for their clients. Her stern expression and rigid posture earned her the epithet "the wooden Indian" from later associates.[5]

Cheryl Crawford had a "healthy, happy childhood" of solid parental guidance, three meals a day with all the family present, a large cookie jar filled and refilled by her grandmother on baking days, and summer travels by car to Turkeyfoot Lake and farther to the West Coast. The Crawford yard was populated with dogs, cats, chickens, and a small horse named Tex. There was surreptitious smoking of hand-rolled corn tassel cigarettes since the smart brand of the day, Violet Murads, was guarded by a storekeeper who would tattle to their parents if children tried to buy them.[6] Even though her father disapproved, she and her grandmother enjoyed movies, especially *The Million Dollar Mystery* and *The Perils of*

Pauline. Her grandmother also required Lydia Pinkham's tonics before meals. Cheryl sampled the restorative tonic water and concluded in later years that it had a fair percentage of alcohol.

Sundays were days observed in strict Congregationalist fashion. After a customary Sunday chicken dinner, her father played a recording of Galli Curci on a phonograph in the parlor. There was no dancing, singing (other than church hymns), or game-playing.

On one occasion, her father, described as a strict disciplinarian, spanked his daughter for some childish infraction. Later, her father came to her room to offer an apology and handed her a dollar to make up for her distress. She was standing by an open window and threw the money out in a childish act of rebellion.[7]

She also recalled a time during her adolescence when a boy she was "in love with" invited her to a party. "I was very excited," she remembered. Nevertheless, her excitement was short-lived. The afternoon before the party, her father allowed her to drive the family car for the first time to the local drugstore to pick up an item. His instructions were to drive directly to the store and back. "I got in the car and went straight on through town," she recalled, "and got stuck in the mud and had to get someone to help get me out." Her father punished her by refusing to allow her to go to the party. "I hated him for that," she recalled, shutting herself in her room for three days and refusing to talk to anyone. "I ate chocolates," she recalled in triumph.[8]

Another thread woven into the fabric of the future producer's constitution was her spirit of independence defined at the time as her inability to conform to "the conventions of virtue."[9] Her brothers' many challenges motivated her to climb trees higher and ride bicycles faster than they did. When Tex, the family horse, threw her, Alden and Newell watched to see if she would remount—all the time whooping "chicken, chicken." Of these early challenges, she admitted that it wasn't easy keeping one step ahead of her brothers and the neighborhood boys. The young men of future years by the names of Harold Clurman, Lee Strasberg, and Elia Kazan would likewise observe her ability to keep step with them on far greater and more significant adventures.

Cheryl Crawford's destiny was cast when her grandmother took her to see *Uncle Tom's Cabin* performed by Akron's professional stock company. Recalling the experience of her first play, she said,

> After flying off to heaven on perfectly perceptible wires, Little Eva walked out into the audience hawking pictures of herself. That was the first time I

criticized a performance. I stood in my seat and cried out, "Grandma, she can't do that! She's dead!" Even then I knew that the illusion must not be broken.[10]

The miracle of Little Eva's revival was sanctioned by her parents' mutual enjoyment of dramatics. After college, Cheryl's mother had attended the Emerson School of Elocution in Boston, where she learned elegant pronunciation and the Dalcroze method of meaningful gestures. In Akron, she earned pocket money by teaching Akron youth in search of culture. She arranged her daughter's piano, violin, and voice lessons, guitar playing, swimming, and horseback riding. There were also ballroom dance lessons with a young couple, dubbed "the Castles of Akron" for the top-billed Irene and Vernon Castle. The enterprising Cheryl converted her ballroom dance lessons into a neighborhood business. She charged a quarter a lesson and considered charging more for her popular tango lessons.

She also entertained her neighborhood friends by playing the piano and singing hit songs heard on the radio in a quavering voice while accompanying herself, left-handed, on the ukulele. She was left-handed at everything but writing, an orthodoxy imposed on her by Akron schoolteachers.[11]

When Cheryl was growing up, Akron was a town of over forty thousand people. At dusk each day, a man appeared on his bicycle to light the gas street lamps, and in summer gardeners drove carts through the streets loaded with potatoes, corn, and garden vegetables for sale to neighborhoods. It was a quiet and safe environment for children to grow up in, but Cheryl soon yearned for a more adventurous life beyond Akron.[12]

Before she fulfilled those yearnings, the glamour and excitement of Little Eva's stage adventures were replaced by acting in grammar school plays. Since her parents performed in amateur theatricals and declaimed at the dinner table the Shakespearean verse they had learned in college, Cheryl had some preparation for grammar school enactments with Dalcroze gestures and declamatory delivery. Her father's (and the children's) most cherished dinner-table performance was as Spartacus addressing the "Gladiators at Capua." "He made a frightening Spartacus," Cheryl observed.[13]

By the time she was eight or nine, she was a devoted player in grammar school theatricals. She began acting in a third-grade pageant about the settlement of Jamestown, playing Priscilla Alden complete with spinning wheel. Not satisfied with the role assigned to her, she begged to play Miles Standish or John Alden instead. Their roles were "more dramatic and had many more lines," she declared.[14]

To decode this statement is to begin stripping away the public narrative of Cheryl Crawford, Broadway producer. In her autobiography, *One Naked Individual: My Fifty Years in the Theatre*, she portrayed her early youth as a "tomboy" and recalled the child who resisted the housewifery of a Priscilla Alden in apron and bonnet. In those early years, she preferred the active role of men, who pioneered new-world colonies with guns and horses.

By the third grade, Cheryl was moving away from feminine roles assigned to women by society in the name of family, children, and caretaking. Intuitively, she discerned that the Miles Standishes of the world had more adventurous, meaningful lives—and they also wore more interesting costumes with boots, breeches, hats, and weapons. No Priscilla Aldens for Cheryl Crawford! More dramatic enterprises were out there for her choosing which would not relegate her to secondary roles in life's dramas.

In his fine essay entitled "One Not So Naked Individual," Jay Plum argued that Crawford turned to her middle American background as "proof" of her normalcy. Nevertheless, she characterized her childhood self as rebellious ("I smoked and drank"). She defied in deeds, couched in terms of tomboy behavior, accepted standards of femininity. She appropriated her father's cigars and sipped her grandmother's medicinal "tonic" and her father's sherry. In ballroom classes, she learned both to follow and to lead. Together, she and her brothers first learned about sex from a book her father kept hidden in the bottom of his dresser. "It seemed very dull, and we didn't think it even worth trying," she recalled.[15]

In addition to cursory glimpses into her father's book on sex, there is reason to believe that her grandmother explained the facts-of-life to the adolescent girl. In later years, Crawford confided her memory of returning home one afternoon in a white dress to find her mother and a neighbor in conversation on the front porch. Her mother noticed blood on Cheryl's dress, and her daughter asked, "What's that?" Her mother directed her to Lavinia Parker ("Go ask your grandmother") to be instructed in the changes that occur in the female body during adolescence. It is likely that Luella Crawford did not want to deal with her obstreperous daughter who stubbornly rejected outward forms of femininity.[16]

Crawford's youthful rebellion against parental authority and her refusal to conform to accepted standards of femininity have been cited as early indications of her lesbianism.[17] Her childhood antics—her preference for playing boys' games and excelling her companions of the opposite sex in boxing, climbing trees, and racing bikes—have been read as early clues. In truth, these tomboyish antics fail to prove little more than her boldness, independence, and competitiveness with the opposite sex. ("It wasn't easy trying to keep one step ahead of two active boys," Crawford recalled.)[18] These childhood traits that Crawford sustained in her personal narrative were repeated in various guises in later experiences with quixotic male partners in the Group Theatre and on Broadway.[19]

On graduation day, Cheryl performed the most memorable role of her school days—Lady Macbeth's sleepwalking scene, a role that notoriously argued, "Come, you spirits/That tend on mortal thoughts, unsex me here,/ and fill me from crown to the toe top-full/Of direst cruelty!" She recalled her performance: "I stood on the podium with flowing hair and a lighted candle and began the monologue. Suddenly my hair caught fire. I could hear Mother scream from the audience. I blew out the candle, grabbed my hair with both hands and put the fire out. Then I continued to the end."[20] Variations on this no-nonsense approach to problem-solving character-ized Crawford's adult demeanor and working methods throughout her years as a producer.

She also remembered her high school dates in Akron, including going to dances, fumbling kisses in cars, and flasks filled with straight alcohol. "I smoked and I drank," she recalled as proof of her triumph over Mid-western modes of conventional virtue.[21]

Only by escaping the "tame Midwest" at age eighteen was she, over time, able to reassess the peaceful street in Akron where she grew up. She came to realize that the pleasant tree-lined street on Merriman Road masked the pain and disappointment of several of its families and the children with whom Cheryl had played. She found corners of darkness in childhood memories that came to her in later years when she produced the plays of Tennessee Williams. Once, she gave a speech to a women's group in a suburb of Pittsburgh where she was challenged by a matron to explain how she could have produced plays about such "sick, neurotic people." In answer, she did not defend the playwright but rather told a story about a peaceful Akron street and what happened to some of its residents:

> On the corner was a family who had two children with whom I played. After
> I left home their father absconded with a considerable amount of money and
> was never found. Next to them lived a doctor with his wife and two lovely
> boys of whom I was very fond. The older one married and went West to live.
> One day he drove back to Akron, parked his car on the high bridge over the
> Cuyahoga River and jumped off. Just down the street lived another family
> whose father was found hanging from a pipe in the basement. On our side
> of the street another family had two sons; the younger one was my bosom

friend with whom I talked poetry and listened to music. In early manhood he was placed in an asylum.

The last scene of this dark memory was perhaps the closest to circumstances that Cheryl would have lived had she been more conventional. She recalled the piano-playing girl next door with whom she had sung popular songs.

> . . . [She] grew up to work for the city and care for her ailing parents, which she did for the rest of her life. She was pleasingly plump with a sweet disposition and should have been a wife and mother. But the gentlemen who called didn't return after they observed what their responsibilities would be. I remember the last time I saw her, rocking on the porch in a squeaky swing in the summer twilight—alone.[22]

These Akron neighbors recalled the absent husband-father who fell in love with long distances in *The Glass Menagerie* and the vulnerable women and men with such names as Blanche DuBois, Allan Grey, Alma Winemiller, and Catharine Holly of *A Streetcar Named Desire, Summer and Smoke*, and *Suddenly Last Summer*. Speaking to the suburban women of Pittsburgh, Cheryl Crawford concluded that "Tennessee's people" were not so far from reality.[23]

At age eighteen, Cheryl Crawford exchanged the tame Midwest for the hills of New England and replaced parental supervision with the freedoms of Smith College in Northampton, Massachusetts. She had dreamed of a more adventurous life. ("I always knew I'd get out. I didn't know what I'd do but I'd get out.")[24] At Smith, she found unforeseen experiences—and an enduring career.

2

SIGNS OF A CALLING

Somehow I always wanted life to be larger, more spacious, more adventurous.
—Cheryl Crawford

Sometimes in the night she dreamed about a golden Buddha and a mythical goddess dressed in a silver tunic with silver-painted body. She awoke to the reality that she had traveled over a thousand miles to New England and Smith College but the distance from Akron to Northampton proved far greater than mileage. It was a distance measured by personal freedom, intellectual discovery, and artistic challenge.

In 1921, the year Crawford enrolled at Smith, middle-class women arrived from homes all over America to attend Mount Holyoke, Vassar, Wellesley, Bryn Mawr, and Smith. The women's colleges provided educational opportunities for ambitious young women to invent new careers and gain productive employment within a white-collar workforce as lawyers, doctors, bankers, journalists, professors, managers, and producers. In the all-women's college environment, those who dismissed traditional roles of marriage and motherhood found congenial paths into professions and into same-sex relationships where traditional roles were exchanged for equal responsibilities, shared decision-making, and financial autonomy.[1]

At Smith, Crawford discovered an environment that encouraged her independence, ambitions, and same-sex lifestyle. She went so far as to set herself apart from many of her peers whom she described in conventional terms as naïve, virtuous, and dedicated to acquiring a higher education—and a husband. Although she sometimes found herself a misfit among her peers, she felt comfortable in the New England hills more so than in the valleys of Ohio.

Looking back on her first year at Smith, she pronounced herself "a rotten student."[2] Her newfound freedom was too heady to waste on studies, and she indulged her old habits of smoking and drinking, both forbidden by college rules. When her senior counselor asked what she intended as her major extracurricular activity, she surprised herself by answering, "Theatre." Her response surprised her. "I hadn't known I was going to say that. Where was the missionary of yesterday?"[3]

She threw herself into the activities of Smith's Dramatic Association and appeared in various one-acts. She became a campus star as Count de Candale, costumed in white satin breeches and powdered wig, in *A Marriage of Convenience*. The low timbre of her voice, and the ability to ape men she learned from her brothers, won her male roles, exotic costumes, and campus stardom. Fame made her daring. She purchased a secondhand Model T touring car for one hundred dollars (two months of her father's allowance for books and clothes) and toured the countryside with her more daring friends, where for a dollar and a half they dined on steak and baked Alaska at village inns. She rationalized that her allowance was well-used because she could borrow the books and had no interest in clothes. These adventures would get her expelled from Smith but not before she declared English as her major, discovered Plato and Nietzsche, and became entranced with drama and playwriting courses taught by Samuel A. Eliot.

Sam Eliot had been a play reader and stage manager for producer Winthrop Ames, who managed the New Theatre in New York, an ambitious nonprofit repertory theater, and later the three-hundred-seat Little Theatre, where he presented plays in the style of the "new stagecraft," as the European trends were called in the United States. Eliot later joined the Washington Square Players, also in New York, one of several theaters including the Provincetown Players that emulated European independent theaters.

With Eliot as her guide, Crawford came upon "entrancing horizons" in Indian, Greek, and Japanese drama and the great European playwrights.[4] From "Sam," as she soon called him, Crawford also received the dream of the "ideal theatre"—dedicated to experiments in playwriting and simplified stagecraft—and conceived as almost a religious belief. She became his chief acolyte and plunged into reading hundreds of plays in remote corners of the library. When she published her autobiography in 1977, she still possessed the notebooks that she kept on her play readings.

While at Smith, Eliot translated and adapted several volumes of little-known Eastern plays, among them Kalidasa's Indian classic, *Shakuntala*, considered by historians the finest of all Sanskrit plays. It tells the story of the love of King Dushyanta for Shakuntala (the foster daughter of a hermit endowed with a mysterious curse); their love, marriage, and separation (prolonged by the curse); and their eventual reunion brought about by the intercession of the gods who have been moved to pity by Shakuntala's plight. Renowned in part for its beautiful descriptive passages, the epic moved freely between heaven and earth.

Crawford's junior year at Smith settled her destiny. Her leadership skills were acknowledged when the Dramatic Association elected her as head officer, instead of the "socially acceptable girl of solid, Protestant convictions."[5] Crawford calculated that she could not win the election because she had never been a joiner and was "rumored" to smoke and drink. Despite the gossip, she won and appointed her opponent head of makeup—"a harmless position to indulge her in."[6]

Alarmed by their nonconformist successor, the outgoing officers voted to appoint a small committee of professors to approve plays for production. Crawford circumvented their efforts to shackle her by choosing an outlandish play—*Shakuntala*. At first, the committee refused to approve the selection on grounds that it was too difficult to present. The future producer convinced them that the epic was stageable. At the same time she persuaded the president of Smith College, William Alan Neilson, to offer the rear garden of his residence for the production. The garden was near perfect for a late spring evening performance with terrace, sloping ground for the audience, large level space surrounded by trees for the stage backed by a length of grass and arched trees leading down to Paradise Pond.

With preproduction matters in hand, Crawford confronted the requirements of the text. As a child of Akron's proscenium theaters, she assumed a front curtain was necessary. This seemed an insolvable problem until she hit upon a water curtain!

Without informing the Neilsons (Dr. Neilson was occupied with college business and Mrs. Neilson was away on a trip), the players proceeded to dig a trough across the lawn in front of the stage area and promised free tickets to the Northampton fire department for lending a fire hose, to attach to a nearby hydrant; a spray of water about fifteen feet high sprang upward and fell (mostly) into the trough, and colored lights were shown on the water between acts. Hence, a water curtain.

"It worked beautifully and hardly anybody got wet," Crawford told a reporter in later years, adding, "When the Nautch dancer came out in the second act she danced knee deep in mud."[7]

The cast of characters presented special challenges. A golden Buddha (a plump round-faced actress volunteered) was required to sit in lotus position on a small platform covered with a borrowed Oriental rug, while a barefoot dancer performed on grass soaked by the water curtain. Dressed in a golden tunic and with face and body painted in "radiator" gold leaf, Buddha took her place on the small platform. Another actress, playing a mysterious deity, wore a silver tunic and her body and face were painted silver with similar paint. In later years, Crawford realized the folly of the radiator paint: "I am happy to say that both girls survived."[8]

The final scene of the play presented the greatest challenge. The hero and the goddess were supposed to meet on a golden mountain. The stagehands and their director had met the challenge of the water curtain, but how to create a gold-colored mountain? Wooden steps of various sizes were brought onto the president's lawn and stacked up to about twenty feet. They cut thin boards in surrealistic shapes to resemble the sides of a mountain reaching to a pinnacle and painted them gold. To create a mysterious fog, the scene designer borrowed smoke candles from the local railway stationer in exchange for tickets to the performance.

Lying in the grass behind the "mountain," they lit the candles just before the water curtain subsided. When the final scene was revealed, the smoke seeping beneath the painted boards hid all but the top of the mountain lit by a pale blue spotlight ensconced in a tall tree. Crawford recalled the murmurs of delighted surprise from the audience confronted with a golden mountain bathed in blue light on the rear lawn of the Nielsons' house.

Shakuntala was standing room only for the two performances and effectively silenced the faculty committee.

Crawford again took advantage of her copious reading to solve another problem: How to avoid spending another quiet summer in Akron. After the SRO performances of *Shakuntala* and her new campus stardom as director-producer, there was no thought of spending another summer in Ohio.

Influenced once again by Sam Eliot, who had connections with Provincetown through his work with the splinter group called the Playwrights' Theatre, she searched for information on the Provincetown Players on Cape Cod, where such writers as Eugene O'Neill, Edna St. Vincent Millay, Susan Glaspell, John Reed, Harry Kemp, and Mary Heaton Vorse lived and wrote during summer months. Even though Crawford had an offer to work with all expenses paid at a summer theater in

Marblehead, Massachusetts—from its producer, who had been impressed with *Shakuntala*—she found the idea of Provincetown more inviting. Moreover, she had saved a hundred and fifty dollars—again borrowing books and doing without new clothes—to support a new adventure.

Disreputable Delinquents

Cheryl Crawford arrived in Provincetown in the summer of 1924 to find only remnants of the Provincetown Players. Her information had been gleaned from outdated materials. She had learned that a group of artists and writers dissatisfied with the commercialism of Broadway had migrated from their winter homes in Manhattan's Greenwich Village in 1915 and held late-evening discussions in journalist Hutchins Hapgood's house during a summer in Provincetown. They decided to rework the old fish house on Lewis Wharf owned by one of their members, labor journalist and novelist Mary Heaton Vorse, and call their producing group the Provincetown Players (subtitled the Playwrights' Theatre at the suggestion of Eugene O'Neill). The Wharf Theatre at 571 Commercial Street became the first home of the Provincetown Players. By the time Crawford arrived on Cape Cod, the work of the Provincetown Players could be found in a converted space at 139 MacDougal Street in lower Manhattan—a fact that had eluded her.

Vacationing there in Crawford's summer of 1924 were Mary Heaton Vorse, who owned property on the Cape, actor-playwright Harry Kemp, playwright Susan Glaspell, and Frank Shay, owner of the Washington Square Book Shop, who had published nine plays from the first New York season of the Provincetown Players.

When she arrived on the Cape, Crawford attended to essentials. She rented a room in the center of town on Commercial Street for five dollars a week, unpacked her trunk, and set out to find the theater. She walked the length of the thoroughfare fascinated by the informal atmosphere, the bare feet and bohemian clothes of this strange new world. Not spying a theater, she went into an antiques shop to ask the owner where it was located and received a shock. "Good lord," the owner said. "That theatre burned down several years ago." She asked if there was another one and the reply was, "No. Nothing this summer."[9]

Stunned by this reversal, she wired the producer in Marblehead that she accepted her offer, repacked her trunk, and hired a boy to push it in a wheelbarrow to the municipal pier where she waited for the ferry to arrive from Boston. A short, bald-headed man was painting a picture of the shoreline when Crawford approached. In all of her nineteen years, she had never seen anyone paint a picture. She asked if she might watch and they began to talk. She told him of her disappointment, and Auerbach Levy said the magic words: A theater group was gathering that evening to start a new theater. When asked if Harry Kemp was among the group, Levy said that he believed so.

At Smith, Crawford had directed a play, most likely *The Prodigal Son*, by the celebrated "hobo poet." She wrote a hasty note to the playwright asking if she might attend the meeting and waited impatiently for his reply. The answer came, "You are welcome." She corralled the boy with the wheelbarrow to return her trunk to her recently vacated room and turned her back on the boat arriving from Boston.

The meeting was held at the home of a wealthy Chicago patron, Mrs. Mary Aldis, who also wrote plays. Crawford found Mrs. Aldis's house at the far end of Commercial Street where members of the group were gathered in the backyard. A disheveled Harry Kemp in ancient dungarees and checkered wool shirt greeted her cordially and introduced her to Mary Bicknell, the group's president-elect, Frank Shay, Mary Heaton Vorse, and Susan Glaspell, one of the founders of the Provincetown Players together with her husband, George Cram Cook. Glaspell was celebrated for her experiments with expressionistic settings to reveal the state of mind of the "new" woman in search of autonomy. That summer, she was working on her most controversial play, *The Verge*, an experiment in symbolism and expressionism to reveal the state of mind of a woman who goes mad striving for individual fulfillment.

The discussion was a familiar one. How to raise money to build a new theater on a wharf at the other end of town? In the meantime, they planned to use Frank Shay's large barn for their summer productions. This was music to the newcomer's ears. Despite the venerable group, Crawford must have contributed to the discussion because Shay and Kemp walked her to her room and invited her to come to the barn the next day and give them some advice on how to make a theater out of it. Within the week, they extended an invitation to her to spend the summer working on the productions in the makeshift space.

Crawford negotiated her room and board because, as she told them, she had a money problem. Mrs. Aldis agreed that she could stay in a large studio in the rear of her house that looked directly onto the bay and consented to feed her. Crawford set to work with the help of "a large, powerful girl" named Conway Sawyer to construct a stage and curtain at one end of the barn and build scenery for the first production. They begged and borrowed from homes and shops but they needed a car to transport the furniture and props.

For thirty-five dollars, Crawford bought a two-seater Ford with trunk space in the back. Its only problem was that it started under special circumstances. The best technique was to leave it on a rise where it could roll downhill to start, or push it on level ground holding onto the wheel and leaping aboard as it began to move. She reported that she named the car "Desire" for the fact that she parked it at night under an elm tree and for its likely connections to amorous back-seat gropings of memory. Although the allusion to *Desire Under the Elms* has a whiff of the autobiographer's dramatic license, O'Neill's drama was completed sometime in March of 1924. Most likely rumors traveled quickly from New York to Provincetown of the new play about greed, incest, and infanticide.[10]

Despite his absence that summer, the theater people in Provincetown felt Eugene O'Neill's presence. He had joined the playmakers on Cape Cod in 1916 and made the move with them to New York as their most gifted writer, seconded by Susan Glaspell. The unofficial Provincetown players of Crawford's acquaintance restaged his one-act sea plays during the summer of 1924.

Provincetown proved an invaluable training ground for the young apprentice. Crawford graduated from building scenery to a small amount of acting and directing. Of these months she said, "I acquired a more valuable education from my extraordinary associates than college offered me. They were older than I, and they had interests and attitudes quite foreign to anything I knew about."[11]

Among her closest friends that summer were Frank Shay, Harry Kemp, and Mary Heaton Vorse. The journalist was admired by Crawford for putting her idealism into meaningful practice, a trait that informed many of Crawford's later choices. A Provincetown resident since 1907, Vorse owned the wharf where the Provincetown Players first held their public performances. As a first-rate reporter, she specialized in the plight of the underprivileged, and, when she was not engaged in writing a new novel, she wrote scathing, prolabor articles about miners and sweat shops for national magazines.

The experiences that Crawford shared with these three also opened up new vistas of antisocial behavior and drunken sexuality. On one occasion, Mrs. Aldis gave a garden party to interest society matrons in contributing to the building of a new theater. She invited members of the theater's board along with her houseguest who lived on the premises.

Harry Kemp ruined the party for Mrs. Aldis and her society guests by walking, fully clothed, into the pool, where he stood waist-deep and calmly ate his plate of cold cuts, thereby shocking the very people the board hoped to win over. For once, Crawford was taken aback by this behavior and turned the episode into an instructive lesson. She commented,

> I had not seen such unrestrained behavior before, but it did not shock me as it did the proper ladies. It was my first exposure to the way creative people often alienate the very ones who have the means to help them.[12]

Another unrestrained party was given in a house next door by a wealthy young man from Boston to which neither Mrs. Aldis, her guest Alice Gerstenberg (a Chicago playwright), nor her college-age tenant was invited. The party became very noisy, and, about three o'clock in the morning, Alice Gerstenberg, an ample woman, appeared in her nightgown on the second floor balcony overlooking the raucous scene and shouted, "We've called the police. The police are coming." What followed was a wild scramble to vacate the property.[13]

The next morning the remaining members of the scandalized theater committee took action against the partygoers. They determined to separate from the disreputable behavior of Vorse, Shay, and Kemp, and finish the season in a theater set up in the studio. As the youngest member of the group, Crawford was elected to drive to Shay's barn and remove the stage curtain, props, furniture, seats, and anything else that was movable.

Upon reflection, Crawford drew a second lesson from the events: "The rest of the summer was not much fun. It was the 'disreputable delinquents' who had the talent."[14]

At summer's end, Crawford was faced with a brief visit to Akron before returning to Smith. To celebrate the end of the season and her departure, it was decided to have a farewell evening on the beach. She drove the Ford packed with guests, cold food, and drink to Race Point, where for one last time she carefully parked the car on top of a rise. Crawford's companion for the evening was Howard Rubien, an older writer whose face looked like some "Italian painter's soft and gentle face of Jesus."[15]

Crawford's account of the evening with Rubien was little more than the tale of an alcoholic binge: "We spent the night immobilized, gazing at the spinning stars."[16] When they awoke, they staggered to the car, pushed off, and drove back to Commercial Street, where the Ford stopped forever. "I was too wretched to feel bad about abandoning it," she said. Saying goodbye to her companion, she walked cautiously to Susan Glaspell's house, where the playwright immediately diagnosed a colossal hangover. Weak, but willing to live, she walked on to Mrs. Aldis' place, where the matron, dressed in white dimity and wearing her "ubiquitous dog collar of small pearls," greeted the wrinkled, sand-laden, and thoroughly hung-over college girl. She didn't ask where Crawford had been, or what had happened. "I don't think she wanted to know," Crawford surmised. Nonetheless, she was certain that Mrs. Aldis was pleased to see her disheveled tenant leave the Cape that afternoon.[17]

A straggly-haired, ill-dressed Cheryl Crawford appeared in Akron in late August. Sensing a change in their daughter, her parents were perplexed over whether to reprimand her or accept the change. For the most part, they accepted the change. Two weeks later, she returned to Smith for her senior year "cleaned, trimmed, and properly dressed." After Provincetown, she found college life tamer than ever. To ensure her independence, she rented a room in the basement of the Plymouth Inn in Northampton so that she could smoke and drink wine in private and refocus her thoughts on the Dramatic Association and her next project.

Negotiations

At Smith and in Provincetown, Crawford had begun negotiating the boundaries between her public and private selves. She "passes" as a hard-drinking, chain-smoking heterosexual. Her private world in rented quarters and dining rooms of village inns is, nevertheless, impossible to reconstruct. Sexuality, even romantic friendship, is absent in the narrative of her life. There are instances of fumbling kisses with male adolescents on the backseats of their fathers' cars on prom nights. In the freer society of Provincetown, it was possible to admire openly the "large, powerful girl" who was her backstage assistant; idealize the older, accomplished writer Mary Heaton Vorse; and openly name her car "Desire." She described her male companion on that long-ago beach in terms of the Christ-like features that Tennessee Williams later gave to Val Xavier in *Orpheus Descending*. Their alcoholic binge most likely put them off sex; nevertheless, liquor was a code word to obscure the absence of heterosexual activities in the lives of women with same-sex preferences.

When she returned to Smith after the summer in Provincetown, she recounted experiences of a "purple past" with tales of sexual exploits and life among "real" bohemians. A portrait emerges of the college-age Cheryl Crawford as an imaginative, independent, no-nonsense workaholic in the public arena in tandem with the self-absorbed individual sequestered in library corners and rented rooms as protection against the revelation of her difference.

In the early pages of her narrative about her life as a producer, she cited her difference as "rebelliousness," alluding to her tomboyishness, her parental disobedience, her competitiveness, her scruffy appearance, her defiance of social conventions and college rules. As she tested the waters of an active public role in matters theatrical, she continued, like her middle- and upper-class peers in the 1920s, to frame her sexuality in coded narratives of heterosexual romance.[18] *Lesbianism*, according to Lillian Faderman, had not yet become in the mid-twenties as neutral a term as the Victorian "romantic friendship," and labels such as homosexual and lesbian were, as yet, unacceptable to the educated women of Crawford's generation.[19]

Even at age seventy-five, Crawford sustained what, by then, was an "open secret" in the theater community, confirmed by her lifelong unmarried status, same-sex partnerships, and social interchanges with gays and lesbians. In her writing, she held tightly onto the divide between the public and the private, the professional and the personal. As she tells the story of her life as a producer, she says (without irony) that her private life is mentioned "only in passing."[20]

Reluctant to share details about her personal life, she leaves readers of her autobiography with little insight into her subjective appreciation of her development as a female producer—an anomaly in her highly visible professional world. Reviewing *One Naked Individual*, Christopher Lehmann-Haupt faulted Crawford-the-writer for withholding a sense of self from her writing. "We seem to lack the true source of Miss Crawford's pride and pain," the critic wrote cryptically of her memoir.[21]

What she does reveal with great pride is an outstandingly successful career in the professional theater on Broadway and also with forward-looking companies that she helped found and manage for fifty years. As written, her personal history affords only glimpses of a complicated biography, both in tune with her generation and apart from it. Her desire to present herself living a hermitic life fails to address same-sex desire, avoids talking about oppression of sexual minorities, and treats homosexuality as a subject found only in a handful of Broadway productions.

As the first production in her senior year, Crawford turned to John Masefield's Asian-influenced *The Faithful* and cast herself as the male leader of the Ronin warriors waging war under the banner of virtue, fidelity, and righteousness against an evil status quo. A classic in its Japanese version, the Theatre Guild had produced the story of the forty-nine Ronin of Japan in 1919. Crawford methodically followed the progress of the Guild's seasons in *Theatre Arts*, a well-known monthly journal. By graduation, she was determined to introduce herself to Guild administrator Theresa Helburn, with the hope of attending the Guild's new acting school, even though she was fairly certain that she wanted to produce—not act, write, or even direct.[22]

Crawford quickly dispensed with the faculty committee's concerns over the twenty-one roles plus guards, nobles, attendants, and warriors and staged *The Faithful* in an aging and inadequate theater that the students called "Studes." Following Masefield's published note calling for a screen or backcloth representing a Japanese landscape, with hills and water, all wintry and severe, the drama group repainted the theater's worn asbestos front curtain with a monochrome outdoor scene of misty Japanese mountains and valleys. Making her first contact with the venerable Theatre Guild in New York, she rented costumes from their earlier production and refitted the men's measurements to women's sizes.

Even though the show was again a sell-out and Crawford thrilled to renewed stardom, trouble was on the horizon. Inquisitive classmates discovered her hideout at the Plymouth Inn and spread rumors about her tales of sexual exploits and unsavory life among bohemians. In general, her critics pronounced her "obnoxious."[23]

When several faculty members discovered a group of Smith girls, Crawford among them as the driver of the car, having lunch at a country inn and smoking in public, she was called into the office of Laura W. L. Scales, dean of the college, and expelled. For once, Crawford was thrown into a quandary. "I couldn't go home and shock my family," she said, "and I didn't know where else to go." She retreated to the Whale Inn in the hills of Goshen and quelled her panic by writing the play that Sam Eliot had assigned. She decided, "What the hell. I had said I would write it and I would, even if it ended up in the wastebasket."[24] She finished it in two weeks.

In the meantime, President Neilson was also in a quandary. The year 1925 was the fiftieth anniversary of Smith College, and there had to be first-rate entertainment for the alumnae. Having learned of Crawford's whereabouts from her friends, he sent to Goshen's Whale Inn for his prodigal student and chastised her for her behavior. "You are a very foolish girl," she recalled. "Your grades would have won you the honor of Phi Beta Kappa. But that distinction also rests on moral excellence, as you know, so we can't give it to you. I hope you have learned a lesson."

Presenting a contrite face, she assured him that she had learned a lesson. "Because your scholastic record is exceptional, we will let you graduate," he continued before pronouncing her penance. "You will also be allowed to produce the fiftieth anniversary plays at the Academy. You're a bright girl. Behave and don't be foolish."[25]

In a state of penance, she supervised the anniversary productions and joined the cast of Gordon Bottomley's *Gruach*, a tale of a young woman who was to become the future Lady Macbeth, as the Thane of Fortingall.[26] To her amazement, the literary allusions and windy verse appealed to the returning graduates.

When Crawford walked across the stage at commencement to receive her diploma, some of her classmates were convinced that she received a blank piece of paper. Much to Crawford's surprise, she graduated "cum laude."

With intimations of a future producer ever watchful of the financial bottom line, she assessed her Smith years: "And though I may not have had moral excellence, I did have the satisfaction of leaving the Dramatic Association with more money than it has ever made."[27]

A month later, the twenty-three year-old took a deep breath as she crossed the threshold of the building that housed the Theatre Guild's new playhouse and offices on West Fifty-second Street in Manhattan. Squaring her shoulders, she prepared to come face to face with the legendary Theresa Helburn.

3

THE PRODUCER'S APPRENTICE

There are doors to the inevitable everywhere.

—*Shakuntala*

By the time Cheryl Crawford arrived in their offices on the top floor of the building on West Fifty-second Street, the Theatre Guild had been in business for seven years. During her waning days at Smith, she had scrutinized *Theatre Arts* each month and learned that the Guild was starting an acting school in the fall. She thought of the school as an entrée into the fiefdom of the only woman producer known to her in the New York theater. "I was dimly aware that most producers were men," the newly-minted graduate offered, "but Theresa Helburn was a producer, wasn't she?"[1]

In an unimposing office, Crawford came face to face with a short, slender woman with bobbed salt-and-pepper hair and keen hazel eyes. Theresa Helburn listened as Crawford recited her credentials, including graduation from Smith (with *cum laude* casually thrown in), her leadership of the Dramatic Association, and her successful staging of an earlier Guild play. When she offered her résumé, Helburn pushed it aside, saying, "No, no, just tell me." This was Crawford's first lesson from her newly acquired mentor: "Get people you interview to talk. You can tell much more about them from their faces, their gestures, their voices than you can from reading their dossiers."[2]

When Crawford confided her true ambitions ("I really want to produce"), Helburn reminded her that she was interviewing for a place in an acting school. "Yes, I know," she nodded. "I've acted, and I will if I have to, but I really must learn about the professional theatre and I know the Theatre Guild is the best group."[3]

Ever the business manager, Helburn asked if she knew what training cost? Crawford assured her that she had five hundred dollars to cover tuition.[4] At this point, Helburn relented. "Be here by September 15," she advised. "Give my secretary your address on the way out—and your check." As she left the office, Helburn called after her, "And when you get to be a producer, come see me. I'll give you some pointers!"[5]

On cloud nine, Crawford crossed Fifty-second Street, turned to look back at the Guild Theatre, and saw the marquee for the first time. Helen Hayes was playing in George Bernard Shaw's *Caesar and Cleopatra*. Crawford made a promise to herself, Helen Hayes, the playwright, and the Theatre Guild, "I'll be here. My God! I'll be here."[6]

Convergences

What Crawford could not have known at the time of her interview was that she and Theresa Helburn shared much in common in their early development, education, and youthful ambitions. Theresa Helburn (friends called her "Terry") was thirty-eight years old when Crawford met her. The only child of a wealthy family, she was born in the heart of the theater district on Forty-fifth Street two blocks from Broadway. Her parents, Julius and Hannah (Peyser) Helburn, moved the family to Boston, where their daughter attended the fashionable Winsor School. At age nine, she saw her first plays (holiday matinees only): *As You Like It*, *Much Ado About Nothing*, *The Merchant of Venice*, and *The School for Scandal*. They made a deep impression on her and later influenced her decision to seek a career in theater.[7]

Crawford and Helburn attended prestigious women's colleges and both worked with campus drama groups. Here, some of the parallels between the two women diverge in a finely tuned cultural appreciation of dramatic writing on Helburn's part, and a fervent need to create the production from whole cloth on Crawford's. With its Midwestern touring companies, Akron, unlike Boston, did not afford Crawford the experience of the great plays of Western drama presented by first-class companies. Nevertheless, the visible wires of *Uncle Tom's Cabin* had mesmerized the young Crawford, while Helburn developed a finely tuned sensibility to theatrical writing as a reader and frequent theatergoer. At age twenty, Crawford was ambitious to stage plays; the Bryn Mawr graduate, fifteen years older than her future apprentice, wanted to write plays and act in them.

Helburn's postgraduate educational opportunities separated her from most of the women of her day. After graduating from Bryn Mawr, she decided on postgraduate work at Radcliffe College and attended George Pierce Baker's famous English '47 Workshop at Harvard, spent a year in Paris, then moved to New York, where she met a group of like-minded people preparing to start the Washington Square Players and later the Theatre Guild.

Her career as an actress was preempted by her parents, who discovered their daughter in Lawrence Langner's *Licensed*, a one-act play about birth control, a subject not mentioned in polite Boston society in 1915. Subsequently removed by parental authority from the immediate sphere of the stage, she wrote plays and poetry. When she functioned as drama critic for the *Nation* in 1918, she became associated with the newly formed Theatre Guild as play adviser and later executive director (a position she held when Crawford met her). In 1934, she became administrative director with Lawrence Langner, a position she held until her death in 1959.[8] The year Helburn died, her former apprentice was producing a third play by Tennessee Williams on Broadway called *Sweet Bird of Youth*.

In that summer of 1925, Crawford faced another challenge. She returned to Akron to tell her parents of her decision to go to New York. She described the scene in the Crawford household as "Bombs bursting in air!" Her mother wept and her father raged and threatened against allowing his daughter to go to "that wicked city." "It couldn't have been greater," their daughter reported, "if I had told them I was going to enter a brothel or nunnery."[9]

Anticipating her father's refusal to provide financial support, she reminded him of her inheritance from her grandmother. Lavinia Lynn Parker died while Crawford was at Smith and left her twenty-five hundred dollars, perhaps aware that someday her granddaughter would require the price of liberty.

Her mother arrived at a solution to the stalemate between father and daughter. She could possibly share an apartment with another young woman from Akron whose father worked in New York. Once an agreement was reached, Crawford's parents resigned themselves to her departure. As September 15 loomed, Crawford once again turned her back on Akron.

Actress Winifred Lenihan, who had played Saint Joan in the Guild's American premiere of Shaw's play, was in charge of the acting school located in a rehearsal room on the top floor of the Guild Theatre. Various Guild actors gave lessons in voice, dance, and acting. When the graduating class was reduced to twenty-one at mid-year, the multitasking Cheryl Crawford, who had stage-managed the graduation play, was retained as part of the company. The choice became clear when the Guild decided to use the students in a summer stock company for four weeks on the Vanderlip estate in Scarborough, New York.

Crawford was appointed assistant director to Winifred Lenihan, which turned into frustration and a bruised ego for the earnest apprentice. As Lenihan's assistant, she directed the four plays up until three days before their public presentation. Then, Lenihan took over and changed the performances and stage business. "It was frustrating to have all my exciting ideas destroyed and my ego suffered," Crawford admitted.[10]

When she returned to New York in August, Crawford faced the bleak fact that her grandmother's money was almost used up, her roommate had moved out leaving her with the full rent to pay, and the gas and electricity had been cut off for nonpayment of services. Determined to find a job, she made the rounds of producers' offices looking for work as a stage manager and came face to face with gender discrimination. "Females were actresses or nothing" she learned sitting in the outer offices of Broadway producers as she waited for another fruitless interview.[11]

Believing in the Quaker proverb, "When you pray, move your feet," Crawford kept making the rounds from one office to the next. Just as her situation became desperate, a card arrived from Philip Loeb, a Guild actor and later television star as Papa on *The Goldbergs*, informing her that Theresa Helburn wanted to see her. She hurried to the Guild offices, where Helburn opened another door to the inevitable career.

Helburn told the twenty-four year-old, whom she described as having "a slim boyish figure, looking extremely smart in a very attractive dress," that Philip Loeb recommended that she take over his job as casting secretary because he no longer wanted to do anything but act."[12] Crawford wailed that she couldn't take dictation or even type, but Helburn set her mind at ease. "You don't have to type, Helburn assured her. "You only have to interview the hundreds of actors who pour in here, and catalogue them as to types and experience for future reference."[13]

Crawford hesitated. "I don't want a half-time job. I want to work backstage," she plead. Despite Helburn's warning ("Take what you can get!"), Crawford bargained for a second position as third assistant stage manager on the Guild's first fall production. "I will be glad to work in the daytime and at night," Crawford offered. Helburn reconsidered and agreed to give her a try.

In retrospect Crawford thought that she had pushed Helburn too far with her demands. Meditating on what had persuaded Helburn to make the concession, Crawford thought first of gender: Helburn had made it in a man's profession and wanted to give another woman a break. More likely, Helburn confronted a determined young woman capable of multitasking and calculated the cost benefit of a minimum salaried casting secretary (called a casting director today), who combined stage management skills and acting abilities suitable to minor roles.

Crawford did not dwell at length on second-guessing Helburn's decision. *"Whatever the reason," she remarked, "I now had a job—two jobs!"*[14] Despite working day and night, she had the satisfaction of being a *bona fide* member of the Theatre Guild.

A Training Ground

For four years, the Guild was Crawford's training ground. As casting secretary, she interviewed two hundred and fifty actors a day but often had few jobs to hand out because the Guild had developed a cadre of actors and actresses, helmed by Helen Westley, Alfred Lunt, and Lynn Fontanne. Nevertheless, she gained an understanding of casting that stood her in good stead in later enterprises. She compared the process to tea-tasting:

> As a professional tea-taster does not find it easy to explain why one tea tastes better to him than another, so a casting director has difficulty explaining how he knows just the right actors to select for certain parts.[15]

The casting challenges of *Porgy*, written by Dorothy and DuBose Heyward, in the 1926–27 season, and of *Roar China* by S. M. Tretyakov and *Green Grow the Lilacs* by Lynn Riggs in the 1930–31 season, tested Crawford's newly acquired philosophy. The productions sent her wandering about Harlem looking for African Americans to flesh-out the residents of Catfish Row, helmed by actors Frank Wilson and Rose McClendon, to Chinatown in search of Chinese American extras to lend proletarian authenticity to the Russian playwright's anti-imperialistic play, and to Madison Square Garden to employ genuine cowboys recruited from a rodeo exhibition.

Directed by Herbert J. Biberman, later jailed in the McCarthy era as one of the Hollywood Ten, *Roar China* was praised by the pro-communist *Daily Worker* for the sincere acting by the untrained Chinese cast assembled by the creative determination and physical stamina of the Guild's casting secretary.[16]

When the brawny, bespectacled Herbert Biberman objected to the Equity "cowboys" rounded up for *Green Grow the Lilacs* (later transformed into *Oklahoma!*), Crawford went in search of bowlegged, chaps-wearing horsemen at Madison Square Garden. She contacted the impresario for the show and told him that she had employment for "a number of the boys." Shortly after noon the next day, the thunder of heavy boots and the jangle of spurs were heard as thirty "genuine" cowboys strode across the stage. They proved, in Crawford's experience, as temperamental as many actors. Occasionally, she had to hurry to the basement of the theater to stop a quarrel before someone was seriously injured.

Nevertheless, she read with pride the critical praise for the robust production and the "many attractive picturesque performers among the cowboys, farmers, fiddlers, banjo players, and singers."[17]

In those days, the work of stage managers was not restricted by union rules. As stage manager, Crawford also played two roles in *Juarez and Maximilian* as a lady-in-waiting (with one line introducing the entrance of Alfred Lunt into the boudoir of Claire Eames) and later appeared as a Mexican peasant woman with a baby. She marveled at her own improvisations:

> Under a blue smock, one pocket of which held a revolver that I shot off at some point, I wore a green and black hoop skirt and a heavy black wig decorated with green grapes. In this outfit (minus the smock), I said my single line; then I cued in and beat time for a seven-piece orchestra, ran down to the basement where I shot off a cannon, saw to it that the actors got on stage at the proper time, and changed into the peasant costume. I had no time to get to a dressing room, so I changed behind the light board . . . Then, reaching down to the dusty floor, I spread the dust over my face, picked up my baby, cued in the orchestra, and appeared for the final funeral scene to the music of a death march by Beethoven.[18]

Crawford was assigned *Pygmalion* with Lynn Fontanne as Eliza Doolittle and Reginald Mason as Henry Higgins. Despite their public image of idealized heterosexuality, the Lunts were rumored to mask their same-sex relationships in the marital arrangement and maintained close relationships with prominent members of New York's elite gay circles, namely with Noël Coward and Alexander Woollcott. Crawford was intrigued by the rumors and twice witnessed the breakdown of the Lunts's famous onstage discipline. Once, she observed Alfred Lunt, as Mosca in *Volpone*, playing "sexy games" with a basket of oranges and bananas for the entertainment of his friend Noël Coward, who was in the audience. Another time, during *Caprice*, she witnessed Lynn Fontanne become angered by a *sotto voce* remark uttered by Alfred Lunt; she exited the stage and did not return to complete the scene. The stage manager finally gave up and lowered the curtain.[19]

Whether there was an attraction between the two women during *Pygmalion* remains unknown, but Fontanne devised a game during the show to frustrate and annoy the younger woman. The actress was required to take a ring from her finger and angrily throw it at Henry Higgins. As assistant stage manager, Crawford had to find the ring for use in the next performance. During the run of the play, the actress intentionally tossed the ring in more and more obscure places. After a few late evenings spent searching for the jewelry, Crawford bought a number of rings at a local discount store and kept them in the pocket of her smock, thus taking the fun out of the actress's childish game.[20]

The Guild's 1926–27 season was arduous. Once *Pygmalion* opened, the Guild put into practice their long-held dream of playing repertory with a permanent acting company. As the repertory of plays rolled forward in two theaters, the redoubtable Cheryl Crawford grew concerned about her physical and mental health. She sat at a desk during the day interviewing desperate actors to whom she could give no hope (even Mrs. Patrick Campbell, Shaw's original Eliza Doolittle, was turned away empty-handed). At night, she worked among high-strung temperaments. At age twenty-six, she concluded that this was not "a healthy way to live."[21]

In the spring, Crawford was promoted to full stage manager but continued to work in the casting office five days a week. Her salary was raised to one hundred dollars a week to compensate for her day and night employment. The Guild needed their multitasker since a decision had been made to open a second repertory of two plays at the Garrick Theatre: *Right You Are If You Think You Are*, and a revival of their earlier success, *Mr. Pim Passes By*. Actors were now moving between theaters and special matinees. Even the super-efficient Theresa Helburn had difficulty keeping up with the rotating schedules of plays and actors. Historian Roy S. Waldau reported that Helburn once found actor Edward G. Robinson scheduled to be in two different theaters at the same time.[22]

Crawford was learning a great deal, but she betrayed her doubts and insecurities about a career in the cauldron of the New York professional theater in letters written to Sam Eliot. "It is so difficult to keep clear of the clouds in order to remember just why I am here and for what," she confessed.

The disconcerting pressure of more experienced lives and a more sophisticated environment frequently leaves me wobbly and uneasy. It is only by the sheerest bravado that I can fight them, for at times I even forget the inner certainty that assures me I should go on as I began. What mental and physical force it takes to stand inside and outside of this monster New York. And yet I would feel a very second-rate person if I once contemplated leaving. Rather the danger is in losing focus and perspective and your memory of me serves inestimably in recalling me to myself. I am grateful.[23]

Crawford was approaching burnout, but the Guild production of *Porgy* and a young Moscow-trained Armenian director, Rouben Mamoulian, brought relief to her relentless routine.

Porgy became one of Crawford's most satisfying experiences. "The company and I had a long love affair," she said. Entranced by their uninhibited exuberance, their sense of fun, and their ability to live for the day, she expanded her social life by joining the actors who went once a week to Harlem to sing and dance in Small's Paradise or the Lennox Club. In the twenties, Harlem had become a center of sexual rebellion and freedom where clubs and speakeasies welcomed whites, largely for economic reasons, into an "anything goes" party atmosphere. Whether Crawford took advantage of the sexually permissive license to explore what was forbidden in her "white" world is suspected, but unknown. In her writing, she avoids the parallels between the social discomfort of black people in white society with possibly her own discomfort as a sexual minority in that same world. She frames the Harlem experience as joining in the camaraderie of the *Porgy* cast in Harlem's clubs, rent parties, and apartments to sing and dance "as if there were no tomorrow."[24]

As *Porgy* played continuously at the Guild Theatre, its director asked Crawford to assist him on *Marco Millions*, the first play by Eugene O'Neill to be produced by the Guild. Having missed O'Neill at Provincetown, Crawford was delighted to meet the playwright. She described the forty-year-old dramatist as

a very handsome, laconic man who always seemed to be under great pressure. When he sat far back in the auditorium during rehearsals I noticed that he couldn't stay still for long. He would wander out to the back and disappear. It was obvious that his nerves couldn't take the trial and error, the fumbles, the actors protesting a line they insisted they could not speak.[25]

Marco Millions was a moderate success but was swiftly followed by *Strange Interlude*, which set a Guild record of four hundred and thirty-two performances and was awarded a Pulitzer Prize. Crawford did not work on *Strange Interlude*, but her reading of O'Neill's script was instructive. She puzzled over the dark, brooding play: "I could not see how it could possibly work and I had no great admiration for the writing." As she reached the end, she felt her heart beating wildly and concluded, "Obviously, my heart was smarter than my head."[26]

During the daytime hours in the fall of 1928, she developed the casting for *Faust Part I*, *Major Barbara*, *Wings over Europe*, and *Caprice*. Early in 1929, she was rewarded for her hard work. She was asked to take charge of the *Porgy* company during a transfer of the production to London for a limited run.

Taking Charge

Crawford was guide, den-mother, stage manager, and producer's representative for the *Porgy* company at His Majesty's Theatre in the Haymarket. Many in the company, including their leader, had never been to England, nor sailed on an ocean liner.[27] The eleven-day trip in the second-class cabins and lounge of the S. S. *Columbus* proved a windfall of poker winnings, camaraderie, and dancing.

In London, she rehearsed the actors with an effort to slow the tempo of the Gullah speech, indigenous to Charleston, South Carolina, so that English audiences could understand the dialect. When she was not working, she went shopping on Bond Street with her poker winnings. She was determined that if *Porgy* was not a success, she would at least return to New York in sartorial splendor.

The London presenter, Charles B. Cochran, made amiable visits to rehearsals and invited Crawford to a celebrity party on opening night. On the evening of the final dress rehearsal, she picked up a program from a stack in the rear of the theater and was shocked to read that Charles Cochran was presenting *Porgy* without mention of the Theatre Guild. When Cochran arrived at the theater, she confronted him with the playbill, and he promised to correct the omission before the opening.

The next evening, Crawford arrived early to find that the playbills had not been reprinted. She proceeded to orchestrate a no-holds-barred confrontation with Cochran. She ordered the company to remain in their dressing rooms until they heard from her. Next, she instructed the stage manager to hold the curtain until she gave the green light to start the show. Cochran had not foreseen that the gambler from Akron, Ohio, held the winning hand at curtain time.

Crawford described the sequence of events:

The house was packed with men in black tie and women in evening clothes. Jewels flashed as I peeked through the opening. Ten minutes passed. Then fifteen. The audience became restless. Finally, Mr. Cochran appeared backstage to inquire what was wrong. I told him I could not permit the show to go on unless he went before the curtain and explained that there was an error in the program: the Theatre Guild had produced *Porgy*. He said he had never appeared before a curtain and wasn't going to do it. I just stood where I was, saying nothing. I was scared, but I couldn't let Cochran take all the credit. Finally, after pacing the stage in anger, listening to the audience noises, Cochran said, "All right!"[28]

She drew the curtain aside to allow him to pass through. He made the acknowledgment and she ordered the curtain up. Charles Cochran hissed in her ear, "I hope you are satisfied, Miss."[29] Although he never spoke to her again, she returned triumphantly to New York with a playbill that announced,

Charles Cochran
presents
The Theatre Guild Production of
Porgy

The haunting story of the sad love affair between the physically impaired Porgy and the beautiful addict had a mixed reception on London's West End. Many complained that they could not understand the dialect, but the London reviewer for the *New York Times* praised the actors for the beauty and dignity of their collective performances: "Never in my life have I seen a company so little stage-conscious [but] absorbed in a distant and authentic life disconnected with the stage."[30]

During this period, Crawford's extracurricular activities included closely guarded same-sex relationships and not so guarded bootlegging. She expressed her attraction to an unnamed woman who shared her romantic interests, but she blamed her readings in Eastern asceticism for her reluctance to reciprocate. "Physical attraction was deplorable to the sages I was reading," she coyly explained, concluding that she had been "an idiot."[31]

In this same timeframe, she referred openly to a well-to-do, unmarried stockbroker who invested her small portfolio in the stock market, bought dinners at neighborhood speakeasies, and supplied champagne and bourbon to friends in her brownstone apartment on West Forty-ninth Street. She maintained that this relationship was platonic.[32] While the Good Samaritan remains nameless, there is no reason to suspect her veracity since she was straightforward about her relationships with Sam Eliot and Howard Rubien.

Crawford also supplemented her small income from the Guild with bootlegging and poker. Combining alcohol with distilled water and juniper berries, she made, what was euphemistically known during Prohibition as bathtub gin, which she poured into Gordon gin bottles and sold for twenty-five cents each. On Sundays, her only free day, she loaded five or six cases of booze into her secondhand Mercer and drove to Amherst and Northampton, where she sold a bottle for a respectable profit of two dollars and fifty cents.

On other occasions Crawford enhanced her income with poker. Having sharpened her skills with the *Porgy* cast, Crawford had become an unusually successful poker player. She exhibited an icy nerve and wooden expression at the poker table, thereby betraying no clue as to the value of the cards she held in her hand. Her gaming skills, honed at the poker table, were an important part of her apprenticeship for the world of the independent producer.

Then, as a number of women before her, Crawford became infatuated with the great Russian-born actress Alla Nazimova, who appeared in the Guild production of Ivan Turgenev's *A Month in the Country* in 1930. Crawford described Nazimova as "a most enchanting person with sex appeal galore and a mischievous sense of humor."[33] Although Nazimova made a fortune in Hollywood and built the famous mansion the Garden of Allah, later turned into a hotel, her film career in Hollywood declined by the late twenties along with her image as a *femme fatale*. Eva Le Gallienne brought her to New York to star as Madame Ranevskaya in the revival of *The Cherry Orchard* at the Civic Repertory Theatre, which Le Gallienne founded and operated on Fourteenth Street during Crawford's years with the Guild.

Nevertheless, another seduction from unexpected quarters temporarily altered Crawford's career path. The Guild's board, encouraged by Theresa Helburn, who believed the managers should "inject new blood" into the organization, resulted in the hiring of young, socially committed artists and the creation of the Theatre Guild Studio, a forum for developing young talent.[34]

Theresa Helburn was mindful that the Guild's middle-aged managers had once been a young group of idealists. She formed a production committee of three Guild associates: their casting secretary, Cheryl Crawford; a member of the play-reading department, Harold Clurman, who had a doctorate from the Sorbonne; and stage manager Herbert J. Biberman, who had attended the Yale School of Drama and studied with Vsevolod Meyerhold in the Soviet Union. Helburn was encouraged to form the Guild Studio by the success of the *Garrick Gaieties*, a special Sunday night performance at the Garrick Theatre, contrived by youthful composer Richard Rodgers and lyricist Lorenz Hart and stage managed by Lee Strasberg. It was such a success that the Guild offered the revue to their subscribers. It became an annual event for several years until Rodgers and Hart, as their collaboration was soon called, were writing successful musicals.

With an eye to adding a youthful infusion of energy and talent into the normal work of the Guild, Helburn called Clurman to her office and told him that the Guild had taken an option on *Red Rust* by V. Kirchov and A. Ouspensky. The Soviet play became a landmark production for the Guild and the soon-to-be Group Theatre. Critics lauded the production as one of the Guild's more interesting experiments. It opened in December of 1929 and ran for sixty-five performances. Unknown to the Guild managers at the time, the cast of forty-three actors and extras was a roll call of future members of the Group Theatre, including Herbert Biberman, Lionel Stander, Lee Strasberg, Luther Adler, Gale Sondergaard, Ruth Nelson, Franchot Tone, Ruth Chorpenning, and Eunice Stoddard, with Julian (John) Garfield among the extras.

The Studio galvanized the group of young idealists to engage in discussions of socially committed theater and eventually to create their own experiments in acting and staging. Crawford had never been around people her age who talked so fervently about the theater. The loquacious Clurman inspired Crawford and others by holding forth during midnight sessions with views that Crawford called "an unlikely synthesis of Jeremiah and Walt Whitman." As she explained, Clurman's "jeremiads deplored the state of the theater and his Whitmanesque moods painted the ideal, what it could be."[35]

Clurman argued for a permanent company producing plays reflecting modern social and cultural life. In quiet moments, Lee Strasberg injected his ideas on Stanislavski's methods of acting as the ideal approach to training a unified company without tricks and clichés. Herbert Biberman urged a test of their ideas in a workshop. More and more they referred to themselves as the Group Theatre, and, by the spring of 1931, the Group was solidified with three self-appointed director-managers—Harold Clurman, Lee Strasberg, and Cheryl Crawford.

During the turmoil, her two friends, who were scornful of her job with the Guild, pressured Crawford to leave. "This isn't what you really want, is it?" Clurman repeatedly insisted. Strasberg was frequently silent, but equally disapproving. Part of their argument was self-serving. For the Group to succeed, they needed Crawford's executive abilities to spearhead the work. "Someone like you," Clurman urged, "someone who believes in our approach and *who knows how to get things done.*"[36]

Clurman admired Crawford, whom he had once called "a sturdy girl," as a practical, shrewd, and tactful person with executive experience who also possessed the social skills to deal with the Guild's board and was capable of being roused to fine action when she was confronted with a sound idea or a noble motive. He also admired her "determination, moral perception, and desire to learn and grow."[37] Teetering on the verge of a decision to leave her well-paying job, Crawford saw herself as often swept away by the "bit-in-mouth idealism" of her friends.[38]

With the success of *Red Rust*, the three managers planned a second Studio production. Crawford began directing *Dead or Alive* by Philip Barber, but the board attended a rehearsal of the seriously flawed play and "autocratically ruled against it."[39] Furthermore, the board acted precipitously and dissolved the Guild Studio at the end of the 1930–31 season as a financial measure more so than an artistic one.

Disheartened by the closing of the Studio, Crawford nonetheless renewed her contract for the 1931–32 season. "Ideals or no, it was a good job," she reasoned. Under her new contract, she received one hundred and fifty dollars a week with three weeks' paid vacation. ("A handsome salary for the time," Crawford remarked.) She was named to the board as an assistant director. Helburn cautioned, "You may say what you think, but you are not allowed to vote."[40]

Once inside the Board's deliberations, Crawford observed the dynamics of artistic people lead by a female executive and tempered her disappointment over the loss of the Studio. She came to appreciate the contributions of the "extraordinary and diverse" group. Believing fervently in "the play's the thing," they had proceeded in a high-minded fashion quite unlike the casting-couch, cigar-smoking producers of the day. In Crawford's view, they put on many unusual plays that no other producer in her or his right mind would have chosen—*Strange Interlude*, for example. Moreover, they believed with George Bernard Shaw that "The theatre should make people feel, make them think and make them suffer."[41]

A Splinter Group

Faced with a splinter organization and encouraged by remembrances of their own youthful arrogance and disrespect for elders, Helburn persuaded the board to release two plays to the emerging company (Paul Green's *The House of Connelly* and Claire and Paul Sifton's *1931*), along with actors Franchot Tone and Morris Carnovsky and seventy-five hundred dollars for production costs.[42]

One of Crawford's jobs as Group codirector was to work on new scripts. *The House of Connelly*, the story of post–Civil War adjustments facing plantation owners, their freed slaves, and local "white trash," became a formidable challenge to shape into a workable script. There were two versions of differing lengths (one over two hundred pages and another under one hundred). Moreover, the tragic ending was a point of contention with the Group's leaders.

In March, Helburn notified Paul Green that the Theatre Guild planned to launch its 1931–32 season with younger members of the Guild who added "an impassioned social conscience to their passion for the theatre."[43] In May, Crawford reported difficulties with the cumbersome script, and Helburn wrote the playwright to suggest that her assistant, one of the leaders of the Group, visit him in Chapel Hill, North Carolina, to discuss the script and also invite him to rehearsals in Connecticut over the summer.[44]

Within two days of the receipt of Helburn's letter, Paul Green responded:

Chapel Hill, N. C.
10 May 1931

My dear Miss Helburn:

I shall be very glad for Miss Crawford to come down here in connection with *The House of Connelly*. I can see, of course, both the advantages and disadvantages in such a tryout as is outlined in your letter. Since I am not able to comprehend, perhaps, the disadvantages as well as I am the advantages, and accordingly I say let's go ahead. If the company is good and the production means adequate—and I have no doubt they will be—then it seems to me that a preview such as this will make it possible to eradicate certain faults which everybody seems to feel are present in the play. As a first step in whatever direction I strongly suggest that Miss Crawford come down for a few days where we can talk and look things over.

I don't know about my being able to go to Danbury [Connecticut] for rehearsals, but if my affairs are in order so that I can, I certainly will want to go.

Cordially yours,[45]

Crawford made the trip to Chapel Hill to go over the script and discuss the play's ending. In the Group's view, a play's *message* was paramount. "If the play did not provide the proper message," Helburn observed, "they felt justified in changing it to suit their needs. They did this with *The House of Connelly*, changing the author's intent and the ending from tragedy to 'a helpful message.'"[46] This fervor of ideological conviction among the Group's members (Green fingered it as "communist ideology") eventually brought the association between the Theatre Guild and the Group Theatre to an end.[47]

At the outset in 1931, the Group faced the reality that to form a true company and prepare their first production they needed to spend a summer in the country. They also needed money to finance the interval. Just as Crawford had searched for out-of-the-way inns during her Smith days, she now toured the countryside in her Mercer and found a "country enclave" in Brookfield Center, near Danbury, Connecticut. The property had a large barn and numerous houses, including one with a large kitchen and dining room. There, twenty-eight actors, three managing directors, wives, children, and assorted dogs lived for twelve weeks. The *New York Times* reported that the assembly included "twenty-one Victrolas, three radios, fourteen motor cars, a complete library of symphony records, a lot of books on theatre . . . and Alexander Kirkland's dog."[48]

Once in Brookfield, a division of labor evolved that would remain problematic for Cheryl Crawford throughout her years with the Group Theatre. Strasberg directed the play, Clurman worked with individual actors, and Crawford worked on the script, finances, scheduling, and "calming tempers." The delegation of duties preempted by her male cohorts ignored her creative ambitions and her expectations to be treated as an equal partner in artistic decisions. Such was not to be the case.

Paul Green arrived in Brookfield, and, at the urging of the Group's directors, revised the last scene of the play, so that Patsy Tate, a symbol of life in the new South, can "live rather than die."[49] In Green's original ending, two black women placed a sack over the heroine's head and murdered her. As Crawford explained, "There has got to be some hope."

> The whole thing just can't go down the drain. The heroine was a young daughter of a tenant farmer who had come into the old plantation that was going to pot. She saved it by falling in love with the young man who was the inheritor of the plantation. So we persuaded Paul [Green], with some difficulty, to write a new ending. It did not say that everything was going to be happy ever after,

but it did say that with the girl's energy and enthusiasm and vision, there was a chance that this plantation and its people could be saved.[50]

Despite his reservations, Green settled upon a "yea-saying" ending that satisfied the fervor of his constituents.[51] In this version, Will Connolly tears his father's portrait from the wall and figuratively tramps on it, and he and Patsy remain in "Our house, not yours."[52]

Nonetheless, Paul Green never came fully to terms with his decision. When Crawford invited him to reminisce about *The House of Connelly* for her autobiography, he wrote a four-page letter in which he addressed the revised ending:

> From my experience with its production, I became convinced more than ever that life should not control art but that art in its interpretation of life will the more work its control over life. The original tragic ending of the play was the right one. It came out of the nature of the material, out of the author's seeing and feeling, and it should have been kept. . . .[53]

At summer's end, the Guild's board attended a run-through at the Martin Beck Theatre, whereupon they expressed outrage over the violation of the author's original intention to give the play a tragic ending. ("You have murdered the play," they declared.)[54] Despite their objections, *The House of Connelly* was successful ("It actually made money for us," Crawford chortled.), and the Group Theatre became a separate organization.[55]

With Harold Clurman's resignation from the Guild, Crawford faced her reluctance to dissolve her association with her mentor, friends, and the job she had dreamed of six years earlier. Moreover, she and Helburn had developed a friendship that, in Helburn's words, "survived the tensions of show business and even the high emotions generated by the Group Theatre."[56]

In her final two years with the Guild, Crawford took over many of the executive duties when Theresa Helburn took a leave of absence to work in Hollywood as a screenwriter. In fact, Crawford was being groomed to replace Helburn when she joined Langner as co–administrative head. Despite her skills, Crawford found herself engaged in serious (and even embarrassing) conflicts of interest that eventually persuaded her to offer her resignation. She was making artistic contacts with playwrights for the Guild at the same time she was making contacts with the same writers for the Group. The board soon asked Crawford to decide which of two masters she wanted to serve.

With deep personal distress, Crawford resigned her affiliation with the Guild in 1931. "I feel there is more creative work for me to project and accomplish within the Group," she said. "I think it is a shame that the organization which brought me up should not have the benefit of what I might do but I have puzzled and found no solution within the Guild."[57]

From her various observation posts over six years, she had identified the Guild's Achilles heel: "The extra activities the Guild undertook never lasted." The acting school, which she had attended in its first year of operation, was abandoned two years later. The Studio, an interesting concept for developing young talent, who might have contributed fresh ideas and methods to the older group, lasted for one production. "In other words," Crawford concluded with her usual succinctness, " . . . the Guild's fuse was too short. The fires they lit burned out too quickly."[58]

When the board learned that Crawford intended to leave, they offered her full board membership with an increased salary. She declined the offer. Her two Old Testament prophets, as she called Harold Clurman and Lee Strasberg, had persuaded her to take up their dream of a new kind of theater. "It had taken four years," she confessed, "but Harold and Lee had seduced my mind."[59]

As she crossed Fifty-second Street and glanced up at the strangely prophetic title *Too Good to Be True* of another Shaw play on the marquee, she experienced a sense of déjà vu. Her missionary spirit had taken her to Smith, where her directing experiences with *Shakuntala* and *The Faithful* had resulted in her awareness of a production as a translation of words on a page into physical form and live action.[60] Her six-year apprenticeship with the Theatre Guild had begun beneath the marquee of *Caesar and Cleopatra*, where she promised herself, Helen Hayes, and George Bernard Shaw that she would make it in the business. The Guild had educated her in the ways and means of that business and provided reliable guides in the choosing of plays. Theresa Helburn had offered a single rule: "We have had . . . only one criterion in choosing a play, and that is—does it say enough to us and say it well enough to be worth the effort of production."[61]

As she turned away from the institution that had been her creative home for almost a decade, she was keenly aware that she was taking an "irreversible step, dangerous to security but in its way inevitable."[62]

4

RAISING THE ROOF

Not for nothing had I daydreamed as a child of being a missionary. All that had changed was the religion.

—Cheryl Crawford

Three years into the Group experiment, Cheryl Crawford sat among a stack of unread scripts in theater owner Lee Shubert's office on West Forty-fourth Street. For weeks, she read dull plays until she came across *Crisis*, a medical drama by Sidney Kingsley, soon to be known for his realistic social melodramas. Crawford was already facing the fact that the idealistic Group enterprise was a failed experiment. After the failures of *1931*, *Night Over Taos*, *Big Night*, and the minor triumph of *Success Story*, they were overdrawn at the bank, had no house playwright, and no new plays to produce. In consolation, Crawford thought, "We may have been broke, but we were famous."[1]

Three years earlier, a smartly dressed, determined Cheryl Crawford approached Lee Shubert who, with his brother Jacob J., owned most of the theaters in New York City in the late thirties. With script in hand, she wanted "Mr. Lee," as the theater mogul was known, to finance John Howard Lawson's new play, *Success Story*. Nevertheless, she was aware from Clurman's friendship with the Shuberts that they were not fans of the Group's nontheatrical activities; namely, they thought they were all communists engaged in communal living.[2]

As Crawford entered Lee Shubert's office, she faced a small, dapperly dressed gentleman with impenetrable brown eyes and a simianlike face. Although feared and disliked by many theater people (his detractors dubbed him "Lee Shylock") for his fierce business acumen and rough-

and-tumble deals, Crawford established a rapport with him and reported that he was invariably kind to her.[3]

It was to Crawford's advantage that Lee Shubert liked no-nonsense theater people. He was also prone to favor individuals who had severed connections with the Theatre Guild. He was scornful of Lawrence Langner's "long-haired bunch of jerks" who valued art over money.[4] Nevertheless, he held notions about "serious" theater and favored the Group because, not only had they split from the Guild but they called for a new, impassioned American style of writing and acting. When Cheryl Crawford approached Lee Shubert as an investor, she was honest and forthright with him and he responded to his unconventional emissary by investing in a number of the Group's plays and allowing them to perform in Shubert theaters.[5]

As part of her strategy to get a commitment of sixty-five hundred dollars to produce *Success Story*, Crawford invited Shubert to see a rehearsal at Dover Furnace, their second summer retreat in upstate New York. When Shubert arrived at the rehearsal barn, he was seated on a thronelike red velvet chair, and the actors played around him. This was a new experience for a man who usually sat removed from performers in a far off seat on the aisle. Crawford thought he was particularly taken with Luther Adler's portrait of an ambitious young Jew on the make, a character in her view whose story was not unlike Shubert's own. The theater owner was impressed and promised to put up the financing and install the show in the Maxine Elliot Theatre. *Success Story* opened in September 1932 and survived for one hundred and twenty-eight performances. Shubert took "first money" for operating expenses and was satisfied with his investment.

Nevertheless, Crawford's professional directing debut with *Big Night* was a nine-performance disaster. During rehearsals for the bitter social comedy, Crawford lost confidence in her abilities as a stage director and business woman. She concluded that her direction was indifferent and her efforts to secure money haphazard. Confiding to her diary, she wrote, "Worried about finances for the play. Hard to work with that pressing on me all the time. Don't think I'm a really good businesswoman. Must get the money or we're washed up. Nerves jangly. We're trying to run a business like a philanthropy." On the day of the opening, she wrote again, "No matter how tired I am, I've got to stick. I don't know what to do. Work, another year, another time, we must go on.[6]

Crawford's meditations echo the ending of Chekhov's *The Three Sisters*, where the sisters look toward a bleak future of habitual work and loneliness. Crawford's frustrations were not just with the constant pleading for money. As the Group's manager and principal money-raiser, she felt that she was trapped in "women's work," as she called her theatrical housekeeping. When she abandoned the security of the Theatre Guild and a salary of nine thousand dollars a year ("then large money for a Miss of twenty-six"), she had hoped to begin a directing career.[7] She mistakenly thought that she would share, as an equal partner, directing responsibilities with Clurman and Strasberg. Nevertheless, her compatriots took the plum scripts for themselves, and, when Crawford objected, Clurman told her that her ego was getting in the way of her artistic and political commitments.[8]

For six years, Crawford handled the Group's fundraising and business affairs, search for new scripts, scheduling, and summer retreats. In short, she performed the tasks that failed to inspire her male colleagues, including staging plays in which they had little interest. Despite efforts to view her treatment as gender discrimination or ethnic bias against the "shiksa" in their midst, her codirectors' choices were ego-driven and short-sighted. Although there were many Jews among the Group, Clurman and Strasberg swept aside prejudice, along with the opinions and ambitions of men *and* women, in pursuit of their shared vision of an ideal theater. In time, they were criticized for their failure to develop outstanding actresses to equal the men of the company and the same could be said for the neglect of Cheryl Crawford's potential as a stage director. Crawford's pride most likely prevented her from rebelling against the neglect of her creative ambitions and returning to the Guild.

Claiming little time for her private life, Crawford debunked the myth that theater people enjoyed a hotbed of sexual experience.[9] The truth lay somewhere between the strictly business efforts that absorbed her energies and the sexual freedoms of communal living. The Group's summer retreats were notorious for their "communal, al-fresco summer life" where, after rehearsals, they had midnight suppers of crackers and milk, along with enthusiastic conversations that lasted till dawn.[10] Crawford's diary entry for June 26, 1933, hinted that there was more to her experience than work and conversation: "I was in a bad temper all day—rain, problems, of financing, housing difficulties, sex."[11]

Away from her collaborators and Group matters, she indulged her love of books, records, "some intermittent love life," and intimate dinners with friends. "Come to dinner and bring a book to read," she would say.[12] Nevertheless, a glamorous actress from the state of Tennessee, who had been part of the Theatre Guild's young company and became one of the original members of the Group, revealed the sham of Crawford's self-imposed image as a heterosexual woman married to her career. Crawford's romantic interest was actress Dorothy Patten, whose family wealth came from Coco-Cola bottling companies.

Three years younger than Crawford, Dorothy Patten was a long-legged, stylish brunette, frequently photographed in rowboats, beach and lawn chairs, bathing suits, fur coats, and clever hats. She made her theatrical mark with the Lunts in the Theatre Guild production of *Elizabeth the Queen*. Like Crawford and others, she was seduced by Clurman's and Strasberg's visionary passion for a "different" theater with plays of social importance, a permanent acting company, and a common technique derived from Stanislavski's theories. Like others, she burned her bridges with the Guild to join in the experiment. She stayed with the Group for seven years and played in eleven productions, including *Big Night* and *Till the Day I Die*, both directed by Crawford.

When the company fell on hard times, Crawford, living on money she had saved while working for the Guild, sublet her apartment to composer Aaron Copland "at a small profit" and moved into Patten's Eastside apartment overlooking the river. Crawford claimed somewhat disingenuously that she occupied "the maid's room." Lost in the fiction was the fact that a live-in Swedish maid cooked and cleaned for Dorothy Patten and her guests.[13]

During the period Crawford was without financial resources, the women lived together and traveled to family homes in Akron and Chattanooga. Patten remained behind when Crawford resigned from the Group and was among the original members shunted aside when Odets's *Golden Boy* was cast. Thereafter, she was hospitalized with clinical depression. During her recuperation, she was attended by Cecelia McMahon who became a lifelong companion.[14]

Groupstroy

In 1932, the Depression was in full swing, and the Group's fortunes mirrored the state of the nation—economically and emotionally depressed, discouraged by life and art, living from hand to mouth, and not knowing where the next dime (or script) would come from. To save expenses, some of the company rented a ten-room coldwater flat on West Fifty-seventh Street near Tenth Avenue for collective living in a building near the railroad tracks. Crawford referred to the Soviet-style living arrangements as *Groupstroy—stroy* or *stroï* being a Russian word for "unit"—but Clurman tagged it the "poorhouse."[15] Members lived in "uncomfortable abrasion," sometimes getting odd jobs, sometimes eating from "CARE" baskets provided by more fortunate members, namely Margaret Barker, whose father had a medical practice in Baltimore, and Dorothy Patten, whose packages of cooked foods were prepared by her housekeeper.[16]

One rainy afternoon, Crawford was seated in the Group's business office located on the top floor of the Shuberts' Forty-eighth Street Theatre, pondering the funding for their next retreat, when two young men knocked on the door and announced they were Yale graduates wanting to join the Group Theatre. The two petitioners were Alan Baxter, a tall, handsome, juvenile type, who seemed placid and shy. The other young man, shorter than his companion, had burning eyes and a fidgety energy. He introduced himself by his college nickname Gadge (short for "Gadget") Kazan.[17]

On that rainy afternoon, Cheryl Crawford came face to face with the future stage and film director Elia Kazan. Their careers converged in that makeshift office high above the stage of a Broadway theater on Forty-eighth Street, and, unknown to them on that day, they would work together, off and on, for the next thirty years.

Despite hard times, Crawford was determined to find a script that conformed to the Group's mandate to do contemporary plays on social issues with appeal to audiences. She haunted Lee Shubert's office and read through an enormous "woodpile" of manuscripts made available with the understanding that the theater owner would receive compensation from any profits. She came across a medical drama that she described to Helen Thompson, the Group's press agent, who later invented the successful Play of the Month Club: "It's a hell of a subject and it hasn't been treated in the theatre. I think we could make a fascinating production of it."[18]

When Clurman and Strasberg were unenthusiastic about the new script, she took it to Theresa Helburn, who offered to produce it with her. Her codirectors refused her request to work outside the Group, and, once again, she bowed to their autocratic decision-making.

Crawford arranged accommodations for the Group's third retreat at a large adult camp, named Green Mansions, near Lake George in Warrensburg, New York. For bed and board they entertained the paying guests with revues, solo acts, comic turns, and even the second act of a new play by Clifford Odets, called *I've Got the Blues*—an early incarnation of *Awake and Sing*. With time passing, her two partners agreed that, with no other play on the horizon, Crawford should negotiate the rights to *Crisis*. At that point, she discovered that two young producers, Sidney Harmon and James Ullman, had optioned Kingsley's play. Not to be denied, Crawford worked out a coproduction with the Group performing the play and assuming half the financing and proceeds.

With the deal made, Crawford set herself the task of finding six thousand dollars to cover production costs. By happenstance, Doris Warner of the Hollywood Warners, who owned the film studio, was in New York City learning part of the film business. She came to Green Mansions to see a run-through of the play, and, after returning to Manhattan, she read Kingsley's script and agreed to put up the money.[19]

Reminiscent of the Group's disaffection for the original ending of *The House of Connelly*, they viewed the ending of *Crisis* as another "downer."[20] Engaged to a wealthy fiancée, who cannot understand his dedication to medicine, Kingsley's idealistic intern falls in love with a young woman who dies following an abortion. Upon discovering the affair, his fiancée tells him that she is breaking their engagement. As the curtain falls, the doctor stands alone in abject misery.

When Strasberg discussed the unsatisfactory ending with Crawford, she remembered that earlier in the play there had been a telephone conversation between the doctor and an elderly Italian woman worrying about her injured son. In the earlier dialogue, the doctor said to the mother, "Don't worry, your boy is going to live. He's going to be all right. He's really going to live." The dialogue failed to advance the story and was excised from the second act. Crawford suggested restoring the conversation to the final scene played by Alexander Kirkland:

> After the fiancée deserted the young doctor, and the phone rang, Bill Kirkland, who was playing the part, picked it up and talked to the Italian mother. . . . You knew that the young doctor was going to go on and do his job no matter what happened to him. That gave the play the kind of up-beat ending that seemed right to us.[21]

Sidney Kingsley's *Crisis* opened as *Men in White* in the Shuberts' Majestic Theatre on September 26, 1933, and played over three hundred performances. Much of the success was attributed to the graphically realistic production and the fresh theme that was discussed years before television's popular medical shows. One critic called it "an honest, tricky, and propaganda show that can be attended without a sacrifice of intelligence."[22] Kingsley won the Pulitzer Prize for Drama, and the Group had their first unqualified hit.

After the first preview, Lee Shubert came up to Crawford in the lobby and said, "Too bad. It's a wonderfully interesting play, but, of course, it won't make any money." She gave a half-hearted but cocky reply: "Mr.

Lee, after we open, you will thank me on your knees that we are in your theatre." He was thankful with his sizable return but he never "knelt," she later joked.[23]

With faith in her business acumen and artistic judgment restored, Crawford nurtured *Men in White* at night and during the day searched for new plays. She encouraged author Melvin Levy, who was eager to write a play on an American theme, to develop the story of a power-hungry robber baron in San Francisco. *Gold Eagle Guy* spoke to a constant Group theme: the American dream's obsession with power and money.

Nevertheless, Crawford was growing weary of her routine: reading unsuitable plays, looking for summer quarters in faraway places, and seeking backers for the next season. During the summer of 1934 in an abandoned camp near Ellenville in upstate New York, she found the arguments of newly radicalized members tiresome. They accused the Group's management of exploiting actors, designers, and kitchen help—"in fact, everyone except the animals."[24]

Crawford admitted that she, unlike Clurman and Strasberg, was never able to stand up well to criticism and became impatient with the actors' demands for more money and better scripts. While Clurman enjoyed returning the brickbats and Strasberg hammered the members speechless with his "Gotterdammerung violence," Crawford simply walked out for a week. Someone asked, "Won't you be lonesome?" She answered, "I hope so."[25]

The frissons among the members were partially healed by the slightly-frayed-around-the-collar actor-turned-playwright Clifford Odets, who appeared with a rewritten *Awake and Sing*. Crawford found the frenetic style completely foreign to her but liked the vivid dialogue and unusual characters. While Clurman and Strasberg delayed a decision on Odets's play, she and Helen Thompson were occupied with setting up a six-week tour in the fall to Boston with *Men in White*, *Success Story*, and *Gold Eagle Guy*. The adventure was jeopardized by a change in booking that forced them into a large, musty theater unsuitable for intimate productions.

Crawford ameliorated her unhappiness in Goodspeed's Bookshop, where she bought rare books by Thoreau, Whitman, and Emerson and photographs of all three, which she hung in her bedroom. Greeting her three Bostonians each morning, she felt spiritually regenerated at the start of the day for the next forty-five years.

Her disappointments with the huge theater and an unenthusiastic Boston press were set aside when Odets, clutching yellow sheets of paper to his chest, appeared at her side after a matinee and announced that he had just finished a long one-act called *Waiting for Lefty*.[26] As the first to read Odets's groundbreaking play, Crawford thought it was dynamite, but did not anticipate the enormous effect it would have on audiences and on the fortunes of the Group Theatre.

Crawford's political education derived largely from the Group's socially conscious plays and the nationally known women political activists of her day. Before meeting the remarkable Mother Bloor (the former Ella Reeve, who was a labor organizer and founding member of the American Communist Party), Crawford derived her politics by way of the social conscience of the plays selected by the Group to make statements about current political and social themes. Issues of racism, health care, poverty, discrimination, unionization, rising fascism, and mortal pressures derived from *The House of Connelly, Men in White, Success Story, Gold Eagle Guy, Awake and Sing, Till the Day I Die*, and *Waiting for Lefty* shaped Crawford's liberal politics. At the time, Crawford did not suspect there was a communist cell within the Group Theatre.[27]

Sometime in 1935, Crawford met Mother Bloor through the activist's son-in-law, actor Will Geer. Described by her new admirer as "a tiny, gray-haired bundle of energy, who worked to radicalize the dispossessed farmers in the 'dust bowl' region," Mother Bloor (women radicals of the day were almost always called "Mother") told stories about poverty and injustice that were revelations to the Akron-born Cheryl Crawford.[28] Noted for holding mass meetings of striking miners and unemployed workers, Bloor began her speeches with the salutation, "Friends, Comrades, and Stoolpigeons." She was usually arrested. When Crawford met her in New York City, she was between incarcerations.

Crawford's politicization took place on the cusp of Hallie Flanagan's struggles to administer the Federal Theatre Project for the Roosevelt administration and her head-on confrontation with the Martin Dies Special House Committee on Un-American Activities, authorized by the U.S. Congress. The year Flanagan was invited to administer the new theater program, established under the Works Progress Administration, the Group Theatre produced Odets's trilogy—*Awake and Sing, Waiting for Lefty*, and *Paradise Lost*.

It can be surmised that Crawford's introduction to Mother Bloor and her trip to the headquarters of the Communist Party—USA were background to staging *Till the Day I Die*, written as a curtain-raiser for *Waiting for Lefty*. Odets's short anti-Nazi play argued the virtues of the communist brotherhood. Critics found the play inferior in technique and "best suited to the party ear."[29]

Unlike many in the Group, Crawford did not dwell in the thirties on communism as a "redemptive force in a troubled world."[30] As a marginal idealist, her liberalism never translated into political activism, peace marches, or speech-making.[31] Her social conscience was derived from her Congregationalist upbringing and the message-laden plays of her day. Her trip to the Soviet Union in 1935 had little to do with her political tendencies, or her sympathies for the Russian people, and had everything to do with the highly praised theater productions in Moscow and the major artists there.

Four years into the Group experiment, there were no suitable new plays on the horizon, and many of the actors were finding opportunities in Hollywood, thus draining the Group's talent pool. The phoenix struggled from the ashes once more when Clurman announced that he would direct *Awake and Sing*. Odets read the play to the company, and their enthusiasm was contagious. The Group's internal dissensions temporarily abated.

A House Playwright

The year 1935 was known as the Clifford Odets year among the Group's adherents. Parallel to rehearsals for *Awake and Sing*, Sanford Meisner and Clifford Odets staged *Waiting for Lefty*. Uncertain how audiences would respond to the union play, based on a New York taxi strike of the previous year, the Group arranged benefit performances in the Civic Repertory Theatre in lower Manhattan. During a Sunday evening performance, the play received a tumultuous response from the audience. Both plays by Odets reaffirmed Crawford's personal and political creed; namely, to be at the center of a theatrical enterprise that spoke to the social conscience of America.

In mid-February, *Awake and Sing*, the drama of Jewish life in the Bronx, opened to legendary notices and played over one hundred performances. The play examined a lower-middle-class Jewish family in the uneasy climate of the Depression. Taking its title from the prophet Isaiah, "Awake and sing, ye who dwell in the dust," the awakening of Odets's hero, played by John Garfield, resolved to go forth as a leftwing agitator and change the world. *Awake and Sing* mirrored the period's "inchoate longing for personal and political triumph" and fulfilled the Group's passion for a meaningful "American" play.[32]

In a bold move, the Group's coproducers made the decision to bring *Waiting for Lefty* to Broadway with a hastily written anti-Nazi curtain-raiser to go with it. Crawford directed *Till the Day I Die*, a cautionary tale that argued the evils of Nazism and the need for a united front to fight Germany. The double bill opened at the Longacre Theatre on March 26, 1935, and played for 136 performances. At a time when many Americans were polarized politically, *Waiting for Lefty* was that rare breed: a theatrically effective drama and a propaganda piece on behalf of unionization. At a meeting of a taxi drivers' union (the Longacre served as the meeting hall), members await the return of their committeeman, Lefty Costello. Several address the union, urging them not to strike, but agitators harangue the members to use the strike as a weapon against capitalism, seen as a corrupt and dying political system. When the news arrives that Lefty has been killed, the drivers vote to strike—shouting in unison, "STRIKE, STRIKE, STRIKE!!!"[33] Crawford rejoiced in the tumultuous reaction of the audience to the pro-union play. "The response was wild, fantastic," she said. "It raised the roof."[34]

With productions running on Broadway and the Group the talk of the town, Crawford decided to coast on her hard-won laurels. With a guaranteed fifty dollars a week in her pocket, she proposed traveling to the Soviet Union to see the highly praised productions that Strasberg and Clurman had seen a year earlier in Moscow. Crawford persuaded Clurman to accompany her on the five-week trip.[35]

Soviet Giants

In April of 1935, Crawford and Clurman sailed to Europe aboard the *Ile de France* and made their way by train to Moscow and to the old Hermitage building on *Kamergerskil pereulok*, the home of the legendary Moscow Art Theatre. They proceeded to see twenty-nine shows and interview such theater and film notables as Edward Gordon Craig, Sergei Eisenstein, Konstantin Stanislavski, and Vsevolod Meyerhold. During their sojourn, the travelers were ignorant of Soviet oppressive measures and had no knowledge of the "labor camps or of the vicious trampling of human rights" that later resulted in Meyerhold's disappearance into Lubyanka Prison and his wife's murder in their Moscow apartment.[36]

Although productions at the Moscow Art Theatre were sometimes disappointing, Crawford and Clurman's interview with Stanislavski was not. They learned from an official at the theater that Stanislavski had been in Moscow for the last five months recovering from a heart attack. An appointment was arranged, and, when they arrived at Stanislavski's home, they were surprised to enter a private house with servants, since Moscow was so "overcrowded in those days that scarcely anyone had a private house." They judged the house as a sign of the government's respect for its famous artist.[37]

As Stanislavski greeted them, Crawford noted that, despite his illness, he was "a most impressive figure, very tall, with a handsome face now lined with signs of pain; the full, red lips suggested a sensual nature. I felt it was an actor's face, capable of instant emotional reactions."[38]

Mesmerized by the presence of the first artist to devise a complete method for training actors, they took their leave as they observed Stanislavski growing tired. Crawford noted in her journal that it had been one of the "most memorable visits of my life."[39]

Their second appointment of the day was with Vsevolod Meyerhold, whose "almost Mephistophelian face" furrowed with heavy lines and offset with a very large nose suggested to his observer emotional extremes of love and hate.[40] They talked about his famous "biomechanic" method required of his actors and his staging innovations labeled constructivism and theatricalism. Meyerhold's riveting productions of *The Inspector General* and *The Lady of the Camellias* prompted Crawford's decision to urge the Group to reconsider the classics—"an original concept, expertly carried out," was the key, as she had witnessed, to refocusing the old texts onto present-day society.[41]

During their return trip to New York, Crawford and Clurman assessed the lessons applicable to the Group. Measuring the Moscow Art Theatre's criterion to recreate true-to-life experience that in its naturalism killed theatricality and Meyerhold's stylizations that abandoned truthful acting, they concluded that the goal of the Group should be to move an audience in the ethical and aesthetic sense, and not necessarily in a political sense.[42]

As the travelers approached New York harbor, their spirits soared. From the ship's deck, they saw several members of the company waving greetings. With rejuvenated spirits, their first tasks came in the form of *Paradise Lost, Weep for the Virgins, The Case of Clyde Griffiths,* and *Johnny Johnson*. Their spirits were soon dampened, and the lessons learned in Moscow for greater personal and theatrical discipline were set aside in the face of dissatisfactions voiced by members of the company.

Wolf at the Door

Two years following the trip to Moscow, Crawford contemplated resigning from the Group. She was motivated by the failures of her coproducers to

approve two shows (later Broadway hits) that she urged them to under-
take, namely Maxwell Anderson's *Winterset* and Sidney Kingsley's *Dead
End*, and by the clamoring dissension among the company. She decided
to finish the projects scheduled for their fifth season before making a
decision on her future course.

Increasingly dissatisfied with their leaders' inability to mount a successful production and guarantee steady employment, twelve members,
including Clifford Odets, Elia Kazan, and Robert Lewis, created a docu-
ment in the fall of 1935, called "Development of a Studio," demanding
reappraisal of the Group's management and mission, the development
of a studio, and new strategies for securing plays to be directed solely
by Lee Strasberg. Deep in her heart Crawford knew their requests had
merit but there was not a lot the codirectors could do without infusions
of money and energy.

In order to shore up a producing organization adrift under "loose
leadership," Clurman proposed "a single managing director" in combination with centralized leadership. He nominated himself to assume
the job of managing director and Crawford and Strasberg agreed to the
new arrangement.[43]

Despite the reorganization, the company did not have a script at the
close of the short-lived *The Case of Clyde Griffiths*, Erwin Piscator's dramatization of Theodore Dreiser's *An American Tragedy*. Because of the
Group's commitment to stage the Dreiser play, they had missed, to Crawford's chagrin, the opportunity to produce Irwin Shaw's *Bury the Dead*.
"That's the play we should have done," she remarked in disappointment.[44]

Without funds or scripts, attrition began to afflict the core company,
and Crawford remarked on the dire situation: "The wolf was at the door
again, and this time the door was open."[45]

Composer Kurt Weill stepped into the breach. Persuaded by her friend
Janet Flanner, European correspondent with *The New Yorker* who wrote
under the penname Genêt and admired Kurt Weill's early works, Crawford sought out the composer of *The Threepenny Opera* and his wife,
actress Lotte Lenya. The couple fled Nazi Germany in 1933 by way of
Paris and came to New York, where Max Reinhardt was producing *The
Eternal Road* with score by Weill. When she learned that Weill wanted to
work on an American subject, Crawford thought of the most American
writer she knew—Paul Green.[46]

Crawford telephoned to ask if she and Weill could come to North Carolina to talk with the writer about a new work. After lengthy discussions,

the material that seemed most promising was based on the subject of the First World War. The three derived inspiration from Jaroslav Hašêk's *The Good Soldier Schweik*, Georg Büchner's *Woyzeck*, Carl Zuckmayer's *The Captain of Köpenick*, and from the American folk hero Will Rogers. The collaborators planned a revue-style, antiwar musical named after an ordinary soldier to be presented with elements of vaudeville, fantasy, and lyricism.

The rough outline of *Johnny Johnson* was the story of an unworldly idealist who enlisted in the U.S. Army when President Woodrow Wilson described the conflict as the war to end all wars. Green set out to write a morality play, an *Everyman*, whose picaresque journey takes him from basic training to the battlefield, where he befriends a German sniper and nearly stops the war.[47] To protect the rest of the world in its madness, Johnny is committed to a mental institution, where his natural goodness cannot be distinguished by medical personnel from the virulent manias of other patients.[48] Eventually restored to society, he peddles toys to children and exits whistling the show's theme tune as a prowar rally echoes in the distance.

The Group worked on *Johnny Johnson* in the summer of 1936 at Pinebrook Club Camp in Nichols, Connecticut, near Bridgeport. Crawford, Green, Weill, and Lenya stayed about two miles from the camp in an old house on Trumbull Avenue. Green set up his typewriter in a room on the top floor.[49] Crawford took the second floor bedroom above Weill's piano and listened to his music day and night. She had had her fill of living "packed like a sardine with the vacationing, fun-loving guests" and was supremely happy with the arrangement.[50]

At summer's end, Crawford, Dorothy Patten, and the Weills decided to economize by sharing an apartment overlooking the East River at Fifty-first Street. Film legends Lillian and Dorothy Gish had previously lived in the apartment, which had two separate wings with a common kitchen and dining alcove. Crawford relished the peaceful living, which served as a refuge from the agonies she suffered searching for backers to fund the Group's most expensive production.

As Strasberg rehearsed *Johnny Johnson*, Crawford approached arts patron Mrs. Motty (Bess) Eitingon for funding. An admirer of Kurt Weill, she agreed to put up forty thousand of the sixty thousand dollar budget. Crawford turned next to John Hay ("Jock") Whitney, who sent Robert Benchley of *New Yorker* fame to see a run-through. Benchley was charmed by the show presented in a small space without scenery.

Following Benchley's encouraging report, Whitney's lawyers arranged a meeting with Crawford. Although Clurman had praised her for knowing how to deal with members of the Theatre Guild board, Crawford was intimidated by the four businessmen in expensive dark suits seated around a large table in the wood-paneled room. They wanted to know what the Group was prepared to offer in return for an investment of twenty thousand dollars. Crawford spoke directly to Whitney. "This is nothing I can haggle over. We need the money desperately, so whatever you think is fair we will accept." She apparently touched a nerve in the philanthropist for he agreed to provide the money. For the moment, Crawford was relieved that *Johnny Johnson* ("her baby," as she called the musical) had been given a chance to survive for a Broadway opening.[51]

For the debacle that ensued, Crawford blamed the huge 1400-seat theater and the nineteen heavy sets designed by Donald Oenslager. To her surprise opening night went smoothly. The three huge cannons, singing sweetly to the sleeping soldier, arrived on cue; and the large Statue of Liberty appeared promptly to sing to Johnny as he stood onboard a troop ship leaving for France. Kurt Weill expressed his appreciation by dedicating the score to Crawford with a hand-written inscription:

> It will always carry these few words: For Cheryl Crawford, but they include all the love and admiration and thankfulness which I feel for you.
>
> This is your evening, more than anybody else.
>
> Success or failure. We have our friendship, you and I. That is worth it.
>
> I kiss you,
>
> Kurt [52]

The audience response was enthusiastic, but the reviews were less so. Brooks Atkinson complained that Paul Green was "an honest and exultant poet but not a virtuoso theatre man." [53] Without "money notices," the show lasted sixty-five performances. With the Group's cupboard bare, an exhausted Crawford remarked, "It was a heavy blow to me. I had believed that *Johnny* was a truly fresh form of musical. I didn't think I could endure much more." [54] Her friend Dorothy Patten was more forthcoming. She said that *Johnny Johnson* was a "near fatal blow" to the Group, and its failure precipitated Crawford's decision to try her skills as an independent producer—an activity she described as agreeably devoid of "group" discussion.[55]

Before she could compose her letter of resignation, members of the Group presented their leaders with a "White Paper" citing their personal defects and shortcomings: Clurman's failures as managing director, Strasberg's personal coldness and cruelty, and Crawford's character and commercial interests. She considered their criticism harsh but with kernels of truth:

> *Cheryl Crawford:* She's had six years of dirty jobs. We appreciate this, but she strikes us as a disappointed artist. She always feels she is wasting her life, that she is a "martyr" to the Group, that without her the Group would fold in a minute, and worst of all that no one appreciates her. . . . [56]

Stung by the criticisms, the codirectors resolved to resign. Startled by the reality of a leaderless company, stop-gap measures were proposed to reorganize with a new directorate composed of the three former directors and three company members. Since there were no new plays and no funding prospects, the chosen course of action was to stop all activities "to get back our health and sanity and find easier ways to survive."[57] In early January, Clurman announced in the *New York Times* that the Group Theatre would produce no more plays that season.[58]

Never, Never Land

For a short time, Hollywood held out false solutions. Film producer Walter Wanger was interested in employing Group actors as a kind of stock company for his films. Crawford traveled to the West Coast to meet with the head of Warner Brothers and was stunned to receive a job offer from Mervyn LeRoy at an astronomical salary. As she studied the successful film people and weighed the Hollywood atmosphere and ubiquitous swimming pools that dotted the landscape, she determined that she probably could not survive in "never, never land." "It wasn't the way I wanted to spend my life," she concluded. "I wanted to prove myself in the theatre, as a producer.[59]

Once back in New York in an inexpensive office set up to search for scripts for the future revival of the Group Theatre, she stared at the handwriting on the wall: "The seven-year marriage of Harold Clurman, Lee Strasberg, and Cheryl Crawford was dissolving."[60] While she debated with herself over how to make it as a producer (with or without a business partner), she received two letters from friends in Hollywood that propelled her toward a decision. The first was from Clifford Odets, with a check for five hundred dollars to be divided among the remaining actors and information that he was working on a new play called *Golden Boy*. With an Odets play in their future, Crawford surmised that the Group could continue without her.

The second letter, from Kurt Weill, urged her to do another show with him: "Please write me often—and let's do a fine show!"[61] The way was now paved for her entry into the world as an independent producer.

Crawford sat down at her typewriter in March of 1937 to draft her letter of resignation. She began, "After the most serious consideration I feel that I must leave the Group."

> I had thought I would write you a long explanation of my reasons, but I think at this time they would not serve their purpose of making myself clear to you; and besides the difficulty of writing exactly what I mean on paper is very great. The shock and surprise of my determination is perhaps greater to me than it will be to you, but I have tried to deal with my problems logically and sanely and unsentimentally.
>
> I plan to stay in the theatre and consequently will have to make an announcement of my leaving within a short time. . . . I hope very much that you will not feel I am failing in responsibility to the Group in making this step, for if my interpretation of the reports I have received from the Coast is correct, I have not done so.
>
> I would like to say that I still believe with all my heart in a Group Theatre and that the objective or outside situations have caused us so much strain and difficulty *can* be slowly solved, but the inner situation seems to me incapable of solution at least at this time.

She ended with heartfelt regret: "Believe me that I more deeply regret this than anything I have ever had to do, but it truly seems to be necessary and inevitable.[62]

Lee Strasberg's resignation followed, and Harold Clurman accepted their two resignations with "a kind of friendly fatalism and no argument."[63] The Group Theatre continued as a producing office for another four years and eight plays.

Postmortem

From the beginning, the tensions among the three codirectors ranged from polite assent to icy bitterness to doleful withdrawal. Their disgruntled relationship, in Crawford's view, gave new meaning to the old Abbott and Costello routine "Who's on first." Regardless of their dissatisfactions with one another, the troika had failed to secure continuous employment for the company and develop new plays to reflect what the Group wanted to say about life in America.

As she reflected on her previous seven years, she counted among their mistakes the rejection of the classics. "I realized that we could have done some classic plays, finding a point of view to make them vital and relevant to our time."[64] In hindsight, the insufficient financial funding still seemed insurmountable. Absent a National Endowment for the Arts and a New York State Arts Council, which became realities only some thirty years later, there were few willing patrons interested in a leftwing nonprofit theater. The Federal Theatre Project, subsidized by the U.S. Congress through the Works Progress Administration, found brief stability but disappeared from the cultural landscape when Congress voted against reauthorizing funds in 1939. In contrast, the Theatre Guild and the Civic Repertory Theatre found benefactors, but they did not try to sustain acting companies. Moreover, they produced "known" plays, largely classics by Shakespeare, Molière, and Ibsen, and such established modern writers as Chekhov, Shaw, and O'Neill.

At first, Crawford looked at her years with the Group as a glass half empty. In time, she revised her opinion of the Group's place in American theatrical history. As she told historian Foster Hirsch, "People don't remember the Theatre Guild anymore, but the Group is still very famous."[65]

PART TWO

DOORS TO EVERYWHERE, 1937–1961

5

DIZZY SPELLS

The American theatre is an uncertain gamble from start to finish.
—*Theresa Helburn*

By March of 1937, Crawford was without prophets or signposts pointing her to the next open door. At thirty-five, disconnected and alone, she reassessed her tenuous foothold on a theatrical career:

> I had lost my religion in college. Then for seven years my religion had been my faith in the ideals and values of the Group. Now that had dissolved, and I was thrown back on myself, a solitary individual. It was scary. I needed some support, some guidance.[1]

The idealistic woman, described by Lee Strasberg as "gentile, midwestern, and nonverbal," soon found her direction without her two Old Testament prophets.[2] She made a to-do list: secure an inexpensive office, locate a resourceful assistant, find playwrights, and discover "the emotional wherewithal to go it alone."[3] She rented a two-room office in the St. James Theatre on Forty-fourth Street where the Maurice Evans-Eddie Dowling management team had a suite of offices. Next, as her assistant producer, she enlisted the Theatre Guild's Elizabeth Hull, whose personal income paid the secretary's salary and oftentimes fifty dollars a month for rent. She then explored the theater district in search of scripts to make her mark as a commercial producer.

Playing Solitaire

The commercial theater district in 1937 was drab and dirty. It extended along the thoroughfare between Fortieth and Sixtieth streets and teemed with traffic, noise, jostling crowds, garish neon marquees, and enormous billboards. The number of Broadway productions had been shrinking due to tight money during the depression and the burgeoning film industry. The 1937–38 season was a low point, with fewer than one hundred new productions controlled by male producers and investors. This was the climate in which Crawford set out to prove herself.

She succeeded in presenting three failures one right after the other. The first closed after the final run-through in New York, during which the fledgling producer told her bewildered backer that "the show was hopeless and he had better cut his losses."[4] The second production, *Yankee Fable* by Lewis Meltzer, with blond, peaches-and-cream-complexioned Ina Claire, closed in Boston. The third, *All the Living*, broke the cycle of disappointing flops.

Brooks Atkinson praised the "high priestess of the Group Theatre" for offering a play about mental illness as her first independent production to reach Broadway.[5] *All the Living*, directed by Lee Strasberg, opened in March of 1938. Citing Strasberg's versatile direction, the critic applauded as "sheer perfection in stagecraft" Hardie Albright's medical drama about "a dark corner of modern life" that takes place in a hospital for the mentally ill. Atkinson called the production one of the foremost achievements of the season.[6] Crawford modestly confessed herself proud of the production: "I think it was the first time a play was located in an insane asylum, and for the first time on stage a young catatonic was cured by the injection of a newly discovered medicine."[7]

The favorable reviews brought attention to the newly minted "producer in skirts"—a euphemism for women working on Broadway in traditional male roles. A newspaper article at the time featured a photograph of a self-satisfied Crawford. The caption quoted her as saying: "A play producer takes more chances than anyone on earth and winds up with more wooden nickels. We stick to it only because it's in our blood, I guess." Commenting further for the reporter, she explained: "What did I have to get me here? A ton of nerve and the same philosophy a gambler has."[8]

Another theater artist "in skirts" was a member of Maurice Evans's production team. Stage director Margaret Webster had come from London in 1937 to direct *Richard II* with Evans in the title role. For her fourth production as an independent producer, Crawford enlisted Webster to stage *Family Portrait*, a serious play about the humble Judean family of Jesus of Nazareth with Mary, the mother of Jesus, as the central figure.

Family Portrait succeeded in reminding Crawford about the five pitfalls a producer faces on Broadway: investors, stars, writers, directors, and critics. The producer's major task—the play's financing and budget preparations—were daunting in the post-Depression climate. By the late thirties, it was rare for producers to put up their own money, unlike in previous times when David Belasco, Gilbert Miller, and John Golden financed their own shows. By the time Crawford arrived on the scene in 1938, a straight play, that potentially cost twenty-five thousand dollars, was sold to investors in "units" (a unit was one percent of the projected costs). Once the play opened, investors received all profits until their full investment was returned. In the meantime, the producer took a minimum of one percent of the weekly gross until the show paid off, at which time the profits were divided between investors and producer with each receiving fifty percent. Many variables affected the profit margin: reliable investors, strong or weak plays, available stars, and "money" reviews.

The financing for *Family Portrait* attracted investors who were either moved by the play or lured by the star performer. In order to solve the problem of who would play the role of Mary, Crawford contacted, in turn, Helen Hayes, Katharine Cornell, and Laurette Taylor. Hayes was afraid to follow Queen Victoria (in *Victoria Regina*) with Mary, mother of Christ, and declined. Cornell did not want to do a show that was not directed by her husband Guthrie McClintic; and Laurette Taylor remembered that she was a Catholic and begged off.[9]

To Crawford's astonishment, the glamorous Judith Anderson agreed to forego her customary star salary and accept an Actors' Equity minimum wage, then one hundred and ten dollars a week. Moreover, her performance as a humble, soft-spoken woman was an argument *against* typecasting. Audiences saw a small mousy woman in peasant dress walk onstage, not the sexy starlet of *As You Desire Me*.

With director, star, cast, and designer hired, "things looked rosy." The downturn came two weeks before rehearsals began. Crawford's major backer telephoned to request a meeting and announced that he had changed his mind based on some unfortunate financial investments he had made. "Where were we going to get the money?" she groaned to Elizabeth Hull in the privacy of their office. Facing the fact that expenditures were already committed, she turned to two young producers, Day Tuttle and Richard Skinner. They liked the script and agreed to raise the money. Crawford's relief was "inexpressible."[10]

Once the show went into rehearsals, she faced another unwelcome fact. The husband-and-wife writing team of Leonore Coffee and William Cowen was intractable when it came to rewriting scenes or lines of dialogue; moreover, they had wanted Katharine Cornell or Jane Cowl for the lead and expressed dissatisfaction with Judith Anderson from the outset. Crawford recalled that "rehearsals were not very friendly" and resulted in numerous blow-ups.[11]

By the time Crawford hired Margaret Webster, the Anglo-American, born in New York City to British actors and three years younger than her producer, she was a seasoned Broadway director. Within a period of two years, she had directed Maurice Evans to critical acclaim in *Richard II* and *Hamlet*, and played Masha in the Lunts' production of *The Sea Gull* for the Theatre Guild. When Crawford approached her with the script of *Family Portrait*, she was between engagements, having signed with the Guild to direct *Twelfth Night* with Helen Hayes and Maurice Evans as soon as the national tour of *Hamlet* closed.

The women knew one another because of the proximity of their offices on the upper floors of the St. James Theatre. They met briefly in elevators and hallways, and Webster admired Crawford for her theatrical ideals and courage to go into management ("not easy for a woman, even then") following the breakup of the Group Theatre.[12] Moreover, the women shared a great deal in common. First, they were singular women in a profession inimical to female producers, directors, designers, and playwrights. They shared ambition, courage, street-smarts, and theatrical ideals. They also shared their sexual orientation (Webster's partner at the time was actress Eva Le Gallienne) and a lesbian subculture scorned by the professional men who controlled the pocketbooks of Broadway. As independent women, they sought support among other lesbians and bisexual women of their acquaintance within the theater world and masked their private desires and sexual preferences behind a façade of work, work, and more work.[13] The legend that they were faithful workaholics was their mainstay as they navigated the shoals of the commercial theater's sexual politics, which favored heterosexual relationships and male-dominated business practices.

Crawford's *passing* as a heterosexual enhanced her business opportunities but negated public expression about her life outside the theater. Even though she called the shows her "babies," only rarely did she portray the theater business as a source of private pleasure and sexual desire. During *Yankee Fable* in Boston, her infatuation with Ina Claire was couched in terms of worrying about the actress's reluctance to learn her lines, all the while admiring her blue eyes, peaches-and-cream complexion, and beguiling smile. "She was allergic to learning lines," Crawford wrote as preface to the revelation of her infatuation for the beauty lounging in her hotel room in a pink lace peignoir:

> Steeled by many cups of coffee, I would go to her room determined to let her have it. She was always in bed in a lovely peignoir of pink and lace, her blond hair curling around her peaches-and-cream face, her saucy blue Irish eyes twinkling and a beguiling smile playing around her perfect white teeth. I would melt. The most devastating remark I could produce was "Oh, Ina, come on now. You must learn your lines."[14]

Nevertheless, these moments were cold comfort for a woman of Crawford's sexual interests, who maneuvered to carve out a career in the Broadway theater.

Rehearsals for *Family Portrait* were perilous. Crawford remarked upon the growing tensions as writers and star did not see eye to eye, and their director was at a loss to negotiate between them. In the play's final scene, the child has been born, and Mary, contemplating his name, says the last line: "I'd like him not to be forgotten." With producer and director in agreement, Judith Anderson argued that the words were artificial and pedantic. The actress suggested rewriting the line to say, "I wouldn't like him to be forgotten." A bitter stalemate ensued between actress and authors, and Webster tried in vain to reconcile the parties. Finally, Webster, not known for her lady-like demeanor, blazed with fury and flung her fur coat on the stage floor, stamped up and down on it in helpless rage, before leaving the theater to cool off. "It was an extraordinary example of what we now call primal therapy," Crawford caustically observed. "Why her fur coat should have substituted for the bodies of the writers, I never knew." [15]

Despite the sound and fury, Judith Anderson had the last word. On opening night, she brought the curtain down with "I *wouldn't* like him to be forgotten," and continued to do so throughout the run. The authors got their revenge by refusing to sign a contract for the show's national tour, and Crawford lost an opportunity to tour her first production in her new role as a Broadway producer.

After opening night at the Morosco Theatre, the cast, director, and producer went to composer Lehman Engel's apartment on East Fifty-fourth Street to celebrate. Around two o'clock, the show's press agent telephoned to tell Crawford that the reviews were lukewarm. As Webster put it, "They were magnificent for Judith, pretty good for the production and death to the box office on the familiar principle of damning with faint praise."[16]

Brooks Atkinson called the play "an intoxicating dramatic idea" but found the Cowens inadequate to the task of telling the story of Christ through the family's eyes.[17] In turn, Crawford faulted the director's lack of invention. With memories of what the Moscow Art Theatre accomplished in *The Lower Depths* by showing ordinary village life with simple detail and inventiveness, she felt the Broadway production was "bloodless" and lacking "unusual details that would prick an audience into unexpected recognitions." Finally, it was "nice—too nice," she remarked.[18]

Crawford praised Webster as "one of the most intelligent women I ever knew." "She was a no-nonsense director, a 'get on with it' director trained in the English repertory system, a facile and adroit craftsman with great technical knowledge. But she was not innovative."[19]

Despite their disappointment in the show, which closed after three months, both women knew that they shared the blame for the failed production. They had not defused the hostility between the writers and the leading actress, and they had not addressed the need for local color and realistic detail. Their mutual failures had stymied the future of the production on Broadway and elsewhere.[20]

Cold Comfort

Despite financial problems, Crawford proceeded to produce a fifth failure. *Another Sun*, written by world-famous journalist Dorothy Thompson, concerned German intellectuals forced to flee their country and take refuge in the United States. Although she found the writing mediocre, Crawford was attracted to the material ("the theme was on the side of the angels") and to the journalist's political passion as well.[21] Through Thompson's connection, German director Fritz Kortner was signed to direct *Another Sun*, and Celeste Holm made her Broadway debut in the play.

At forty-five, Dorothy Thompson was, in her new admirer's estimation, a "hard-hitting, no holds-barred, powerful crusader against all injustice and evil." After evening rehearsals, the two women often went to a small bar near the National Theatre where they talked about their careers in a man's world. Neither felt that she had suffered from being a woman in male-dominated professions, partly because they were just "too determined and engrossed" in their careers to notice. "I'm not sure we really cared whose world it was as long as we could pursue our careers," Crawford said.[22]

In the barroom atmosphere, Crawford detected that Thompson, who was ruthless in exposing the political diseases of her time, was insecure about her femininity and felt the need of the attentions of strong, talented men. Crawford shared with her Edna Ferber's lesson in cold comfort. At twenty-seven, the would-be producer had nervily asked the coauthor of *The Royal Family* and *Dinner at Eight*, "Miss Ferber, how does it feel to be an old maid?"

"Well, Cheryl," Ferber promptly replied, "it's rather like drowning—and not bad once you stop struggling."[23]

Even though Thompson laughed at the anecdote, she endured Fritz Kortner's bad-tempered outbursts and verbal abuse during rehearsals. Even though Kortner was a physically intimidating man with a wild temper, Crawford was astonished that the writer tolerated his outbursts. On one occasion, as he strode up the aisle with eyes bulging and bellowing that he was "through, through!" Crawford called his bluff with the same ferocity she had exhibited with Charles Cochran in London. "'Okay! Okay!' she shouted at Kortner. "Let's quit! Let's forget it!" *Another Sun* was his first job in New York, and, the last thing he wanted to do, Crawford had surmised, was to acquire a reputation for quitting a show.[24]

Even though she had gambled that Kortner would not walk out on the show, the static drama closed quickly and Crawford found that she had exhausted her resources. "By 1940, even if I had found a play," she mused, "it seemed impossible to excavate any more unenlightened investors."[25] To make matters worse, Elizabeth Hull retired to her farm in Connecticut and Crawford found herself ten thousand dollars in debt and without the wherewithal to pay the office rent.

Crawford consoled herself with a story that she had heard at a revival meeting. The preacher told the congregation of a man who one dark night fell off a cliff, but managed to cling to a branch to stop his fall. He hung on for hours in misery until he simply had to loosen his hold. With a despairing farewell to life, he dropped and fell six inches onto a ledge.[26]

A telephone call from John J. ("Jack") Wildberg, a copyright attorney turned producer and Crawford's soon-to-be business partner, involving the Maplewood Theatre in New Jersey, constituted the ledge that stayed her plunge into financial disaster. The tall, attractive, and well-dressed Wildberg had discovered a large movie house in Maplewood, formerly used as a summer theater. He proposed that Crawford join him in producing a season of summer stock, with a different play each week, in a location opposite the train and bus stations and close enough to Manhattan for actors to rehearse in Maplewood and still live in the city. Wildberg also found a plastic surgeon "devoutly addicted to the theater" to back the enterprise. The surgeon's only drawback, as far as Crawford could see, was the fact that he authored plays which she would be required to read and criticize.[27]

Reenergized by the prospect of bringing Broadway shows at the end of their New York engagements to Maplewood for a week, Crawford rebounded from her misery. She hired professional designers, so that the shows looked first-rate, and proceeded to plan a first season of twenty-six weeks. Beginning in July of 1940, she proved her catholic tastes with plays ranging from *The School for Scandal* and *The Royal Family* to *The Emperor Jones* and *Watch on the Rhine*. The stars varied from Ethel Barrymore, Tallulah Bankhead, and Ingrid Bergman to Maurice Evans, Eddie Dowling, and Paul Robeson. Crawford threw herself into promoting the theater with appearances before political and church groups, Rotarians and Elks clubs, church suppers and sewing circles. At first, speaking in public was a painful experience, but she soon evolved into a ham, "full of funny stories collected from every possible source." When she addressed the Maplewood audience at the opening of the second season, she told them, "When I got to New York this winter, I had to go into hiding, due to the erroneous and Fifth Column reports that you made me a millionaire!"[28]

In two and a half seasons of over fifty productions, Crawford described herself as "a busy lady," and bragged to *New Yorker* writer Janet Flanner that the Maplewood project made money, from the moment it started.[29] Nevertheless, she complained about having "no private life to speak of, just occasional evenings with colleagues. A social life, not to mention a love life, takes time, and I had none to spare. It was a high price to pay."[30]

In her public expression of life outside the theater, she neglected to say that Dorothy Patten had joined her in Maplewood.[31] Patten's revelation that she "renewed her acquaintance" with Crawford at the summer theater contradicted Crawford's legend of the lonely workaholic with only a dog for companionship. A publicity photograph taken of Crawford in Maplewood with "woman's best friend" showed her with close-cropped, coiffed hair and striped dress with low-heel black shoes. A terrier stood beside her on the park bench where she sat studying a script. "Trying it on the dog," the caption read. "Cheryl Crawford, in a moment of *what passes for leisure*, goes over the script of a new play that may appear on the boards of the Maplewood Theater."[32] The writer of the caption unwittingly reinforced Crawford's public insistence that even her free time was solely occupied by work with only her dog as companion.

When Crawford realized that Maplewood's third season in 1942 would be shortened to five weeks due to wartime gasoline rationing (most of the audiences came by car), she decided to produce "something big" and to "close with a bang." Recalling George and Ira Gershwin's last work together, she set her mind to stage *Porgy and Bess*, produced by the Theatre Guild in 1935. Wildberg agreed that the Gershwin musical would "close Maplewood with fireworks!"[33]

With permission from Lawrence Langner to revive *Porgy and Bess* (with an option to produce it after Maplewood in New York and elsewhere), they hired the original conductor, Alexander Smallens, and located most of the original cast, including Todd Duncan and Anne Brown, who had played the title roles in the Guild production. With the blessing of the Gershwin family, Crawford worked diligently with Smallens to cut the recitative passages which, she felt, "were out of keeping with the black milieu." The show, flowing "swiftly and tunefully," was joyfully received by Maplewood audiences. Crawford exulted, "We blazed happily out of Maplewood."[34]

Needing a theater for a Broadway revival of the triumphant Maplewood production, Crawford found herself seated, once again, in Lee Shubert's office. "You will have the Majestic," he pronounced, prompting woeful memories of *Johnny Johnson*. With tears in her eyes (she cried "easily, usually over injustice or anything I find beautiful and moving"), she wailed, "Oh, Mr. Lee, that big old barn has been a jinx house for years. Please don't put us there."[35] Even as she protested opening in the "flop-house," as she called the Majestic, she knew that they would have to take the barn-like theater on Forty-fourth Street.[36]

Despite the Majestic, *Porgy and Bess* got sensational notices, broke even, toured the country, and returned to New York twice for repeat engagements.

With confidence in her business acumen restored, Cheryl Crawford found her theatrical glass half full rather than half empty. "My success with *Porgy and Bess* and my failure with straight plays made me think that my fortunes lay in the musical theatre," she mused.[37] So, she began a search for something unusual and found *One Touch of Venus*.

6 _____

NO WOODEN NICKELS

Music seemed to have changed her luck.

—Janet Flanner

The adult Cheryl Crawford in 1942 was no longer the sturdy girl of Harold Clurman's recollection. With the Broadway success of *Porgy and Bess*, she was interviewed, photographed, and featured in *About Town* sitting languidly in an armchair dressed for the evening in white silk blouse, long black skirt, and silver evening slippers. In another publication, she revealed that her suits were made by Marlene Dietrich's tailor, although at five feet, four inches tall, she would not "look like Marlene in slacks," nor, like the blond, silken-haired Veronica Lake in "plunging neckline," seeing that female producers never wore low-cut blouses.[1]

In the early forties, Crawford was described as having "close-cropped light brown hair, gray-blue eyes, a soap and water face, small thrifty-looking hands, and a very firm handclasp." "In fact, Miss Crawford," the writer observed, "is very firm in a quiet, unobtrusive way."[2]

On the cusp of fame and fortune with *One Touch of Venus*, Crawford was regarded as a no-nonsense producer in search of original, meaningful, and entertaining material to make her mark on Broadway.

Ensconced in offices with business partner Jack Wildberg, Crawford sat at a Chippendale desk surrounded by framed stage designs from *Porgy and Bess* on the walls and searched for material for a new musical.[3] Despite her many contacts with agents and writers in New York and Hollywood, she found nothing that appealed to her. She recalled Kurt Weill's plaintive letter to her from Hollywood in the late thirties ("Let's do a fine show together"), his "unofficial" advice on *Porgy and Bess*, and his "walloping" new hit *Lady in the Dark*. Crawford approached the composer and learned that he had been "playing around" with music based on an obscure novella, written in 1885 by British humorist and former contributor to *Punch* Thomas Anstey Guthrie (who signed himself "F. Anstey"). *Tinted Venus* was the story of another goddess. Instead of the silver-painted deity of *Shakuntala* fame, this one was more akin to Galatea in the Pygmalion legend. The tinted Venus is a statue brought accidentally to life by an ordinary barber who impulsively slips his fiancée's engagement ring on the statue's finger. The goddess comes to life and becomes involved in the romantic entanglements of mortals in "Ozone Heights" before returning to her heavenly realm.

Crawford was intrigued by the story that involved two conflicting views of experience ("the world of mundane, conventional human behavior, and the free untrammeled world of the gods") that promised social meaning and musical entertainment.[4] With Weill's approval, she enlisted Sam and Bella Spewack to write the book (Sam dropped out early on) and hired humorist Ogden Nash, who referred to himself as a "worsifier," instead of a "versifier," to write the lyrics with a "light touch and just the right social punch." With Wildberg onboard as associate producer to look after the financing, she was soon jarred out of her complacency by Spewack's unfocused script, called *One Man's Venus*, written with Marlene Dietrich in mind.

Crawford and Kurt Weill had doubts about Spewack's writing, but their enthusiasm for the film star obscured their appreciation for the script's weaknesses. In September, producer and composer traveled to Hollywood to enlist Dietrich. She invited them to her home and greeted the suppliants at the door in silk lounging pajamas. Crawford marveled that she looked exactly as she did in film. "It was nice to find that a star could live up to one's expectations," Crawford quipped.[5]

Disparate Worlds

As Crawford was spinning the Galatea story to Dietrich, she also had two other shows to monitor. *The Perfect Marriage* by Samson Raphaelson was in rehearsal, and *Porgy and Bess* was running on Broadway to enchanting reviews and audiences humming "Summer Time" and "I Got Plenty O' Nuttin." Despite her demanding schedule, Crawford was as determined as Kurt Weill to interest Dietrich in the musical.

As producer and composer described the musical to the film star, Dietrich was attentive and interested but gave no hint of her inclination one way or the other. "She had, we were soon to find out," Crawford mused, "a most elusive quality."[6]

Accustomed to eccentric behavior from stars, Crawford was startled by Dietrich's interludes with a musical saw to accompany her singing of the Brecht-Weill "Surabaya-Johnny" from *Happy End*. At first, Crawford was mesmerized by the actress' performance on the strange instrument:

[W]hen Marlene placed that huge saw securely between her elegant legs and began to play, I was more than a little startled. It was an ordinary saw about five feet high and was played with a violin bow. We would talk about the show for a while, then Marlene would take up the musical saw and begin to play; that, we soon found out, was the cue that talk was finished for the evening.[7]

Night after night of discussions, followed by Dietrich's musical performances, soon strained Crawford's "mid-western mind."[8] Aware that the film star could not make up her mind ("Marlene couldn't, or wouldn't"), Crawford decided to return to New York to oversee the completion of the script. Dietrich promised to come to New York to give them an answer.

When she eventually arrived in Manhattan, Dietrich telephoned from the St. Regis Hotel on East Fifty-fifth Street and invited Crawford and Weill to her suite for more discussions. Crawford grumbled, "I hoped she'd left that damned musical saw in California, because I didn't plan to spend any more evenings listening to it."[9]

Once they resumed their talks, they were no closer to a commitment from Dietrich in Manhattan than they had been in Hollywood. Each day, the star would go to the Metropolitan Museum of Art to look at paintings and statues of Venus. She bought reproductions of the Venuses and bolts of light gray chiffon that she draped around herself in the style of the latest Venus she had seen during the afternoon. After discovering some twelve or fifteen different Venuses, she developed a fondness for the Callipygian Venus (meaning, in Crawford's opinion, "the Venus with the beautiful buttocks"), she decided that was her "Venus-to-be."[10]

Crawford became more and more frustrated with Dietrich's nightly fashion shows. "She looked divine in all her chiffon creations and poses," the Midwesterner remarked, "but what it had to do with our show was not sufficiently clear for us to express an educated opinion."[11]

Theatrical good sense finally intervened, and Crawford and Weill colluded to bring the film star to the Forty-fourth Street Theatre to listen to Dietrich's voice in a large space. Once on the bare stage, Dietrich sang "Surabaya-Johnny" in a "small voice choked with timidity." Even though producer and composer had difficulty hearing her from the third row, they remained undaunted.[12] Crawford was now aware that "if Marlene was going to do our show we would have to use a mike of some kind—perhaps put microphones in the foots," a practice far from standard in 1943.[13]

Crawford wanted to open the show in the fall and proceeded to force a commitment from the star. With an Equity contract in her pocket, Crawford went to the St. Regis only to find Dietrich's fifteen suitcases assembled for departure. Crawford asked with unmasked surprise, "You're leaving?" "Yes, my darling, I have the most terrible headache," the actress replied. Crawford thought her headache couldn't possibly match the one she was about to have and reached for the unsigned contract in her raincoat pocket. Suddenly, she had a wicked idea![14]

Crawford produced a "pick-me-up" that she kept for use during the long nights of technical rehearsals and gave the caffeine-laced tonic to the wavering star. In a restored condition, Dietrich signed.[15] Crawford justified the use of stimulants as a sign of her own desperation: "We wanted her, thought her perfect for the part, and had to have a commitment to move ahead."[16]

With signed contract in hand, Crawford turned to Spewack's unfinished script—and decided to fire the writer. The playwright had not developed the theme that Crawford wanted: the irreconcilable differences between the world of conventional human beings and the unrestrained world of the gods. Kurt Weill and Ogden Nash agreed with her estimation of the script, and, after serious deliberations, they decided that someone would have to tell the playwright. "What a mess!" Crawford wailed.[17]

Nevertheless, the state of affairs was only going to get messier. Before they involved another writer (Ogden Nash had suggested his friend and New Yorker colleague humorist S. J. "Sid" Perelman), their producer had to tell Bella Spewack that they were terminating her contract.

Crawford summoned Spewack to her office, whereupon she conveyed their decision and the writer fell over on the sofa, where she was seated, "in a dead faint." Rattled by the fainting, Crawford got a glass of water to revive Spewack who recovered and asked, "What did you say? Crawford told her, word for word, whereupon she fainted a second time. Crawford took stronger measures and produced smelling salts from the corner pharmacy. When Spewack revived the second time, she hurled epithets at Crawford, threatened to sue, settled for $10,000 in severance pay, and never again spoke to Cheryl Crawford or to Kurt Weill.[18]

Sid Perelman was hired to write the musical book, and, with the addition of choreographer Agnes de Mille of Oklahoma! fame, the creative team was again complete. Perelman, Nash, and Weill developed a workable script at the Harvard Club between martinis and lunches. The contemporary, New York–based musical book, now called *One Touch of Venus*, clearly set forth the conflict between two disparate worlds.

In her enthusiasm for hiring Marlene Dietrich, Crawford had ignored the fact that the actress also lived astride the disparate worlds of Hollywood and Broadway. When Crawford sent the new script to Dietrich and telephoned the star for her reaction, she learned that Dietrich did not like the musical book at all. The film star called it "vulgar and profane." Crawford talked rapidly about the virtues of the show and made a date to call the star again in a few days for her final answer. "From the way she sounded," Crawford said, "I feared we'd lost her."[19]

Crawford then arranged for Kurt Weill to speak to Dietrich. When the composer asked if she had read the script, she answered in a slow, deliberate voice, "Kurt, I cannot play this play; it is too sexy and profane." She concluded, "It really is impossible for me to play it," adding, "I have a daughter who is nineteen years old, and for me to get up on the stage and exhibit my legs is now impossible." Crawford reported that the enraged composer started screaming in German: "How dare you? Have you lost your sense of values?" Nevertheless, Dietrich remained adamant.[20]

Now they were back to their earlier predicament: they had a script, but no star. Reminded of her Quaker proverb ("When you pray, move your feet"), Crawford began a star-search. She telephoned agents and sent scripts to actresses appropriate for the role—Gertrude Lawrence, Lenora Corbett, and Vera Zorina—and received a variety of responses. Gertrude Lawrence and Lenora Corbett simply did not want to do the show; Vera Zorina wanted her then-husband, George Balanchine, to choreograph, not that "de Mille woman."[21] After her Group Theatre experience, Crawford was not in the habit of letting actors make decisions for her. Forthwith, she declined to release de Mille.

Jean Dalrymple, the show's press agent and Crawford's good friend, encouraged her to consider Mary Martin, whose Broadway-bound show had just closed in Boston. Crawford protested: "That skinny thing with a Texas accent to play Venus?"[22] Although not a Broadway leading lady, Martin had stopped a show on Broadway in 1938 with a sultry rendition of "My Heart Belongs to Daddy" in Cole Porter's *Leave It to Me*.

After two interviews with Crawford's team, Martin was offered the role but had her own reservations. She did not see herself as either Venus de Milo or Marlene Dietrich. Nevertheless, her husband Richard Halliday, a story editor at Paramount and her manager, took her to the

Metropolitan Museum of Art to look at the many physical varieties of the Venus statues, even one "noticeably broad of beam."[23] Once Kurt Weill played the score for her, she fell in love with "That's Him," and the seduction was complete.

Miracle Workers

With Mary Martin and Agnes de Mille onboard, Crawford turned to the missing link in the creative team—the director. Convinced that the show needed a "realist," she telephoned her Group cohort Elia Kazan.[24] Although he had never directed a musical, Kazan had directed plays with large casts, elaborate sets, and complicated movement, and Crawford had "a hunch he'd be good at it."[25] Moreover, he had two successes on Broadway in the 1942–43 season, Thornton Wilder's *The Skin of Her Teeth* with Tallulah Bankhead and Colin Clements' *Harriet* with Helen Hayes, and was intrigued with the idea of a musical to round out his Broadway credits. In addition, he was celebrated for saving difficult plays, as the jingle contrived by the writers of *Harriet* implied: "Kazan, Kazan/The miracle man/Call him in/As soon as you can."[26]

The previous spring *Oklahoma!*—with closely integrated song, dance, and storyline—had revolutionized the musical theater, but Kazan found that *One Touch of Venus* was less promising, with its fabled story about a classical statue that comes to life in New York City and falls in love with a mortal. When Kazan asked Kurt Weill, whom he knew from *Johnny Johnson*, why he should direct the show, the composer argued persuasively that he wanted the musical directed as a drama with the songs as a continuation of the dialogue, not in the old-fashioned, out-front staging of traditional musicals.

Crawford set up a luncheon between Kazan and Mary Martin in the Oak Room of the Plaza Hotel. Toward the end of the luncheon, the director wanted to know how the actress intended to play Venus. "I was afraid you were going to ask me that," she said. "I haven't the vaguest idea." Martin reminded him that she had mostly worked in films and didn't know how to develop a part. "I think in terms of movement, and how I will walk," she said. "If I can work out the walk, the tempo, then everything else comes naturally."[27]

Kazan parried with the suggestion that he would convey Venus' predicament to her in musical terms:

> In our world, everybody is in such a mad rush, and in Agnes' ballet when Venus comes to life, people are like puppets going wild, up and down the streets, rush, rush, rush! Venus is the only sane one in the world, and she

thinks everyone she sees is crazy. . . . they have no joy, no fun, so your tempo and your movement should be absolutely legato. Everything else is staccato.[28]

Eyewitnesses later acknowledged that Kazan's greatest contribution to the show was his work with Mary Martin. He focused on her performance, making her, people said, less-mannered, more down-to-earth, less of a soubrette than she had previously been.[29]

When rehearsals began in August of 1943, the cast was complete, with Kenny Baker, of radio and film, as the male lead; John Boles, also from films, as the art collector who buys the statue of Venus and transports it to New York; Broadway's Paula Laurence, as the second female lead; and Sono Osato, the lead dancer for de Mille's choreography.

Kazan gave the star the same notes in rehearsal ("Your tempo, your movement, should be legato, slow and graceful") that he imparted to her during their lunch at the Plaza. He also imbued her with the freedom to find the role as well.[30] He was not as nurturing with the writers and made enemies of Perelman and Nash. At one point, Kazan stopped the rehearsal to think through the staging, but his thought-process was interrupted by the writers who pointed to their half-page, single-spaced description of business for the scene set down in the script. Kazan turned on them: "What do you think my business is in being here? I'm the director; I have to think of the business!"[31] Crawford observed Perelman and Nash retreat without further argument.

The Boston tryout brought hostilities into the open. Kazan was dissatisfied with Perelman's book. (He called it "foolish and boring.") In turn, the writer insisted that Kazan lacked a sense of humor, and Agnes de Mille found that he had no visual sense. "He has a wonderful ear," the choreographer remarked, although "not for music, but for speech."[32] Many in the company (actors and dancers) feared and disliked the director, calling him "an arrogant bully" and "common and vulgar with women."[33]

Despite the hostilities and backbiting, the show was an enormous success by the time it reached Broadway. Critics agreed that *One Touch of Venus* was the best new musical to open on Broadway since *Oklahoma!*[34] Kazan credited their success, not to himself, the "miracle man," but to the "real miracle workers" of the show: Mary Martin ("She did everything asked of her better than any of us could have hoped"), Agnes de Mille ("the most strong-minded stage artist I've known"), and Sono Osato ("a poem in movement").[35]

Crawford had already hired de Mille when she and Weill went to New Haven to see a tryout of *Away We Go* (later changed to *Oklahoma!*). They were enchanted with the choreography, even though they thought the show would fail. "So much for our judgment of one of America's biggest hits!" Crawford chuckled. Later, she took pride in the fact that "engaging Agnes was one of my better decisions."[36]

The strong-minded de Mille soon gave orders to Kazan to clear the stage of all scenery for her dances. "She wanted space! And she knew what to do with it," Kazan recalled.[37] Moreover, he soon realized that for her fanciful ballets, de Mille would not tolerate the show directed as if it were a drama, and not a musical. De Mille contributed "Forty Minutes for Lunch" in the first act, where Venus meets New York workers in Rockefeller Center, and the second-act dream ballet, "Venus in Ozone Heights," where Venus discovers suburbia.[38]

Once she put the creative team together and found them a mismatched, fractious bunch, Crawford kept a low profile. In fact, she turned her attention to what she could reasonably influence with Jack Wildberg—the show's financing.

Venus Rising

One Touch of Venus set the model for a Crawford production: talented artists and cost-saving measures. The notoriously frugal Crawford (when courting Marlene Dietrich, Kurt Weill stayed at the luxurious Beverly Hills Hotel, while Crawford found more modest accommodations for herself) established a budget for *One Touch of Venus* at one hundred and forty thousand dollars with the intention of bringing the show into New York for less. Moreover, in order to get the actress to sign a contract, she promised that her costumes would be "marvelous," and, "we'd solve her concern about her long neck."[39]

The famous couturier Mainbocher, who had never worked on Broadway, was enlisted to solve the problem. When first approached, the fashion designer, who looked like a businessman instead of a "tall, effete, very grand" couturier, insisted that he had never designed clothes for a theatrical production, and refused outright.[40] Crawford urged him to listen to the score, unaware that Mainbocher adored music and had wanted to be an opera singer. They gathered in Kurt Weill's apartment, and, when Martin sang "That's Him," she picked up a small chair and placed it in front of the designer. She turned the chair around backwards, and, sitting sideways, sang to him. When she ended the song, Mainbocher said, "I will do your clothes for the show if you will promise me one thing. Promise me you'll always sing this song that way. Take the chair down to the footlights, sing across the orchestra to the audience as if it were just one person." For the next two years, Mary Martin sang "That's Him" exactly as she had rendered the song in Mainbocher's presence.[41]

Martin's fourteen costume changes and hats plus the black velvet ribbon that the designer placed around the actress' neck, cost, by Crawford's calculations, between fifteen to twenty thousand dollars—"small change by current standards," she later remarked.[42] At the time she complained that she paid more for Mary Martin's costumes than any producer had ever paid for costumes in a musical. When audiences applauded Martin's entrances, some of Crawford's pain over the extravagance was alleviated.

Convinced that the show would be a hit, Crawford put some of her earnings from *Porgy and Bess* into the financing, which was "easy for a change," but she had spoken *before* the Boston tryout.[43] Crawford's adroit management of the ensuing problems with the scenery (the coffinlike gray velveteen drapes were discarded for a slender portal adorned by doves), the set piece (the barber's house looked like a "troglodyte outhouse" and was redesigned), the "vulgar" line of dialogue that Mary Martin had been saying for weeks and now objected to, and an ending that lacked "something upbeat," resulted in an award-winning display of ego-strength and teeth-gritting determination on Crawford's part. Only the fact that she needed to throw in another twenty-five thousand dollars to make the changes rattled the penurious Crawford. John Wildberg borrowed the money from Lee Shubert, who had seen the Boston opening, found the show agreeable, and offered a cash loan and the Imperial Theatre.

Dissatisfied with the show's downbeat finale, Crawford implemented de Mille's idea that Venus return as an "ordinary" young girl, an art student, dressed in a simple Mainbocher dress and hat—a sort of down-home reincarnation. In the final version, "a clap of thunder sounds," Venus disappears, and the stage goes dark for a brief transition. When the lights come back up, Venus is standing on the pedestal as a statue once again. The barber speaks to the statue, asking, "Why did you leave? You said I'd never be alone again." Then he sings a refrain from their love ballad, "Speak low to me, speak love to me."[44]

At that moment, the young girl, who might be Venus' country cousin, enters. The barber looks at the statue of Venus and then he looks at the girl. He asks her where she comes from and she tells him Ozone Heights. He asks if she likes it there and she says she wouldn't think of living any place else, thus validating the audience's world. He tells her his name, and, when she starts to say her name, he stops her. "You don't have to tell me, I know," he says. She takes his arm, their eyes meet, and they walk off, looking into each other's eyes as the curtain falls. A satisfied Cheryl Crawford pronounced the ending "marvelous!" Others viewed the happy ending in which love transcends death as a subliminal offering to wartime audiences.[45]

With new, airier settings and further cuts in the book and score, the show opened on Broadway in early October and ran for 567 performances. Its satisfied producer said, "I had the hit I had wanted: the show *was* original, meaningful, and entertaining."[46] Moreover, the musical established Mary Martin as a Broadway star and made a profit of two hundred thousand dollars. Although not the sole producer (Lee Shubert took first money), Crawford received enough money from the show to declare that, with the roll of the *Venus* dice, her luck had changed.

Despite stunning reviews and a show settling in for a long run, Cheryl Crawford was homeless. She had given up her apartment when she went to Boston and was waiting to move into a new one. It was the height of wartime, New York was overcrowded, and hotels had three-day restrictions. Upon returning to New York for the load-in at the theater, she checked into a hotel in the East Forties and promptly forgot about the restriction. The day before the opening, she was evicted.

"I begged a bed in someone's apartment," she reported without identifying the Samaritan.[47] She recalled that she slept most of the day on October 7. In the late afternoon, a friend called to make certain she did not sleep through the opening. Although she didn't plan to attend the performance, she offered to cook dinner, if someone would bring over a chicken and potatoes.

Famous for her "one-dish meals," Crawford was once described as a "misplaced home economics teacher" and often photographed standing in her kitchen wearing an apron and preparing her favorite dishes—ham and noodle casserole or pot-roasted chicken basted with a quarter pound of butter.[48] On the eve of the Broadway opening of *One Touch of Venus*, the chicken pot-roast served as comfort food prepared by the producer facing a momentous opening night.

Crawford timed her appearance at the theater to coincide with the final scene and the enthusiastic applause. She then went to a party on Park Avenue, given by friends of Mary Martin. When asked by an enthusiastic couple, "How was opening night?," the show's producer answered, "I don't know. I wasn't there," and detected the disbelief in their faces that silently asked, "What kind of producer are you?" Crawford made no effort to explain the theater's opening-night traditions. "There's nothing on earth you can do any more," she mused, "and you might as well rest your nervous system for whatever fate may be when the papers hit the street."[49]

Nevertheless, the reviews guaranteed long lines at the Imperial box office the next day. Lewis Nichols, writing for the *New York Times* in Brooks Atkinson's place (he had been reassigned to Europe as a war correspondent), called the show "complete with freshness, an adult manner and lavishness of display," and Louis Kronenberger compared it to "a trick perfume." There were paeans to Kurt Weill ("his best"), Mary Martin ("wit, grace, endearing charm"), Agnes de Mille ("impish, imaginative, beautiful dances"), and Sono Osato ("graceful, alive, beautiful, the toast of autumn").[50] With one exception, all agreed that *One Touch of Venus* was certain to be a smash hit. Only Burton Rascoe expressed disappointment that the creators had never agreed on whether *One Touch of Venus* would be "something arty, sophisticated and abstract," or "something like a Minsky burlesque only more literate."[51]

Most remarkable among all of the words written that October about the new show in town was the attention given to its producer. Ward Morehouse summed up Crawford's contribution: "Cheryl Crawford has performed Broadway a service in bringing along a musical show that breaks sharply away from pattern and accepted routine." He concluded that her taste and courage brought "new and needed life to a season that has been fearfully meager."[52]

At season's end, Crawford' efforts were vindicated. *One Touch of Venus* garnered the first Donaldson Awards given by the profession for best musical direction (Kazan), best female lead performance (Martin), best male supporting performance (Baker), best choreography (de Mille), and best dancer (Osato).

Sexual Politics

Mary Martin, on the other hand, spoke of Crawford as one of the special women in her professional life—"a brilliant, creative veteran of Broadway and of theater."[53] The actress's close working relationships and personal friendships with three women—Cheryl Crawford (soon to be a Connecticut neighbor) and actresses Janet Gaynor and Jean Arthur (whom she succeeded as Peter Pan)—have been scrutinized in recent feminist writings. Martin's onstage and offstage performances have been seen as enabling her to conceal her life as a "closeted bisexual."[54]

Even theater people, celebrated for dismissing middle-class mores, were cautious in the 1940s and 1950s about their public images. Those like Mary Martin, Margaret Webster, and Cheryl Crawford, who achieved fame in those decades, walked a careful line, because the public equated homosexuality with moral weakness and with communism. One solution to such opprobrium was the passing marriage. Katharine Cornell and Guthrie McClintic (and also the Lunts) successfully sustained the legend of the happily married couple in which the male partner enabled the actress-wife to carry on her work without hindrances of rumor and gossip columnists. When writing about *One Touch of Venus*, Kazan suggested that Martin and Halliday had a passing marriage. He represented the view of the theatrical community when he said, "I cannot believe the sexual aspects of these unions are of great importance; that energy passes into their work."[55]

Another solution adopted by the Mary Martins of stage and film to assure success in their careers was to perform only straight roles. Martin's performances as Venus (*One Touch of Venus*), Nellie Forbush (*South Pacific*), Annie Oakley (*Annie Get Your Gun*), Maria von Trapp (*The Sound of Music*), and her signature role of Peter Pan (the boy who wouldn't grow up) masked her offstage life and made the nature of her romantic friendships with women difficult to penetrate. As Stacy Wolf reasoned, "Martin's money, her well-publicized marriage to Halliday, her child, and her visibility in one of theater's most popular forms could both protect her and insulate her."[56]

Cheryl Crawford, on the other hand, made no effort to conceal the fact that there was no man in her life, and her sexual preference was commonly known among professional associates. Actress Anne Jackson, married to Eli Wallach, described her former producer as "tom-boyish" with a peculiar habit of opening doors for younger women.[57] Another associate recalled surprise upon first hearing her "deep voice" on the telephone. "When she answered, I always thought it was a man," playwright Romulus Linney recalled. "It wasn't, it was Cheryl, a woman I came to admire as a person as well as a legend."[58]

Despite her "butch" mannerisms and lesbian lifestyle, Crawford's *public* image signaled to the entertainment world that her work as a producer was her entire existence. Her strategy, unlike a musical comedy star's legend, was a simpler achievement. Her commercial independence and avoidance of public displays of romantic attachments precluded the need for more elaborate protective mechanisms, such as marriage and children. Crawford's behind-the-scenes work as a producer essentially kept her out of the limelight. With the exception of show-time interviews and opening-night appearances, she remained out of the public eye. Nevertheless, within the inner circle of professional associates, who knew her dual identities, she was vulnerable. Smarting over her late decision not to produce *West Side Story*, playwright Arthur Laurents described her as "the stereotypical butch lesbian: short and stocky, mannish garb and hair, dry and humorless, with an alert eye for a pretty, available girl."[59]

Backstage Politics

Another well-known fact held sacred by the theater community is that very little ends with opening night. Despite excellent reviews, clamorous audiences, long box-office lines, and prestigious awards, the backstage atmosphere at the Imperial Theatre continued to be fractious. Ill will and bruised egos were in abundance. Perelman loathed Kenny Baker for his anti-Semitic remarks; Mary Martin and Jean Dalrymple tossed invectives at one another; Elia Kazan's disinterest in the show provoked hurt feelings among the cast; and Kurt Weill blamed Crawford's stinginess for the show's less than satisfactory publicity.[60]

Crawford downplayed the backstage strife as "a few personality clashes." She was sanguine about the fact that musicals were "apt to have more problems and more temperaments" among their large casts of actors, chorus, dancers, and musicians.[61] Whenever she inquired if all was running smoothly, the production stage manager always assured her that *One Touch of Venus* was a cakewalk in contrast to his previous job on the *Ziegfeld Follies*. Even her business partner praised her coolness during the ups and downs surrounding *One Touch of Venus*. "I think you have done a magnificent job," Wildberg wrote to her after the episodes with Bella Spewack and Marlene Dietrich, "handling the many difficult temperaments you have had to deal with."[62]

In her role as producer, Crawford had developed a technique for dealing with bruised egos and festering ill will among creative personalities. "When the shouting would get loud and the reasoning impossible," she explained, "I'd just retire to my hotel room or apartment and read Walt Whitman . . . until the dust settled." With some exaggeration, she added, "Sometimes it took a few days, but when I figured the adversaries had tired out, I'd go down and make a decision.[63]

Despite the supportive tone of Wildberg's earlier letter, he had grown concerned for Crawford's seeming lack of gratitude for his work as partner and associate producer. He had, after all, established her at Maplewood and developed the funding for *Porgy and Bess* to move to Broadway. In

September of 1942, while *Venus* was still in development, he reminded her that he had entered into the partnership "in good faith because I think you are one of the smartest woman in the theatre." He went so far as to remind her that "a partnership is like a marriage—you enter into it for better or for worse—and certainly in our case we entered into it with our eyes wide open." He ends with an invitation to sit down and discuss if "we really haven't captured the Bluebird without knowing it."[64]

By the following June, as the partners were projecting *Venus* to be a potential mega-hit, Crawford moved to renegotiate their partnership agreement. Whereas their original contract called for a fifty-fifty split on all direct profits after $10,000 on a venture, Crawford now asked for a seventy-thirty split in her favor based upon the fact that she had raised $90,000 of the *Venus* money and worked on casting, contracts, budgeting and planning for both *Porgy and Bess* and *Venus*.[65] Wildberg countered with a sixty-forty split on *Venus* and fifty-fifty on the indirect profits (souvenir programs, etc.). In the terms of the new contract, he asked for and was given the freedom to produce with others, and not exclusively with Crawford, as had been the case.

In his letter to her, written four months before *Venus* opened, Wildberg expressed concern for Crawford's health and warned that he doesn't think she can produce a large show, like *One Touch of Venus*, by herself. "It is just too big an undertaking for any one person who isn't completely strong and 100% healthy," he advised.[66]

By January 29, 1944, the partners had renegotiated a new partnership to be billed as "Cheryl Crawford presents." [67] They would continue to quarrel over financial matters until their partnership was effectively dissolved in January 1946, and Crawford would not enter into another business partnership for another twenty years.

Crawford ignored, as best she could, the internecine conflicts backstage at the Forty-sixth Street Theatre where the show had moved to accommodate its long run. In the summer of 1944, she had more important concerns: the health of her star. New York theaters were not air-conditioned and many shows routinely closed during the summer months, or went on tour. The Forty-sixth Street Theatre was cooled by a fan and ice system, but, on stage, the temperature, with heat generated by the stage lights, could reach 112 degrees. Mary Martin collapsed with heat prostration following one matinee when the ice for the system had not been delivered to the theater. Crawford, the ever-diligent problem-solver, removed an air-conditioner from her new apartment and installed it in the star's dressing room. [68] During another performance, Martin, allergic to the stage dust stirred up by the trailing folds of her Mainbocher negligee, lost her voice while singing "That's Him." Crawford summoned the house doctor, who prescribed allergy shots to restore the singer's voice.[69]

While attending to her star and avoiding the backstage bickering, Crawford worked on her next independent production, Samson Raphaelson's *The Perfect Marriage*, with Miriam Hopkins and Victor Jory, and on the coast-to-coast tour of *Venus*. Crawford persuaded Mary Martin, who was now a big musical star, that the road was still important to building a theatrical career, as it had been for the Lunts, Katharine Cornell, Helen Hayes, and Jessica Tandy.

For a going-away present, Crawford gave Mary Martin a trunk full of books. As a serious collector of books, many she unearthed in out-of-the-way bookstalls, Crawford often presented gifts of prose and poetry to friends on special occasions. Martin's gift featured two biographies of Sarah Bernhardt, plays by George Bernard Shaw, pamphlets on the Moscow Art Theatre and the genius of Eleonora Duse, and essays on the art of acting by London's famous actor-manager Henry Irving and French drama critic Françisque Sarcey. The actress volunteered that it took two years to "wade" through the many tomes.[70]

With *One Touch of Venus* and *Porgy and Bess* both making handsome profits and matters settled for a time with Jack Wildberg, Crawford decided to live like the Hollywood stereotype of a Broadway producer. She rented a spacious apartment overlooking the East River on Fifty-second Street, bought a fine car and new clothes, and acquired packets of books in first editions. She ordered a smart black dress from Valentina to enhance her new image as a successful New York producer. She also bought six expensive hats from Fifth Avenue shops. She wore the dress once, looked imposing in it, and retired it to a closet in favor of her tailored suits in sky or field colors. Detaching herself from the hats took longer, she wryly suggested. Although she never wore any of the hats, she went about carrying them in hand as she went about her affairs until one by one she left all six in taxicabs.[71]

Uppermost in Cheryl Crawford's mind was the fact that her success with musical theater had not been a onetime thing. The Venus touch had reinforced her reputation as a singular producer of musicals. *Brigadoon* was in her future, but not before she veered into the noncommercial arena to join forces with two other producers-in-skirts to stage Shakespeare and modern classics as experiments in repertory.

7

PRODUCERS IN SKIRTS

... I was never cured of my dream.

—*Cheryl Crawford*

The coy label awarded by male producers to the distaff side applied to very few women in the New York theater in the forties.[1] Cheryl Crawford was virtually alone as an independent producer, shortly to be joined by Margaret Webster and Eva Le Gallienne in a doomed enterprise called the American Repertory Theatre. Crawford's collaboration with the Anglo-American director and the London-born actress grew out of boredom with her long-running "cash" machines—*Porgy and Bess* and *One Touch of Venus*. She mused, "So I was living well. I had money in the bank; *Venus* and *Porgy* were flourishing. It was lovely. And it was dull."[2]

She was lifted out of her doldrums by an unexpected encounter with Carson McCullers. They shared the same dentist and their friendship evolved over several visits in the waiting room. Even though Crawford was fifteen years older than the Southern novelist, McCullers liked her immensely and received her first taste of the "baffling and mysterious new world" of the theater from Crawford's many tales of theatrical shenanigans.[3]

Within a few months of their acquaintance, the novelist described her feelings for her special friend as a disquieting infatuation, although she ascribed no sexual feelings toward her on the part of the older woman. Virginia Spencer Carr attributed the writer's discomfort over being "once again attracted to a female" as an emotional holdover from the unhappy end of her love affair with Swiss-born writer Annemarie Clarac-Schwarzenbach, who died in an automobile accident. McCullers was fearful that she would ruin her new friendship by an unwarranted display of affection.[4]

The tall, thin, and chronically ill author of *The Heart Is a Lonely Hunter* and *Reflections in a Golden Eye* introduced Cheryl Crawford to the unconventional world of 7 Middagh Street in Brooklyn Heights. The three-story brownstone with elaborate Tudor trim was leased by George Davis, novelist and former fiction editor for *Harper's Bazaar*, and turned into a home where writers, artists, and friends could live and work for a modest fee. The assortment of writers and artists, living and working at one time or another in "February House," as the brownstone was dubbed by diarist Anaïs Nin for its many residents born in that month, included in 1940, Wystan ("W. H.") Auden, George Davis, Carson McCullers, Gypsy Rose Lee, Oliver Smith, Benjamin Britten, and Peter Pears.[5]

Always on the lookout for new (and affordable} talent, Crawford was taken with the paintings and sketches of the young designer living in the attic of the Middagh Street house. She hired Oliver Smith, who was also engaged by Agnes de Mille's dance company in the early forties, to design scenery for *The Perfect Marriage* and later *Brigadoon*. Throughout his long career, he would design a stream of musicals that included *My Fair Lady*, *West Side Story*, and *Hello, Dolly!*

Carson's ill health and Crawford's all-consuming efforts to satisfy the needs of the new production of *The Tempest* and the a-borning American Repertory Theatre temporarily eroded the emotional connection between the women. Crawford did not lose touch entirely with McCullers, who was stricken with the first of three strokes in the late forties.

During their work on *The Rose Tattoo*, Tennessee Williams gathered Crawford into his "crew of eccentrics" that included Frank Merlo and Carson McCullers. Crawford warmed to the unique display of friendship between the playwright and the novelist, which mirrored her own close relationship with Williams that developed over the years as she produced a quartet of his plays.[6] Even Crawford's unwillingness to produce *The Member of the Wedding* (she suggested that McCullers "throw it in an ash can") failed to put a quietus to their friendship.[7] Crawford issued invitations to parties, offers of housing in her East River apartment when Crawford traveled abroad, and weekend visits to Crawford's Connecticut home, where McCullers, listening to Mary Martin singing songs around the piano, identified with the singer's "gamine personality."[8]

The Enchanted Island

Although Crawford and Margaret Webster continued to occupy offices on the upper floors of the St. James Theatre, they had not initiated a joint project since *Family Portrait*. Webster's string of successes with Shakespeare plays continually reminded Crawford of the Bard's potential. She mused to herself that she was "fascinated by difficulty, teased by challenge, hungry for something estimable," and the imperfectly written *Perfect Marriage* filled none of those requirements.[9] Moreover, shortly after *Venus* opened, she discovered that Webster was contemplating *The Tempest* as her next project, and, Webster's partner of some years, actress Eva Le Gallienne, had gone so far as to devise a scheme whereby to solve the technical difficulties of staging Prospero's enchanted island. Le Gallienne's design featured a large turntable built up with precipices and caves for Ariel and Caliban's magical appearances.

Once the two women handed her the means of recreating Shakespeare's island, Crawford, in Webster's words, "beetled at it, was abrupt as always, reread the play," and signed on as producer.[10]

Crawford calculated the difficulties (and costs) of recreating the physical demands of *The Tempest*: the ship at sea, a wild storm, Caliban's cave, Prospero's cell, and Ariel's miraculous appearances. Moreover, she knew that casting would be daunting: "How do you find an Ariel you would believe 'could ride on the curl'd clouds,' and a Caliban who is at once 'a monster and pitiable'?"[11]

Perhaps a holdover from her Guild days, Crawford was closely involved in casting. Together, she and Webster chose Arnold Moss to play Prospero; Vera Zorina, the dancer-singer-actress whom Crawford had considered for Venus, for Ariel; and the famous black actor, Canada Lee, who had appeared in Orson Welles's all-black version of *Macbeth* and in Richard Wright's *Native Son*, for Caliban.

At a time when nontraditional casting was unheard of and black actors were stereotyped in servant roles or musical revues, Margaret Webster was engaged in a ground-breaking project with actor–concert singer Paul Robeson that resulted in the first appearance of a black actor on Broadway, in the role of Othello. Determined not to break with the Robeson precedent and with the goal of creating more diverse employment for black actors, Webster, with Crawford's support, cast Canada Lee, who had given up a boxing career following an eye injury to become a film and stage actor.[12] In addition to Robeson's *The Emperor Jones*, Crawford also brought Canada Lee's *Native Son* to Maplewood and was enthusiastic over the resourceful actor, who shared her commitment to a theater of social significance, as "an inevitable Caliban."[13]

Shakespeare's clowns, Trinculo and Stephano, posed the final hurdle. During her clown search, Crawford learned that George Voskovec and Jan Werich, alias "V" and "W," actors and political satirists from Prague who had escaped Hitler's armies, were in residence at the Cleveland Play-house. They auditioned in New York with their "monster," an inspired bit of clown business rendered as a four-legged monster with a "forward and backward" voice. When fully extended, the long green-cloth monster had an actor's head at one end and a second actor in the flat tail that flapped and shouted on cue.

The Broadway production of *The Tempest* paved the way for the American Repertory Theatre. Despite their twenty years of collective experience, Crawford, Webster, and Le Gallienne were deceived by the triumph of *The Tempest* into believing that a classical repertory company was possible within the environs of Broadway. Critics and audiences had been mesmerized by Webster's bold shift of Prospero's famous Act IV speech to the play's end ("Our revels now are ended . . ."). At the close of Prospero's valedictory, the curtain fell on a substantial pageant that ran for three months. Crawford was further comforted by having produced a play of estimable substance.

In her comments written for the souvenir program, Crawford gushed that it had been a "long-cherished dream" of hers to produce *The Tempest* with its strange half-world of monsters and spirits, clowns and wizards, "enlaced" with real-world villainy and love. Reflecting upon the modern-day, gloomily cynical *The Perfect Marriage*, she wrote, "Our theatre is so full of fireplaces with sofas unnaturally placed before them, and with actors whose emotional crises are expressed by lighting cigarettes, that our theatrical imaginations have become stultified."[14]

Union Demands

Crawford met the young composer David Diamond at February House and heard the premiere of his "Second Symphony" conducted by Serge Koussevitzky. With Webster's consent, she invited Diamond to compose the musical score for *The Tempest*, eventually praised as one of the "most strikingly individual and beautiful scores in contemporary incidental music."[15] Nevertheless, the musicians' union was not impressed. "This piece is not a play at all," the union leaders decreed. "It is a musical; and as such it must have a minimum of twenty-two musicians in the pit, as provided in the union's contract for musicals."[16] By declaring the play "a musical," New York Local 802 of the American Federation of Musicians (AFM) required the same number of musicians as *Oklahoma!* and *One Touch of Venus*, even though Diamond had created the musical score for himself as conductor and eight musicians (an appropriate number for an "incidental" Broadway score). Crawford's projected expenses for music would double if she could not reverse the ruling.

Crawford challenged the union's decision, appealed to the head of the national office in Chicago, who deferred to the New York Local. At the end of negotiations, the AFM had devised a new category, called "a play with music," for the Broadway theater. In the new category, productions were required to employ a minimum of eight musicians in the pit, but the total length of the music played by them was not to exceed twenty minutes. The union leader warned Crawford: "If you don't abide by the ruling we close the show."[17]

The music was held to twenty minutes, expenses were met, and *The Tempest* was a box office success. Reflecting upon the affair, Webster said, "We were the pioneer guinea-pigs of this piece of enlightened union legislation."[18] However, the difficulties with the musicians' union fore-shadowed dire things to come for the American Repertory Theatre.

Exhilarated by triumphant reviews and swelling box office receipts, Crawford allowed her fervor to blind her to the perils of operating a rep-ertory company within the control of the trade unions. Unlike Webster and Le Gallienne, Crawford's familiarity with repertory was limited to the appearance of London's Old Vic company, which had staged four plays in rotating repertory on Broadway that same year. Observing Lau-rence Olivier as Henry IV, Oedipus, Dr. Ostrov (in *Uncle Vanya*), and Mr. Puff (in *The Critic*), she described his performances as "a revelation of the actor's art." More so than the ideal of repertory ("with plays ro-tating, actors could stay fresh and develop their talents in the variety of roles"), Crawford bought into the practicalities whereby "a worthy but less popular play would have to close quickly if it played every night."[19]

Crawford soon found herself one of three "middle-aged sirens" woo-ing backers, actors, and unions to little avail.[20] Later, she scorned her idealism and her misreading of the enthusiasm of audiences and critics for *The Tempest* and the Old Vic as their desire for a similar American company. Echoing her associates, she asked, "If England could have an Old Vic, why not the United States?"[21] Within a year, she would have her answer in devastating critical and financial terms.

Crawford also ignored her "mistake book," which she kept during *One Touch of Venus* to remind her of potential pitfalls in the business. Item One: "Don't sign for a theater until the star is signed." With hindsight, she was convinced that she could have gotten better terms from the Shuberts if she had signed Mary Martin *before* negotiating for a theater. Item Two: "Don't budget so closely that there's no leeway for unpredictable expenses." A lesson learned when she was caught short with last-minute scenery and costume changes on *Venus.*[22] In 1945, she ignored her checklist. The A.R.T. women signed for a theater *before* hiring stars and established a budget with no padding for unanticipated expenses.

A Quixotic Dream

At the beginning of the new repertory theater, Crawford welcomed the opportunity to work with two women who shared her artistic values, a lifestyle among a lesbian subculture, and a proven ability to work successfully within the male-dominated commercial theater.[23] As Le Gallienne's biographer suggested, Crawford, in turn, made an attractive partner because she shared the alternative lifestyle of the other women and was also an experienced producer.[24]

In contrast to the austerely countenanced Cheryl Crawford, attired in tailored designer suits, the garrulous Margaret Webster, known to all as "Peggy," was described in a *New Yorker* profile as wearing dowdy clothes and sensible shoes with "mannish" hair and "theatrical eyelashes" and distinguished by a voice that was "full, resonant, and glossy." Writer Barbara Heggie said that Peggy Webster resembled "a high school teacher who has dipped herself giddily into a pot of mascara."[25] In contrast, Eva Le Gallienne, or "Le G" to friends and coworkers, was three years older than the poker-faced producer from Ohio whose reputation for being a canny, close-mouthed manager and "an expert at combining high aspirations with rock-bottom costs" preceded her.[26]

Despite the assembled theatrical talents and years of experience among the three that portended a coequal partnership, Eva Le Gallienne quickly dominated the decision-making process. Described as a "tiny, beautiful, powerful, elegant woman," Le Gallienne, with wavy, short-cropped red hair brushed back from her face and penetrating blue eyes, was known for her assertive personality, self-assurance, and natural authority, although she was only five feet four inches tall.[27] Le Gallienne's strong personality and confidence in her knowledge of theater came to dominate and determine the future of the American Repertory Theatre.

Crawford was not originally included in the discussions for the new repertory theater, but Webster encouraged Le Gallienne to involve her, arguing that they needed an experienced business manager. Remarking on Crawford's appeal, Webster said, " . . . we found the business drive we lacked and a harder head with similar ideals inside it."[28]

In addition to Crawford's business acumen and connections, her theatrical background and alternative lifestyle avoided issues of personal revelations and ingrained prejudices against women spearheading the creation of a theatrical enterprise, or so they thought at the time. Although Le Gallienne knew Crawford only by her professional reputation as a successful, cost-cutting producer, she was impressed with Crawford's handling of *The Tempest.* "Not only did she prove herself a shrewd businesswoman," Le Gallienne observed, "but her calm and consistent good humor, her firmness in the face of trials that would have made most managers lose faith and abandon the struggle, had been invaluable in preserving the high morale of the company and guiding the venture to its ultimate success."[29]

During their preparations for *Family Portrait* and *The Tempest,* Crawford and Webster developed a comfortable and mutually respectful relationship as producer and director. Webster admired Crawford's taste and ability to mount a show with minimal fuss. In turn, Crawford respected Webster's record with Shakespeare's plays in past Broadway seasons. Le Gallienne was known to Crawford as the former producing director of the Civic Repertory Theatre and as an intensely professional actress. Nevertheless, she had little interaction with Le Gallienne prior to launching the new theater and failed to recognize her influence on Peggy Webster.

The success of *The Tempest* set the stage for the precipitous decision to create their ideal theater ten blocks from Broadway. In late-night sessions in Webster's West Twelfth Street apartment, Crawford's coproducers concentrated on choice of repertory and an elaborate touring circuit (an idea shortly scrapped). Crawford focused on the cost of mounting rotating productions, the recruitment of "name actors" to attract audiences, and the renting of a well-located theater. She came up with a figure of $300,000 to mount the six productions with an adequate reserve for operations. She readily admitted that considerable guesswork went into calculating an operating budget based on unnamed plays and unpredictable union demands. Nevertheless, Crawford believed that the various unions would cooperate with the promise of a full season's work for their members. To her everlasting chagrin, she soon learned that she was *wrong.*

As a successful commercial producer, Crawford's involvement as the third member of the undertaking was not entirely fortuitous. She steered the A.R.T. away from a tax exempt, nonprofit status and toward Broadway contracts and ticket prices. She was not altogether wrongheaded to do so. She calculated that Webster had directed seven profitable plays on Broadway. Nevertheless, those plays were not performed in rotating repertory, and, other than the actors' union, there were no union policies in place to accommodate the demands of rotating repertory, nor, operations for a not-for-profit theater.

After much searching, the women acquired the now-demolished International Theatre, formerly the Park Theatre, on Columbus Circle at Broadway and Fifty-ninth Street. (The International was later torn down to make way for the Coliseum, and, more recently, the Time Warner Building.) According to Crawford, the International was the only theater they could acquire "on a four-walls basis." (In the New York theater, the producer rents the building and supplies heat, light, and theatrical equipment.) The International had the advantage of a stage large enough to store scenery and costumes, thereby eliminating trucking costs. Its disadvantage was its location at Columbus Circle. Even though three subway lines converged there and parking lots were nearby, Columbus Circle, in those days, was considered far from Broadway where all theatrical activity was centered.[30] As it so happened, it was not far enough from Broadway, as the women soon learned.

In September 1945, they announced the creation of the A.R.T. to begin in the fall of the 1946–47 season. A twelve-page brochure, titled "Plan for the American Repertory Theatre," described the goals and plans for a permanent company employed for six plays over a forty-week season.[31] The brochure also contained assurances that the A.R.T. would become "a self supporting business enterprise and return to its investors interest on their capital." The women had been persuaded by legal advisors that it was easier to raise funds through an "investment process," rather than through a nonprofit corporation.[32]

The plan ended with testimonials from critics attesting to the "high-minded" and "ambitious" venture, and hailing the "exciting news" of a permanent repertory company for America. Nevertheless, two discordant notes were sounded by *Pictorial Review* columnist Robert Garland: "When all is said and done, you *girls* may have your heads in the clouds of high-class theatrical endeavor, but your feet are planted firmly on the *Broadway* battle-ground."[33] Unwittingly, or not, he identified the issues of gender and commerce that were to plague their efforts through the coming months.

Who's on First?

With Crawford supervising the business end, the women set up a corporation capitalized at $300,000 and offered stock at five hundred dollars a share. At this point in the partnership, Crawford confronted the fact that there was no clear authority established among the three. Crawford had managed the Maplewood Theatre (with John Wildberg) and nine Broadway shows (with investors), and now found herself in a cart-before-the-horse situation, not unlike her experience with the Group Theatre. Just as Harold Clurman and Lee Strasberg dominated the decision-making within the Group, so, too, Eva Le Gallienne and Margaret Webster deferred to their third partner only in business matters and reserved artistic matters as their special province.

Faced with the manager's familiar conundrum—they couldn't choose the plays until they had the actors, but they couldn't get the actors until they selected the plays—they compromised by exploring tentative roles with "name" actors.[34] Webster insisted that they needed a star like Laurence Olivier, who only a short time before thrust the Old Vic into prominence. At different times, they invited thirty-seven "stars" to join the company, but none did. "Wonderful parts," Crawford told actors, "Leading roles in any great classic you might wish to play." She reported the responses as "Great! Great! What I've wanted all my life. A dream come true at last." Nevertheless, when the celebrities learned that the top salary was five hundred dollars a week and they were expected to sign for two seasons, their "sparkling eyes glazed over." "Visions of money they might receive elsewhere, from films, TV, a Broadway smash, won over our quixotic dream," Crawford moaned.[35]

They tried and failed to entice Katharine Hepburn, Vincent Price, Susan Hayward, Michael Chekhov, Marlon Brando, Barbara Bel Geddes, José Ferrer, Montgomery Clift, Geraldine Fitzgerald, Greer Garson, and Mary Martin. Without consultation with her coproducers, Crawford offered Mary Martin the role of Cleopatra in Shaw's *Caesar and Cleopatra* and Rosalind in *As You Like It* and ran afoul of Le Gallienne's *hauteur*. "She herself is nice—but oh God! *Not* Cleopatra," Le Gallienne protested. "She could never be Egypt—except in a musical comedy version. Just a *bonne fille*—with lacquered hair *orange* coloured—Talented and charming in her own medium but I don't think she'll ever get on as a great actress—nor do I think she should—she's fine as she is—why not go on being superlatively good in her own line."[36]

Echoing her partner, Webster wrote a dismissive letter to Crawford about the offer to Mary Martin: "Broadway show business is her meat; it is made for her and she for it. She is brilliant and has a brilliant career firmly set ahead of her . . . Our sort of repertory will curtail her opportunities quite a bit in many ways; she only dimly understands it and is only being persuaded she wants it by the glittering bait you have so skillfully dangled in front of her."[37] Webster and Le Gallienne need not have worried. Mary Martin turned them down, as did Marlon Brando whom they wooed for the title role in *Hamlet*.

At the outset, the three women had not confronted the fact that American actors with training, skill, and experience in the playing of repertory were rare. Those with experience (Maurice Evans, Helen Hayes, Arnold Moss, Basil Rathbone, and José Ferrer) were already engaged on Broadway or in Hollywood. After auditioning hundreds of actors, they eventually recruited a company of experienced "pros" and young unknowns. Anchoring the company was the middle-aged team of Eva Le Gallienne, Margaret Webster, and Victor Jory, who had acted opposite Le Gallienne in *Therese* and in Crawford's *The Perfect Marriage*. He admired the women's skill and idealism and "wholeheartedly agreed" to join the company.[38] Although a fine actor, Victor Jory did not have the star power of Laurence Olivier.

Eli Wallach called the company "a mixture of old pros and young hopefuls."[39] Among the stalwarts were Walter Hampden, Eugene Stuckmann, John Straub, Philip Bourneuf, June Duprez, Richard Waring, Marion Gunnar Evensen, and comedian Ernest Truex. Crawford was proudest of the young group of recruits: Eli Wallach, Anne Jackson, Efrem Zimbalist Jr., William Windom, and later Bambi Linn and Julie Harris, who played Alice and the White Rabbit in *Alice in Wonderland*.

A Stalwart Oak

When the three women wrote their separate accounts of the founding and demise of the theater, they set forth their various motives. As described in her diaries and her autobiography, Le Gallienne wanted to recreate her nonprofit Civic Repertory Theatre.[40] Webster dreamed of an American version of the Old Vic, with its dazzling productions and flawless ensemble playing. Crawford's account was more measured, but her private revelations and letter of resignation tell a different story. Throughout the planning, she was like a stalwart oak enduring the cold winds of uncooperative unions, endless fundraising for a few dollars, and discouraging artistic choices by her business partners. She was felled, at last, by a deficiency of audiences and money.

To raise the $300,000, the three women proceeded to give daily speeches to prospective audiences. Only small increments came out of the countless luncheons, club meetings, radio appeals, and letters of solicitation. Crawford complained that it was "a seemingly endless chore."[41] She got the idea to look beyond New York City. She found enough money among her Hollywood contacts to finance the entire venture, if the film moguls could have voting rights and options on actors and plays. Le Gallienne refused to accept the terms. "I'm scared of that kind of money," she told Crawford. "Those men have been trained all their lives to think in diametrically the opposite way—we don't want them having any 'say' in our theatre."[42]

Clearly a setback, but not dire enough to persuade Crawford to withdraw from her commitment, she continued on the path now set by her collaborators. While she had enjoyed addressing audiences and civic groups at Maplewood with a clear idea of the productions and the names she was bringing to New Jersey from Broadway, she found raising money for the A.R.T. a joyless and draining experience. Mentally exhausted, Crawford wrote a poignant note to Webster: "I find I'm tired, not physically, but my spiritual bin is empty from money-raising, money-cutting, glad-handing and the grinding repetition of our aims."[43] Just as Crawford neared the threshold of defeat, financier and philanthropist Joseph Verner Reed, who had backed the efforts of Maurice Evans and Margaret Webster to bring Shakespeare to Broadway, gave his friend Peggy a check for one hundred thousand dollars over lunch at Voisin's. Crawford pronounced the A.R.T. in business at last!

With the A.R.T. capitalized, the selection of six plays became their first priority. With high-minded determination, Le Gallienne and Webster proposed that "it was not their business to do the best-known plays," but lesser works of Shakespeare and Ibsen.[44] Again, the compromises dripped like water from a leaking faucet. With a company starring middle-aged actors, *Romeo and Juliet* or *As You Like It* was out of the question. Le Gallienne wanted *The Merchant of Venice*, but Crawford considered the play anti-Semitic, and therefore controversial.[45] They settled on *Henry VIII*, one of Shakespeare's lesser-known works. Crawford offered two choices for the "new" play category: Bertolt Brecht's *Mother Courage and Her Children*, not yet seen in the United States, and a first play (called *The Sign of the Archer*) by an unknown playwright named Arthur Miller. Le Gallienne and Webster turned down both scripts. "We didn't think we could cast them well enough," Webster explained somewhat disingenuously, obscuring the fact that the scripts failed to offer roles the actresses wanted to play.[46] *The Sign of the Archer*, renamed *All My Sons*, was subsequently directed by Elia Kazan and ran for 308 performances on Broadway.

After many compromises, the women announced the A.R.T.'s first season: Shakespeare's *Henry VIII*, James M. Barrie's *What Every Woman*

Knows, a double-bill of Sean O'Casey's *Pound on Demand* and George Bernard Shaw's *Androcles and the Lion*, and Le Gallienne's translation of Henrik Ibsen's *John Gabriel Borkman* followed by revivals of Sidney Howard's *Yellow Jack* and *Alice in Wonderland*, based on Lewis Carroll's writings.

As Crawford approached the craft unions for concessions, she found Actors Equity Association amenable to wages below minimums customarily paid in New York City, and to a longer rehearsal period for the preparation of three shows scheduled to open back-to-back. "Actors Equity was the only helpful union," Crawford said.[47] The stagehands and musicians unions were another matter. Even though Le Gallienne had gained concessions from the International Alliance of Theatre and Stage Employees (IATSE) for the Civic Repertory Theatre, neither Le Gallienne nor Crawford was able to persuade the local union council that the A.R.T. was a special case. At the time, there were no established policies within IATSE governing the playing of repertory, or to be exact, the changeover from one production to another. "It was not until we were almost ready to open that Local No. 1 laid down their onerous conditions," Crawford recalled.[48] The councilmen decided that twenty-eight stagehands must be hired for *Henry VIII* and kept on permanently (and idly) for the less elaborate productions.

The musicians' union was equally unforgiving. Even though Crawford had arm-wrestled the union for *The Tempest*'s eight musicians, Local 802 insisted that the number of musicians needed for *Henry VIII*, which they called "a drama with music," must be kept on salary for all the plays, regardless of musical requirements. Composer Lehman Engel had scored *Henry VIII* for eight musicians, and all eight (plus one standby) had to be retained throughout the season.

"All this played hell with my operating estimate," Crawford fumed.[49] Le Gallienne took the moral high-road. "It is not from without that the theatre is in danger," she reasoned, "it is from within . . . I think it is a definite evil to make these unions so hide-bound, so drastic, and at times so ludicrous in their petty rules that they become the greatest impediment and obstacle in the path of sincere and honest stage activities."[50]

As Robert Garland had hinted earlier, *gender* cannot be ignored in the results of the women's attempts to negotiate with the all-male unions in the late forties. Actors Equity had a large number of women on its governing council (Margaret Webster was among them), but the stagehands and musicians unions were male provinces. Le Gallienne reported after one heated session with the stagehands' union that a "gentleman" slapped her on the back and exclaimed, "If we want you to have your little theatre, you'll have it, and if we don't want you to, you won't, see?"[51]

Male chauvinism surfaced in other venues as well. In contrast to press coverage of coequal men, who were queried on their creative influences, professional destinies, and vital beliefs, the distaff producer of *One Touch of Venus* was featured in the pages of the *New York Herald Tribune* presiding over the "tastes of Mr. and Mrs. America." Photographed in her New York kitchen against a backdrop with pots of herbs growing on the windowsill, Cheryl Crawford, wearing an apron, advises on preparing one-dish meals and sugarless desserts.[52] When she was working on *Love Life* five years later, she set aside the apron and the scene of domesticity when she was asked to address the status of women in the world of producing. She minced no words replying to the question—"Is producing a tough world for a woman?" "Sure it is," she responded. "In fact, it's a tough world for anybody."[53]

In a similar, chauvinistic vein, producer and director Norris Houghton wrote a misogynous piece called "It's a Woman's World" for *Theatre Arts* magazine calling attention to the contributions of women to the present-day American theater. Beginning with "our theatre is veritably a woman's world" and naming notable women (actresses, directors, designers, and producers), he reversed his point of view in mid-article and called for the stage to "reacquire its masculinity." Observing the influx of war veterans into drama schools throughout the country as a bright beginning for the new "masculine presence," Houghton called for the men to reclaim key posts usurped by women during the war years, citing "Cheryl Crawford, Eva Le Gallienne, and Margaret Webster [who] run the new American Repertory Theatre with no man to guide them."[54]

On the surface, Norris Houghton, author of *Moscow Rehearsals*, was being tongue-in-cheek, but his reference to veterans reclaiming their positions undercut his amusement at the assertive producers-in-skirts. Garland's "you girls" and the union chief's "your little theatre" were symptomatic of the ingrained prejudice against women in 1946. For the most part, the three producers, who had successfully negotiated around those prejudices in the past, ignored the male chauvinism. It is true that they openly challenged the male establishment when they boldly stated in the A.R.T. brochure: "This will be a theatre conducted by those who love the theatre for its own sake . . . not merely a machinery for getting. It will not be at the mercy of merchandising middle-men . . ."[55]

The three middle-aged women, whose theater was located in the vicinity of Broadway, inadvertently became an irritant to the men in power—

theater producers, managers, and union leaders. Moreover, their lesbianism was a point of contention, especially among backstage crews gossiping about "dykes," and among theatergoers shocked by Lillian Hellman's portrayal of the outing of a lesbian school teacher in *The Children's Hour*. By the mid-forties, politicians tagged homosexuals as "perverts," and equated them with the communist threat to America's national security.

Despite the ingrained prejudices swirling around them, the coming demise of the A.R.T. cannot be laid entirely at the feet of the trade unions, the chauvinism of the theatrical establishment, or the prejudices of society. Multiple factors contributed to the dissolution of the A.R.T. Location, repertoire, union demands, critical umbrage, depleted coffers, and dampened spirits moved the company toward closure after one season. Most importantly, audiences stayed away from Columbus Circle, depriving the theater of earned income.

Tilting at Windmills

When the A.R.T. opened *Henry VIII* on November 6, 1946, with Eva Le Gallienne as Katharine of Aragon and Victor Jory as the King, Crawford's attention was very much divided. As a result of her inability to influence artistic decisions and make the theater solvent, she entertained an offer of a new Broadway musical as she continued to oversee the openings of *Henry VIII*, *What Every Woman Knows*, and *John Gabriel Borkman* with Le Gallienne in the leading female roles.

Disarmed by the favorable comments offered by critics for the introductory brochure, the producers were lulled into thinking that the New York press would appreciate the uniqueness of the repertory theater within a country where none existed. This was not to be the case. Each play was reviewed as a Broadway opening; moreover, the notices were discouraging for *Henry VIII*. Critics found the little-known Shakespeare play an inauspicious start for the new theater. Ward Morehouse called the play an "unwieldly drama," and Howard Barnes added "desultory entertainment." Most were puzzled as to why the new company chose a lesser Shakespearean play of uncertain authorship for its opening attraction.[56] The Barrie play, *What Every Woman Knows*, was tepidly received, but *John Gabriel Borkman*, Ibsen's vengeful dance of death, was an artistic and critical success, but not an audience-pleaser.

Not all reviewers were generous, however. Remarking upon Victor Jory's "unrelenting grimness" as the fanatical Borkman, John Chapman was reminded of a vaudeville routine at the Palace about an old gentleman cooped up in a kitchen who sent word to his hoity-toity daughter,

"Give me another piece of gefulte fish or I'll come out!" George Jean Nathan called the production "a Scandinavian paraphrase of something like 'Madame X.'" Mary McCarthy, who disliked the two actresses intensely, cautioned that the production might have seemed more substantial if "Miss Webster and Miss Le Gallienne . . . dropped the airs of Cassandra, the antiphonal responses, the glare of prophecy, and asked themselves, for a single instant, what a Norwegian housewife was like."[57]

Reading the reviews for the three plays and monitoring the finances, Crawford had nightmares. "In my sleep I clutched for greenbacks," she recalled, "which turned before my eyes into endless bills for stagehands, musicians, costumes and scenery, through which I tried to push, flailing my arms for escape." As the deficit grew, the nightmares continued and she faced the cold fact that "there would never be enough money."[58]

The fourth play, *Androcles and the Lion*, was an unqualified success with critics and audiences, but it came too late to bring about financial stability. The three productions had cost more than their entire capitalization. The critics' consensus (and Crawford's as well) was that the new repertory group had been none too wise in its selection of plays.[59]

Amid the sound and fury of the A.R.T.'s problems, the multitasking Cheryl Crawford, tired of counting pennies on Columbus Circle, but reluctant to resign, found more congenial outlets for her energies. "Distraction also helps," she said of her three-month respite during which the A.R.T. spun out three plays that audiences did not want to see.[60] Sensing that her future lay with musicals, and not with high-toned classics performed in repertory, she signed on to produce a new Lerner and Loewe musical. When le Gallienne and Webster learned that she was producing "*Brigadamndoon*," as they called it, with an advance sale of more than the A.R.T.'s capitalization, long-held tensions came to the fore. Her partners denigrated Crawford's commercial interests and Le Gallienne complained to her diary, "What's the use of trying to do anything fine in this Godforsaken country—all they really want are musicals."[61]

In the period before the A.R.T.'s final shows of the season, Crawford also donated some time to the American National Theatre and Academy (ANTA). Her work for the nonprofit group seemed "like play" because she shared no financial responsibilities. [62] Inactive for ten years, ANTA came to life again in the mid-forties. Chartered earlier by Congress to develop new talents, including playwrights and actors, under the guidance of professionals, ANTA was most likely the source of Crawford's new scripts. During the year the A.R.T. disbanded, she supervised a production of Brecht's *Galileo* with Charles Laughton for ANTA. As a vice-president on ANTA's board, Crawford was instrumental in inaugurating the Experimental Theatre, created to give new plays limited engagements at the small Princess Theatre on Thirty-ninth Street. In February of 1947, Crawford supervised a showcase at the Princess that won the Sidney Howard award as the season's most important development in the theater. Meanwhile, twenty blocks away, the A.R.T. was lumbering along with mediocre to scathing reviews.

As audiences came to Columbus Circle in insufficient numbers, Crawford quarreled again with Le Gallienne over the pricing of tickets. "She wanted a people's theatre with low-priced seats," Crawford complained. While Crawford had no objection to cheap tickets, she knew that, just to break even, they would have to fill the house every night. The bleak fact was, they were not filling the house for any performance. Crawford summed up the situation: "For all our efforts and ideals, we were without audiences and without money. The situation was desperate."[63]

Word leaked out that the A.R.T. was in dire financial straits. In February, Brooks Atkinson addressed three reasons for the theater's difficulties. He called attention to the fact that the A.R.T. was a commercial theater and the unions had no policies in place for repertory. He also took note of the middle-aged actors who dominated the acting company. Finally, he indicted the selection of plays. "Nor has the choice of plays been sufficiently popular for an institution dependent upon public support," he wrote, and ended with, "Of all the arts, the theatre is the most in need of the common touch."[64]

Even though she felt vindicated by the critic's remarks, Crawford could still see no way forward. During January, she retired to her bed with a flu-like virus. She had three recurrences of iritis, a painful inflammation of the eyes, which she described as making the "eyes feel as though a mailed fist were being pounded into them." She diagnosed her recurring illnesses as emanating from a troubled psyche that did not want "to see or face the daily tasks" confronting the A.R.T.[65] Moreover, she blamed herself for miscalculating the finances and the demands of the unions.

The theatrical community rallied to shore up the failing theater. Producer Rita Hassan stepped forward with ninety thousand dollars to subsidize the final two plays, *Yellow Jack* and *Alice in Wonderland*. Internal changes were made to ease the financial situation, including abandoning the repertory schedule and terminating contracts of actors not playing in *Yellow Jack*.

On the surface, *Alice in Wonderland* was the answer to everyone's prayers. Based on Le Gallienne's production fifteen years earlier at the Civic Repertory Company, the recreations of the Tenniel drawings and the masks and marionettes by Remo Bufano were magical. Bambi Linn, remembered for her performance in *Carousel*, played Alice, with thirty-six other actors, including Julie Harris and William Windom, alternating as the White Rabbit. Brooks Atkinson celebrated *Alice* as the "crowning achievement" of the American Repertory Theatre. "O frabjous day!" he rejoiced, "Miss Le Gallienne's jabberwocky is authentic and delightful."[66] Encomiums followed from other members of Broadway's circle of critics, but *Alice* could not save the A.R.T.

For nearly a year, Cheryl Crawford had endured as managing partner. By the opening of *Alice in Wonderland*, she was exhausted from fundraising, from futile efforts to pay the bills, and from her struggles to exercise authority over the finances and the artistic choices. When she assessed her personal dilemma, she admitted to herself that she had had little influence on the artistic choices *within* and the union decisions *without*. "Zealot that I was, I was also a business woman," she said, "and I could not shake the memory of the relentless fund-raising, the unending bills, and the pages of numbers in red ink."[67] Finally, on June 10, 1947, seven months following the opening of *Henry VIII*, and with her associates planning a second season with no assets, Cheryl Crawford resigned.

At the time she became a founding partner in July of 1946, she had written to Peggy Webster with happy anticipation of their future endeavors. "I haven't felt this way," she said, "since I started in the theatre when everything was glittering."[68] Her resignation eleven months later was a mixture of regret for her loss of faith in the enterprise in the face of the harsh fiscal realities and a hardheaded certainty that the A.R.T. needed to regroup as a nonprofit theater. Moreover, she was deeply dissatisfied with her toothless managerial role.

June 10, 1947

Dear Eva and Peggy:

I'm probably a coward to write this instead of telling you, but I am so inarticulate at expressing anything deeply personal that I know I become emotional, involved, and unclear.

In trying to write a statement to our backers, my own position has become more clear to me. For several reasons, I feel I cannot continue with you into the next step you have decided to take. First, because the experience and observation of this year has left me no faith that such a theatre can exist under present conditions and I see no way in which these conditions can be substantially changed. I know that great faith can frequently accomplish the impossible, but I simply don't possess it.

The second reason is that neither artistically nor managerially am I functioning in a way that satisfies me.

My position on both sides is that of advisor, suggestor, consultant, but in no way final in any decisions. And that is very unsatisfying to me. If I have to be responsible for a result, I want to feel responsible for what caused that result, good or bad. This is in no way is a criticism of you. You have both earned the right to pick the plays you wish to do, to cast them and produce them according to your conceptions. In fact, I see no other way in which you could work satisfactorily, but I have very little part in this and don't even believe that a person in my position should have. Only I don't want that person to be me. In the purely business end, which is not my sole interest, I feel a similar lack of authority. My profound admiration and respect for both of you may keep me from asserting myself even to a degree that you could accept but I never could be a fighter against you because I feel your own artistic integrity and knowledge too strongly and besides, I am never sure that I am solely right. It occurs to me that perhaps I am not *strong* enough to work with partners, that I can only be decisive and properly executive when I have to make up my mind alone and stand or fall by that decision. And I don't see how the greatest good will or best intentions can overcome this.

I would like to assist in working out the organization of the non-profit set-up and I have the information from Bill [attorney H. William Fitelson] on how to proceed, with that. A meeting of the important stockholders has to be called and they have to recommend to the other stockholders a transfer of assets and a dissolution of the present corporation. One of the small stockholders is a nationally known tax expert who is willing to assist and advise at such a meeting. I hope you know that I am willing to do anything I can to help except to go on into the next phase.

I know that I have not been the dream partner, able to accomplish all the things I hoped for and dreamed of doing for the A.R.T. so that I have many regrets about my past two years' activities, but I don't want to development any resentments. One thing I have learned is that you are great women.

Love,
Cheryl[69]

Crawford's reluctance to challenge Le Gallienne and Webster has been attributed by those who knew her well to her timidity that sometimes emerged as a measure of self-protection in business negotiations and social situations.[70] Given her track record for business acumen and sharp deals, her shyness was little known among her colleagues. In her letter of resignation, she betrayed an awareness of the character traits that made her an ineffective partner. In the intimidating presence of her partners, she was indecisive and failed to assert her better judgment to challenge their flawed decision-making. Most likely, she was taken off guard. She had anticipated that by joining with two accomplished women, who also shared her same-sex interests, to create a new theater, she would, finally, be treated as an equal partner in a creative enterprise. She soon found that she was peripheral to the decision-making on artistic matters and regulated, once again, to the business end of the endeavor where, this time, she also lacked authority to affect change. She had challenged Le Gallienne's scheme for lower-priced tickets, a minor skirmish in the struggle to wrest concessions from the unions and choose an effective season that investors were interested in and audiences wanted to see. She had been intimated by the women's display of superiority in all things theatrical, and, in the role of bystander had watched helplessly as they announced a deadly season.

During this dark night of her theatrical soul, a note arrived from her close friend Thornton Wilder, whom she had met when *Our Town* opened on Broadway while she was producing *Family Portrait* and whose correspondence through the years was a source of gratification and delight. Wilder advised her to "take three years off from the cultural drama and the better things in the theatre—even the literate shade that skirted *One Touch of Venus*."

> Your doctrinaire tendency has led you down the garden path. Give it
> a vacation. Do popular theatre. Purge yourself in basic theatre, farces,
> melodrama, laughs and shudders. Really, you'd enjoy it. A three year purge.
> Then the big things. By that time all your friends will have deserted you but
> Thornton[71]

Years later, Webster said of Crawford's decision to resign: "She may well have contributed more by cutting her losses with the A.R.T. than Eva and I did by trying to keep it alive."[72] Despite feelings of responsibility to their supporters and actors, Crawford had taken a pragmatic look at the accounts and found that their biggest box office success, *Alice in Wonderland*, reported a profit of $1.22.

In Margaret Webster's valedictory, written twenty-five years later, she returned to the gender issue that had not so silently plagued their efforts: "In the case of the A.R.T. no one had believed that a trio of women could run such an enterprise without arriving rapidly at the point of 'pistols for three and coffee for one.' . . . We disagreed, but we ended, as we had begun, with mutual respect." She admired Crawford's courage and success over the intervening years, "doggedly trying to translate her ideals into hits, doing a man's job in a world where even men can't do it, facing every kind of misfortune with indomitable courage.[73]

In quiet moments following the demise of the A.R.T., Crawford contemplated the incurable dream that had carried her along for a quarter of a century from the Group Theatre to the American Repertory Theatre. "I dreamed of a company," she confessed. "When I was part of a company, I thought of the freedom of being on my own. And, so throughout my career, without quite realizing it at the time, I charted a zigzag course between the two."[74]

Despite her zealotry for serious plays and ensemble companies, what she loved most was the magical world of musicals where pinpoints of light from the musicians' stands in the pit flickered to the swelling of the overture and the rise of the curtain transported audiences into enchanting worlds of Scottish moors and heady gold-rush days.

Cheryl Aileen Crawford, class of
1925, Smith College Yearbook,
1925. Courtesy of Smith College Archives,
Northampton, Massachusetts.

Theresa Helburn of the Theatre
Guild, c. 1930. (Uncredited photograph.)
Billy Rose Theatre Division, the New York Public
Library for the Performing Arts,
Astor, Lenox, and Tilden Foundations.

Cheryl Crawford at the Theatre Guild, c. 1928. (Uncredited photograph.) Billy Rose Theatre Division, the New York Public Library for the Performing Arts, Astor, Lenox, and Tilden Foundations.

Group Theatre Directors, Harold Clurman, Cheryl Crawford, and Lee Strasberg, at Dover Furnace, Connecticut, 1932, during the second season of the Group Theatre. (Photograph by Ralph Steiner.) Courtesy of the Weill-Lenya Research Center, the Kurt Weill Foundation for Music, New York.

Cheryl Crawford as producer of the Maplewood Theatre, New Jersey, 1940. (Photograph by Carl Van Vechten.) Courtesy of the Van Vechten Trust. Billy Rose Theatre Division, the New York Public Library for the Performing Arts, Astor, Lenox, and Tilden Foundations.

Producer Cheryl Crawford with associate producer John J. Wildberg (*standing*) and conductor Alexander Smallen (*seated*) working on the Broadway revival of *Porgy and Bess*, 1942. (Photograph by George Karger/Pix, Inc.) Billy Rose Theatre Division, the New York Public Library for the Performing Arts, Astor, Lenox, and Tilden Foundations.

Mary Martin in designer Mainbocher's gown, singing "That's Him" in *One Touch of Venus*, 1943. (Photograph Vandamm Studio.) Billy Rose Theatre Division, the New York Public Library for the Performing Arts, Astor, Lenox, and Tilden Foundations.

Composer Kurt Weill during *One Touch of Venus*, 1943. Courtesy of the Weill-Lenya Research Center, the Kurt Weill Foundation for Music, New York.

Mary Martin, Cheryl Crawford, and Marlene Dietrich on opening-night of *Kind Sir*, 1953, starring Mary Martin and Charles Boyer. Photofest.

Franco Zeffrelli, Cheryl Crawford, and Roddy McDowell at the Broadway opening of *Good as Gold*, 1957. (Uncredited photograph.) Billy Rose Theatre Division, the New York Public Library for the Performing Arts, Astor, Lenox, and Tilden Foundations.

Cheryl Crawford
and Lee Strasberg
(*right*) with Franco
Zeffrelli and guest
in the foyer during
the opening of
Good as Gold, 1957.
(Photograph by Syeus
Mottel.) Billy Rose
Theatre Division, the
New York Public Library
for the Performing Arts,
Astor, Lenox, and Tilden
Foundations.

Cheryl Crawford with lyricist/
director Tom Jones (*center*)
and composer Harvey Schmidt
overseeing the construction of
the Portfolio Theatre/Work-
shop stage for *Celebration*, 1969.
(Photograph by Robert Alan Gold.) From the
collection of Harvey Schmidt.

Cheryl Crawford and Tennessee Williams at the Gotham Book Mart, 1976. (Photograph by Bill Yoscary.) Courtesy of the Estate of Bill Yoscary. Billy Rose Theatre Division, the New York Public Library for the Performing Arts, Astor, Lenox, and Tilden Foundations.

A late photograph of Cheryl Crawford, c. 1986. (Photograph by Jessie Gilmer.) Billy Rose Theatre Division, the New York Public Library for the Performing Arts, Astor, Lenox, and Tilden Foundations.

8

MUSICAL ADVENTURES

There's magic in a good musical.

—*Cheryl Crawford*

The year 1947 was a very good one for Cheryl Crawford. She produced another smash hit on Broadway and satisfied her zealotry for a good cause by cocreating the Actors Studio with Elia Kazan and Robert Lewis. Queried about her success in a tough profession, she told a feature writer, "I make my decision to produce a play only when it thoroughly pleases me personally. Of course my judgment does err, but that makes the job more challenging."[1] Her judgment did not fail her when attorney William Fitelson, known to friends as "Bill," telephoned to discuss a new project with the unusual title of *Brigadoon*.

On a warm afternoon in late August of 1946, as the A.R.T. was struggling to open its first season, Fitelson invited Crawford to an apartment in the upper fifties at the corner of Broadway. There, in a small living room filled with a grand piano, she met "Alan and Fritz." Crawford described the two young men as rather short and slender. Her portrait of the high-strung Alan Jay Lerner was of a blond, curly-haired young man with wicked blue eyes enlarged by glasses and a profile like those found on Greek coins. The Viennese-born Frederick Loewe had a full head of brown hair which, when he was excited, fell over his steel gray eyes. "And, he was often excited," Crawford reported.[2]

Always a keen observer, Crawford recalled the team of Lerner and Loewe:

> Alan was a chain smoker with a cute habit of twisting a cigarette around his fingers, which gave me a chance to notice that his nails were bitten to the

quick. I thought this might be nervousness about the audition. But no, it was a habit that continued all the years I knew him. On the piano was a balloon glass partially filled with an amber liquid I took to be brandy. This Fritz paused to sip from occasionally, returning to the keys with demonic energy.[3]

The musicians quickly got down to business. Lerner told the story of *Brigadoon* and sang his lyrics in "a sweet, true voice," accompanied by Loewe who played with "passion and authority," as though the piano was a mere extension of his fingers.[4]

Crawford read the script over a weekend on Fire Island, where New Yorkers who were members of the gay community sought refuge from the summer heat among compatible friends.

Cherry Grove

Like the majority of gay vacationers living in Manhattan during the summer months, Crawford and her sexual partner, Ruth Norman, a small woman with auburn hair and Rubenesque skin, known for her great warmth and generous spirit, spent weekends in Cherry Grove, a resort community on Fire Island populated by theater and literary people. Their culinary interests and mutual friends had drawn them together. Ruth Norman was a cooking authority and author with George Bradshaw of *Cook Until Done*. She was also a close friend of James Beard and was affiliated with the James Beard Cooking School in Manhattan. In contrast, Crawford was an aficionado of single-dish meals—what she called "comfort food"—that sustained her through the pressures of Broadway openings. The women met in the late forties, most likely introduced by Janet Flanner, and lived together at 400 East Fifty-second Street in a comfortable setting with book-lined walls and living-room fireplace adorned with sepia tiles, designed by Norman, depicting *commedia dell' arte* scenes based on Jacques Callot's engravings.[5] When they were not in New York City or traveling in Europe, they escaped the summer heat on Cherry Grove among theater and literary people of their acquaintance.

Crawford and writer Janet Flanner were considered "Grovers," since they had spent their wartime summers as tenants on the Grove and were familiar faces among the villagers. Most likely, Crawford met the award-winning Paris correspondent for *The New Yorker* who reported on European cultural and political life at February House. Once the Middagh Street group from Brooklyn Heights discovered Fire Island in the late forties and early fifties, Crawford gravitated to her friends from February House and other celebrity visitors, including W. H. Auden,

Chester Kallman, Carson McCullers, Patricia Highsmith, Jane Bowles, Tennessee Williams, Truman Capote, and Natalia Danesi Murray.[6]

In her sociological study of Cherry Grove, Esther Newton described the uninhibited homosexual ambiance of the island resort and the freedom from exclusion experienced by the men and women bound together as members of a national gay subculture. As they disembarked from the Fire Island ferry, they found themselves in an environment of glorious beaches, homogeneous world views, and uninhibited revelry free of social (and legal) sanctions.[7]

Many of the property owners and newcomers to Cherry Grove were in show business and summer theatricals quickly evolved under the banner of the Arts Project of Cherry Grove. As an escape from the seriousness of the professional theater and as a means of publicly expressing themselves without fear of reprisal, they indulged in theatrical fun and games and set a precedent on Fire Island for gay vacationers engaging in camp presentations. These theatrics featured "witty repartee, parody, double-entendre, and gender reversal."[8]

In tandem with Grove property owners, the Arts Project advisory board, with Cheryl Crawford conspicuous among the group, proceeded to produce the *Cherry Grove Follies of 1948*, a campy revue in the manner of the *Ziegfeld Follies* featuring straight and gay theater professionals in the local community house outfitted with a stage, balcony, and dressing rooms. One script, called "Dismembering the Wedding," was a send up of McCullers's *Member of the Wedding*. In a revue format, devised for the *Grove Follies* and sanctioned by the novelist, a butch-looking woman played the housekeeper Berenice Sadie Brown in gingham apron and eyepatch; a "girl" played the tomboy Frankie Addams in loafers and socks topped by a silver lamé dress and chiffon scarves; and a barelegged "boy" played the young John Henry West in a T-shirt and tutu.[9]

Long after the older generation of Grovers, including Cheryl Crawford, Ruth Norman, and Janet Flanner, passed away, the *Grove Follies* continued as convivial gay theatrics bending in the eighties to accommodate political benefits for AIDS groups and the radical feminism of the New Left.

During one late-summer weekend on the Grove, Crawford read Alan Lerner's script about another escape from city life among the misty hills of the Scottish Highlands peopled by like-minded highlanders who come alive every one hundred years. Analyzing her response to the "touching fantasy," Crawford said, "Perhaps it was the Scottish blood in me that responded so strongly. I realized that *Brigadoon* was probably not for the tired businessman who supposedly supports musicals, but I couldn't let that deter me."[10]

With arts- patron Bea Lawrence committed as a coproducer, Crawford moved ahead, only to learn that impresario Billy Rose was also considering *Brigadoon.* "While he hemmed and hawed, I signed," Crawford chortled.[11] While fulfilling other obligations with the A.R.T. and the Experimental Theatre, Crawford initiated backers' auditions in Lawrence's Eastside apartment.

After holding thirty-two auditions (Crawford recalled getting the money was "like pulling teeth"), they still had not put together the capital needed to produce the musical. Many potential backers feared that the exotic love story with the weird title might not return their investment. Several urged the creators to change the title. "No one will pronounce it properly," they said. Irked by this observation, Crawford replied, "If it's a hit, they'll learn."[12]

Once again, Fitelson came to the rescue. He introduced J. S. Seidman, head of the famous accounting firm, who liked what he heard well enough to gather acquaintances to listen to Lerner and Loewe's creation. The group invested ninety-six thousand dollars. Meanwhile, Lerner and Loewe became so adept at performing the piece that Crawford considered staging *Brigadoon* as "a two-man show!"[13]

Despite the fact that they were short twenty thousand dollars of the total investment needed to capitalize *Brigadoon,* Crawford's gambler's instinct persuaded her to take a risk. She set about putting the creative team together for the musical that combined a well-written book, elements of operetta, and incorporated ballet as the dance form. She chose familiar faces: director Bobby Lewis from her Group Theatre days; Agnes de Mille, choreographer for *One Touch of Venus;* Oliver Smith, set designer for *The Perfect Marriage;* David Folkes, designer of the A.R.T.'s lavish *Henry VIII,* for costumes; and Peggy Clark, lighting designer for de Mille's company. Reasoning that most of the characters were too young to be played by stars, she and Lewis chose actors without star names. She proceeded to rent theaters for out of town try-outs, and arranged for the Ziegfeld Theatre on Broadway.

The Broadway rumor-mills ground out stories about Crawford's gamble and rumors of potential sanctions from the Securities and Exchange Commission that approved contracts for Broadway shows. With Crawford standing on the threshold of personal and professional ruin, the project was rescued by another arts patron, Harriett Ames, whose check bridged the twenty thousand dollar gap.

Crawford exulted over the company assembled for *Brigadoon*. "We were a happy family," she pronounced. The only seemingly false note was the leading female performer, who had an attractive stage presence but lacked an instinct for comedy. "Where was the comedy?" Crawford complained of Pamela Britten's performance during rehearsals and volunteered to work with the actress before the opening in New Haven. As she rehearsed Britten in the ladies' room of the Shubert Theatre, Crawford gave the actress a piece of heather to hold in her hand during her big number, "The Love of My Life," a song about her attempts to attract four men, who subsequently abandoned her.

Pamela Britten's performance was so well received on opening night in New Haven that a number was added in Act Two ("My Mother's Wedding Day"), abetted by a chorus dancing and singing a drunken bacchanal. The show proceeded to Boston and then to Philadelphia, and, by the time the company arrived at the Ziegfeld, Crawford discovered that word of mouth had preceded them and the box office was setting a record. "And the top orchestra ticket was four dollars and fifty cents!" exclaimed *Brigadoon*'s producer. This was the same price that she had set for the American Repertory Theatre with drastically different results.

Wedded to a Hit

For the Broadway opening, Crawford went shopping for "something expensive." "It is my unfortunate habit to predict the success of a production by buying something expensive," the cost-conscious producer said. "It seems to buoy my confidence, though I often regret it after the notices."[14] For the occasion, she bought a party dress and wore it to the theater with great optimism. Then, she sat in the house manager's office reading *The New Yorker* while listening to the applause. Whenever she seemed to tense up, the manager took her to a nearby bar for a drink. By the time the show ended, her anxieties had evaporated. Hearing the enthusiastic applause, and later reading the ecstatic reviews ("epochal," "enchantment," "original," "distinctive."), she was euphoric.[15]

She took her parents, who had arrived from Akron that morning to see the show, their first produced by their daughter, and to the opening-night party in Bea Lawrence's apartment. Crawford recalled the tables were handsomely decorated with colorful tartans, champagne flowed, but the best moment was her father's appraisal of his daughter's achievement. Having seen a matinee performance of *Oklahoma!* Robert Crawford pontificated in his salesman's voice, "I tell you, Cheryl, *Brigadoon* is better."[16]

Crawford's exultation over the show's success was orgasmic. "Even if a honeymoon is all it's cracked up to be," she said, "it can scarcely be more exciting than being wedded to a smash hit."[17] Even as Crawford enjoyed the glowing reviews that rained down on the company and the lines of ticket buyers stretched around the corner from the theater, there were unhappy repercussions. Frederick Loewe and Alan Lerner had a "mysterious falling out," and Loewe retreated to his newly purchased farm in Pound Ridge for four years. Moreover, the joint mismanagement of the American Repertory Theatre lingered in the corners of savvy theatrical minds as the A.R.T. trudged to a permanent close.[18] Adding to the undercurrents, Crawford annoyed her peers among the League of New York Theatres and Producers (now the Broadway League) by setting two new precedents. She raised the salaries of *Brigadoon*'s chorus members and provided, at her expense, health insurance for the entire company for the run of the show. By her own admission, she valued the young people's "admirable and sturdy discipline" and felt that a raise and some security (however brief) were deserved. Rationalizing her generosity, she explained, "Theatre folk lead too insecure a life as it is. Why shouldn't they have the benefits workers in other fields take for granted?"[19]

The appreciative creators gave her an original script and score inscribed with "For our dearie Cheryl Crawford—Thanks!" The cast, who had discovered her love of poetry, presented her with a signed 1861 edition of Walt Whitman's *Leaves of Grass*. It took the place of honor among Crawford's six hundred volumes of poetry collected during her lifetime.

Never one to rest on her laurels, Crawford began strategizing about her next projects that involved Lee Strasberg, Alan Lerner, and Kurt Weill. Strasberg's reappearance in New York, after a stint in Hollywood coaching film actors, led Crawford to invite him to work on acting problems with the *Brigadoon* company. At the time, she saw the "free" acting lessons as an opportunity to extend the work of the company. When she attended their first meeting on the stage of the Ziegfeld Theatre, she found that the "brilliance and perception" of her friend's comments affected her deeply, so much so that in a typical Crawford gesture, she went "home and lay in a hot bath" to reflect upon an idea that was slowly taking shape in her mind for an extended workplace environment for professional actors.[20] By mid-April, the idea of a creative home for actors to stretch their capabilities was being tossed about by Crawford, Kazan, and Bobby Lewis that would shortly develop into a full-blown idea for an Actors Studio.

Crawford had always dreamed of a weekend retreat. By happenstance, Mary Martin was responsible for Crawford's venture into Connecticut real estate. While the actress was on tour with *Annie Get Your Gun*, she loaned her house near Norwalk to Crawford and Ruth Norman for weekends in the countryside. One August afternoon, almost a year after *Brigadoon* opened and was still drawing crowds, Crawford found the perfect (but "much too expensive") house on a small estate about four miles from Norwalk.[21]

Two old houses had been moved from Eastham on Cape Cod and reconstructed on thirteen acres of pasture and woodland. The rooms had been expanded, modern facilities installed, and a garden for vegetables and flowers prepared. The house was surrounded by a rose-covered stone wall in the rear and a picket fence in front covered with pale pink roses. "It was my dream come true," Crawford exclaimed.[22]

The promise of domesticity and rural life in a magical landscape overtook the desk-bound, telephone-in-hand producer. She proceeded to negotiate a price for the house and five acres of property, and set about installing a swimming pool and locating early American furniture from auction houses and local shops. Ruth Norman planted a vegetable garden and cooked with frequent visitor James Beard, a culinary authority who, during the mid-fifties, enlisted Norman as managing partner of a cooking school on West Tenth Street in Manhattan. Crawford credited "Eastham," as she called the place, with saving her "sanity and health."[23]

With money in her pocket from her two Broadway shows and a property owner, Crawford decided to "live it up." She bought a Lincoln Continental and employed a succession of housekeepers to cook and clean for the many weekend guests at Eastham. Those guests, a who's who list from her Group Theatre days, her Broadway contacts, and her Connecticut neighbors, included Tennessee Williams and Frank Merlo, Janet Flanner, Tallulah Bankhead, Thornton Wilder, Harvey Schmidt, Tom Jones, Kurt Weill and Lotte Lenya, Carson McCullers, Solita Solano, Frederick Loewe, Marc Blitzstein, Burl and Helen Ives, and Marilyn Monroe, who came to swim in the pool when she was in the neighborhood. When she was not performing, Mary Martin, Richard Halliday, and their daughter, Heller, also dropped by. Crawford luxuriated in her visitors and the bucolic summer and winter days with hazy summer mists and crackling fires burning in several fireplaces at once.

Weekdays in the city, Crawford strategized in her office at the St. James Theatre. Alan Lerner was eager to begin a new show. Crawford listened to his idea for a story with music based on the history of marriage from colonial times to the present and proceeded to introduce Lerner to the self-contained, bemused, and deeply private Kurt Weill fresh from *Lady in the Dark* and *Street Scene*. Weill was enthusiastic about the lyricist's idea for creating a national allegory as seen through a couple's love life in the face of economic progress that threatens to destroy their relationship. To tell an original story with a large narrative and thematic musical demands necessitated many kinds of popular music. Moreover, the revue-like structure (with vaudeville turns that commented on the dissolution of the Coopers' love life) required that Weill function as cowriter. Together, composer and lyricist set about carving out a story with song, called *A Dish from the Gods*.

By September, they had completed eleven songs and several scenes. Working through many drafts, they decided to frame the musical as a memory play with the device of the Coopers' reminiscing about their life together over one hundred and fifty years. They renamed the show *Love Life*, subtitled "A Vaudeville." It became the prototypical "concept" musical familiar to later Broadway audiences in *Cabaret*, *Company*, *A Chorus Line*, *Chicago*, and *Follies*.

Elia Kazan signed on as director, and Crawford went in search of the leading couple with Mary Martin uppermost in mind, but Martin was not captivated by the score for *Love Life*.[24] Crawford moved forward with two song-and-dance stars from *High Button Shoes* and *Annie Get Your Gun*—Nanette Fabray and Ray Middleton. Critics were misled by the advertising into expecting a joyful vaudeville entertainment helmed by some of the biggest names in show business: composer-lyricists Alan Jay Lerner and Kurt Weill, director Elia Kazan, choreographer Michael Kidd, and designers Boris Aronson, Lucinda Ballard, and Peggy Clark.

When the show opened in early October, critics and audiences were divided. While praising Weill's music, Atkinson expressed disappointment in *Love Life*, calling it an "intellectual idea about showmanship gone wrong." Others called the musical "ingenious," "striking," and "tuneful."[25] George Freedley elevated *Love Life* to "the most intelligent and adult musical yet offered on the American stage."[26]

As a group, the creators were contentious. Kurt Weill blamed Crawford for putting together a "mismatched" team, namely a preeminent "Method" director fresh from the unqualified success of *A Streetcar Named Desire*, who had no ear for music paired with the brilliant, young choreographer Michael Kidd, who would not stand up to Kazan.[27] Lucinda Ballard, Crawford's choice for costume designer, faulted the producer for retreating to her bathroom with the door locked during a crisis with the show's costumes.[28] Delivery of the *Love Life* costumes was held up at the train station until William Fitelson, who was serving as Crawford's legal adviser, in lieu of John Wildberg (the Crawford-Wildberg partnership had terminated two years earlier), stepped in and paid the shipping invoice. Ballard also opposed as an extravagant expense a second-act Punch and Judy ballet, created by Michael Kidd.

Crawford emerged from the bathroom to come to Kidd's defense. She informed the costume designer that she had promised Kidd he could have one ballet, costumed as he wanted it, in the second act. She told the designer that even though it was going to be expensive, she would take the chance."[29]

Elated by her support, Kidd was then devastated by the silence that followed his ballet on opening night in New Haven. He fled the theater, rather than face Crawford's disappointment, only to encounter her hours later in a hotel elevator where she gently explained that the audience had been "spellbound" by the ballet, so much so that they were unable to applaud. "It was one of the most successful things I have ever seen on stage," she assured the choreographer with total candor.[30]

Crawford attributed the show's "respectable" run to its fresh theme, unusual form, delightful settings, and exceptional cast. "But, it has no heart, no passion," she sighed. She observed that audiences could not get emotionally involved in the couple's problems and, with tongue in cheek, she blamed Lerner's marital history. In 1948, he had been "married only twice," she wryly observed.[31]

Hers was an excuse, not an explanation. In 1948, the unusual revue-like format prevented audiences from empathizing with the characters' domestic predicaments. The vaudeville turns injected the creators' ironic social commentaries and prevented audiences from becoming emotionally involved with the Coopers. Not until she encountered *Cabaret*, *Company*, and *Follies* in the late sixties and early seventies did Crawford acknowledge *Love Life*'s groundbreaking significance as one of the first *concept* musicals on Broadway.

Nevertheless, she did not dwell on the new musical's mixed reception because the London production of *Brigadoon* was beckoning.

West End Revisited

Crawford had been in London's West End with *Porgy and Bess* and again with *One Touch of Venus*. To her surprise, *Brigadoon*, with its Scottish connections and American song-and-dance flair, was an instant crowd-pleaser with British audiences. In February of 1949, she met Alan Lerner, Frederick Loewe, and Robert Lewis in London for casting and rehearsals. They booked rooms at the Savoy, where Crawford complained that her "small" room stood in great contrast to Loewe's large suite overlooking the Thames. She vowed that someday she would occupy such a suite, if only for a few days.[32]

As the show toured the provincial theaters, Crawford flew to Rome, where she was introduced by her Italian friend and broadcast journalist for Voice of America Natalia Danesi Murray, to her sister, Lea Danesi Tolnay, who was Tennessee Williams' literary agent in Italy.[33] Within the year, Crawford returned to Rome and sought the agent's help during her campaign to persuade the playwright, who was vacillating in his choice of producers for *The Rose Tattoo*, to convince him to choose her.[34]

Crawford returned to London to watch a technical rehearsal of *Brigadoon*, only to discover that the lights were haywire: "The forest glade, instead of having green shadows, glowed a deep red, looking like Dante's Inferno."[35] The take-charge producer and the distraught director worked through the night with the theater's electricians to duplicate Peggy Clark's lighting.

The London critics praised the musical, calling it a "light-hearted, beguilingly sentimental statement of a fantastic idea," and the show settled in for a long run on the West End.[36] Secure in the knowledge that she had a success, Crawford set out to enjoy herself among London's shops, pubs, and restaurants, including Marks and Spencer's for lingerie, Fortnum and Mason's for homecoming gifts, and the Ivy for first-rate dining.

Crawford already had her next project in hand. Before leaving for London, she had optioned *Regina*, Marc Blitzstein's musical version of *The Little Foxes*, Lillian Hellman's play about ruthless greed and familial conniving in the post-Reconstruction South. Impressed with the power and originality of Blitzstein's music, Crawford persuaded Bobby Lewis to direct the musical, which was more operatic than traditional Broadway fare.

Wonderful but Too Special

In a Broadway season with *Lost in the Stars*, *South Pacific*, and *Kiss Me, Kate*, *Regina* was an anomaly. At the outset, Crawford acknowledged that the material was not in the "traditional style of Broadway musical theatre."[37] Critics labeled it a "musical drama," to define the snatches of spoken dialogue—unexpected interruptions to Blitzstein's music—taken from the original play and woven into the fabric of the score. In a moment of near-interference, Crawford urged the composer to write a sweet song to contrast with his thunderous music, and Blitzstein wrote the enduring "Listen to the Rain."[38]

As she struggled to raise the money for the unconventional musical, Crawford met Clinton Wilder, who was undaunted by *Regina*'s "nonconformity."[39] She provided Wilder with the production's financial sheet, and, several days later, he left a check for eight thousand dollars on her desk. Moreover, Wilder offered his home for backers' auditions and became Crawford's associate producer on the show.

The Georgia-born Jane Pickens, who had been part of radio's singing Pickens sisters, sang the title role, created by the incomparable Tallulah Bankhead, who commented ungraciously on the choice of Pickens. "I didn't even like her when she was one of the Andrews Sisters," she snarled.[40]

Hellman's biographer said that the playwright, a friend and political ally of the composer-librettist of the pro-labor *The Cradle Will Rock*, approved of the "exotic transformation" of her play. Rather than take a fiercely protective stance about the musical treatment of *The Little Foxes*, as was feared, Hellman was "apparently flattered that her work was deemed material for opera and decided that the ambitious project was in good hands."[41]

During the New Haven tryout, Fitelson came up to Cheryl Crawford in the foyer of the Shubert Theatre to express his concerns. He very much wanted her to have a "sure-fire success" but thought that *Regina* was "simply not commercial."[42] The next day, she wrote a rebuttal:

> Just want to go on record about *Regina*. How anyone ever knows what will be commercial is beyond me. I recall all the wiseacres in New Haven at *Streetcar*. "Wonderful but too special." "Not enough people will want to see this morbid thing and these sad, ugly people." Even Gadg and Irene were dubious with all their appreciation of the work.
>
> If I want to stay in the theatre, I have to firmly believe that a sense of truth, coupled with theatrical talent, has an audience, a big one! If you tingle with a sudden awareness of things you only dimly felt before, of evil, of compassion, so that you know more about life after such an experience, that is all I ask.
>
> I'm going to see to it that the audience sitting before *Regina* has an emotional experience they won't forget. That is theatre. That's why I'm in it. Gags and sugarstick romance have a place in a public's entertainment, but I'd like to give them something richer, truer, deeper.
>
> As a play, this must have had a considerable catharsis for an audience or it wouldn't have run so long. I think the music adds bigger values—more emotion, more passion, more tenderness.[43]

Regina opened on October 31, 1949, to minor praise and closed after a disappointing two-month run. Despite Broadway's discomfort with opera, Blitzstein's score was praised as "brilliant," "sharp," and "astringent." Nevertheless, critics spoke wistfully of the power and appeal of Hellman's original drama. The headline in the *Daily News* put the matter more succinctly: "'The Little Foxes' Loses Its Wallop in New Musical Version."[44]

Crawford thought all the critics "got it wrong" until she received a belated letter from John Martin, dance critic for the *New York Times*. He wrote an unabashed fan letter in praise of Blitzstein's bold music written to heighten the show's theatrical values, the inspired casting, and Bobby Lewis's sensitive direction. In an effort to comfort Crawford for the lack of critical appreciation for the work, he acknowledged that by producing *Regina*, she had advanced the theater by fusing realism with the tragic grandeur of the Greeks.[45]

Regina survived for enthusiasts in an original cast recording. Moreover, the recent operatic versions of *A Streetcar Named Desire* at the San Francisco Opera House and *A View from the Bridge*, first seen at the Lyric Opera of Chicago, have served as reminders that *Regina* was staged in the wrong venue, but the only one available to Broadway types in 1949.

Zigzag Course

As vice-president of ANTA's board in the late forties, Crawford supervised the controversial premiere of Brecht's *Galileo*, which opened in New York under the Experimental Theatre's banner on December 7, an iconic date for Americans recalling the Japanese bombing of Pearl Harbor.

Against the historical backdrop of Hiroshima and Nagasaki, which inaugurated the nuclear age, *Galileo* represented the conflict between individual truth and reactionary authority. Charles Laughton gave a remarkable performance as the scientist torn between, in Crawford's words, "the revolutionary conviction that the earth moved around the sun and his recantation of that knowledge to save his skin."[46] As Crawford observed Laughton's efforts during rehearsals to fill out Galileo's humanness with the business of everyday living, she expressed prudish concern over one piece of business. Laughton took "an excessive amount of time bathing the top half of his naked, flabby body, a large pudding of a belly which I found most unattractive," she complained. "To my regret, I was never able to convince him to cut one moment of his public bath."[47] Nevertheless, those in the audience did not easily forget Laughton's showmanship, described as "a constant irradiation of expression by voice, hands, face, eyes, and shoulders."[48]

The show opened four days after the unprecedented *A Streetcar Named Desire* in 1947, and the *New York Times* critic found Brecht's dialectical arguments, interspersed with Hanns Eisler's austere music, "pretentious," "enigmatic," and "a cross between a religious masque and a carnival."[49]

By 1949, it was apparent that ANTA needed a permanent theater. The City Investment Company, consisting of real estate moguls Robert Dowling and Roger L. Stevens, also members of ANTA's board, purchased the Theatre Guild Theatre on Fifty-second Street and turned it over to ANTA to be used for nonprofit theatrical activity. Crawford presented the second production in the newly acquired playhouse. Even though Crawford had persuaded Paul Green to modernize (and Americanize) Ibsen's *Peer Gynt*, John Garfield to play Peer, and Lee Strasberg to direct, the new version had limited appeal. Ibsen's picaresque morality tale of an opportunist's journey from youth to old age was dismissed in one reviewer's headline as, "This Is for Garfield and Ibsen Fans Only." The critical endorsements were qualified for the play ("not truly formidable"), and for Garfield's performance ("not a stage actor of sufficient stature").[50]

Crawford was her harshest critic. She wrote to Paul Green in North Carolina, saying that she was "very unhappy that PG [*Peer Gynt*] didn't turn out as I hoped."[51] Upon learning that *Peer Gynt* was closing, the playwright told Crawford that the play had been a "brave adventure" and offered a home-spun analogy that pin-pointed the subdued spirit of the performance: "the leaping, soaring poetic spirit of Peer never really gets loose to do its stuff in the play. Actually we have a football game. Our star is on the team. The spectators expect him to get loose for a touchdown run. The minutes pass, the game draws on toward the end—he never does. Well, the simile's not exactly accurate, but you know what I mean."[52]

In private, Crawford remarked that "Garfield was good but not astonishing; the production worked only in parts—and not in very many parts." With the clarity of hindsight, she concluded, "Perhaps it is not a produceable play; I have never heard of it being unusually successful."[53]

Contemplating her resignation from the ANTA Board, she experienced a sense of déjà vu. The mixed reviews and subscriber reactions to Robinson Jeffers' *The Tower Beyond Tragedy* with Judith Anderson and *Peer Gynt* mirrored, in her mind, the responses to the A.R.T.'s *Henry VIII* and *John Gabriel Borkman*. Moreover, ANTA's goals were likewise high-minded ideals detached from the realities of financing and theatrically effective playwriting. Nevertheless, they had done some things right. They had negotiated a nonprofit status with the unions (Garfield and Laughton played for ten dollars and eight dollars a week respectively), and they had avoided the expenses of playing repertory, substituting instead individual financing of productions with separate casts. Nevertheless, they had not found a way to establish a company of actors.

Crawford's zigzag course through the worlds of for-profit and nonprofit theater underscored her pioneering spirit. When an interviewer asked where she derived her boundless energy, she answered slyly: "On light days, I sometimes have a double orange juice in a drugstore."[54] Nevertheless, in 1951, she was tired and disheartened. She gave up on the ANTA operation for the same reasons expressed in her letter of resignation from the A.R.T. Expenses consistently outran income—and there was never enough money. "The fabulous balloon of a nonprofit theatre had been injected with gas to little purpose. Enough was enough," Crawford concluded. The two organizations, for which she had the highest hopes, had failed, and her disappointment was profound. She said, "Ever since the Group days I had truly wanted to be involved in theatre that had a core and continuity, theatre that enriched the theatre itself. When the A.R.T. and ANTA's Experimental Theatre died a-borning, I became again that naked individual I had tried to avoid."[55] But not quite. She persevered a third time and was rewarded. The years she spent alongside Elia Kazan and Lee Strasberg shaping the Actors Studio altered the character of the American theater.

9

THE OYSTER BED

In a way all theatre people are lunatics—in a good sense, revolutionary.
—Cheryl Crawford

The Actors Studio, or the oyster bed for cultivating pearls as Cheryl Crawford referred to the new workshop, was the third phase of her adventures in 1947. The Studio opened on October 5, 1947, in a room in the old Union Methodist Church on West Forty-eighth Street, later demolished and converted into a parking lot for Mama Leone's restaurant. Juggling her responsibilities to ANTA and to the new Lerner-Weill musical, Crawford assumed an administrative position within the Studio. At the time, Crawford was comfortable with her managerial role in a workshop wholly focused on the actor's process.

The Back Story

Crawford recalled a critical lunch with Elia Kazan in a Westside restaurant on April 17, 1947. Their conversation began with congratulations on their successes with *Brigadoon* and *All My Sons*, which lead to memories of their struggles during the Group Theatre days and to the current plight of young professionals caught up in long runs on Broadway with nowhere to burnish aspects of their craft or rediscover sources of inspiration.[1]

As reconstructed by Crawford, the conversation went something like this: "It's a damn shame that they have so few opportunities to learn their craft," she remarked. "If they're good in a role, they get cast in another just like it. They're only part of a labor pool."[2]

In her version, Kazan replied: "It's not just the kids. The more experienced ones need a place where they can stretch. Who has time to train them? You know how it is. When I'm directing a play, I'm on a schedule."

He paused to reach for a grand scheme. "We ought to do something about it, get a bunch together, get 'em out of that goddamned Walgreen's drugstore. I've been talking to Bobby Lewis. He's all for it."[3]

Recollections of how the Studio was born take on *Rashōmon*-like proportions in the contradictory memories of the principals. Harold Clurman claimed that he suggested the idea to Kazan and Lewis several years after the Group ended. Kazan had no recollection of Clurman's remarks, nor of his conversation with Crawford in a Westside restaurant. However, he did recall a talk with Lewis during a leisurely walk in Central Park. Bobby Lewis described the subtext of their dialogue as "the yearning we felt for something like the 'home' we had had in the Group Theatre—a place where we could explore and expand our theatrical ideas." In Lewis' account, Kazan wanted a place to train talented actors for the kind of plays and films he would direct. In turn, Lewis wanted a place where he could work with actors on problems of style.[4]

The director of *All My Sons* believed that Bobby Lewis was the ideal partner to begin a studio for actors in the early stages of their professional careers. He admired Lewis's personal simplicity, clarity, and sense of humor, and the fact that his teaching stressed the bolder, imaginative side of acting, rather than the interior emotional side.[5] Lewis was enthusiastic and agreed to teach the craft to the more experienced actors, and Kazan consented to work with the less experienced ones. When they discussed a need for an administrator, who would understand their ideals and not try to convert a free studio into a money-making proposition, they both thought of the same person—their Group comrade, Cheryl Crawford.

In an interview with critic Mel Gussow, Lewis spoke with customary frankness about the founding of the Studio and disputed Crawford's version of where and when her discussion with Kazan took place. "There was no coffee shop, there was no talk, and Cheryl was brought in by Kazan and me because we were lousy at business, and Cheryl was a very good businesswoman."[6]

In Kazan's version, he introduced the subject of a three-way partnership in Crawford's office. With the disclaimer that she was not a teacher, she volunteered to administer the workshop and offered the names of talented young actors from the A.R.T., namely, Julie Harris, Anne Jackson, and Eli Wallach from *Alice in Wonderland* and *Yellow Jack*.

Despite the conflicting views on the germination of the Studio, the three moved forward to establish the workshop. Nevertheless, Kazan's commitments in Hollywood postponed any actual beginning of a studio until October of 1947.

Over endless cups of coffee, the threesome sketched out an artistic home for young professionals who wanted to stretch their capabilities and tackle their limitations in a sympathetic environment. The codirectors also agreed to a financial plan. They would work without compensation, raise money for basic expenses, and forego tuition fees. They concurred that *talent* was the only qualification for membership.

Unlike the trio that launched the Group Theatre, the triumvirate this time was made up of Kazan, Lewis, and Crawford, even though in later years many associated Lee Strasberg with the creation of the Studio. In their early discussions, Kazan and Lewis rejected inviting Strasberg to teach because they considered his manner of dealing with young actors light years removed from their own approach, which discouraged working for emotion for its own sake, and emphasized, instead, its relevance to the character and the play.[7] Strasberg did not come onboard until 1951, four years later, and after Bobby Lewis departed.

To launch the "studio," named for the Group's former workshop (the Group Theatre Studio), they turned to attorney William Fitelson (who at various times represented all three). He set up a tax-exempt organization with a board of directors that included arts patron and philanthropist Dorothy Willard, and Fitelson himself. In the beginning, Kazan and Lewis conceived of classes with approximately twenty actors each. Crawford's role in the mix, as she herself said, was "a vague one of coordinating classes and giving general help where it was needed."[8] Meanwhile, she was juggling the Experimental Theatre production of *Galileo* and the future London production of *Brigadoon*.

The trio spent the next few months talking to familiar actors and interviewing others recommended by agents. Several potential members learned of the Studio by word-of-mouth. The overwhelming response immediately forced them to revise their original idea for two small classes. Bobby Lewis's more experienced group eventually numbered fifty-two and met three times a week and included Herbert Berghof, Marlon Brando, Montgomery Clift, Mildred Dunnock, Tom Ewell, John Forsythe, Anne Jackson, Sidney Lumet, Kevin McCarthy, Karl Malden, E. G. Marshall, Patricia Neal, William Redford, Jerome Robbins, Maureen Stapleton, Beatrice Straight, Eli Wallach, and David Wayne. Kazan's group of twenty-six met twice a week and brought together Tom Avera, Edward Binns, Rudy Bond, Jocelyn Brando (Marlon's sister), Joan Copeland (Arthur Miller's sister), Lou Gilbert, Julie Harris, Anne Hegira, Steven Hill, Peg Hillias, Cloris Leachman, Lenka Peterson, James Whitmore, and, after a time, Kim Hunter.[9]

Enchanted by the actors' responses, Crawford bragged: "From the outset it was a nest of the finest talent of its time."[10]

The first meeting was held in a dingy room on the top floor of what was originally the Princess Theatre, called by then the Labor Stage. Kazan assumed the role of chief spokesman and explained the policies and expectations, namely, that there would be no tuition charges, but all involved were expected to work. If they missed two classes in a row, they would be asked to leave. Since there was no space owned by the Studio and no available funds to rent one, the actors agreed to contribute two dollars a week for a place to work. In early October, the Actors Studio began in a rented room in the old church on West Forty-eighth Street.

With Kazan dividing his time between film projects in Hollywood and preparations for the national tour of *All My Sons*, classes began at the Studio under Crawford's watchful management and Bobby Lewis's methods based on his own interpretation of Stanislavski's theories.

In the early months of the workshop, Crawford was a studious observer. As she described the classes, she recalled that the general procedure required an actor to prepare a scene or an exercise, perform it before colleagues, and engage in discussion afterwards. Lewis exhibited a "quirky, original humor" exemplified in the brochure prepared for his private teaching that offered one hundred and twenty-nine classes, including "Theatre of Sexual Shock, Horse Opera, and Poor Theatre."[11] He asked his group to work mainly on scenes and prepare roles that they could not expect to play on Broadway. Dancer-choreographer Jerome Robbins, for example, was given a scene from *Waiting for Lefty* in which he played a young Jewish intern who was a victim of anti-Semitism in the hospital where he worked, and, Tom Ewell, who was playing a lead in the Broadway comedy *John Loves Mary*, prepared the part of the mentally challenged Lenny in *Of Mice and Men*. At the end of his scene, comedian Ewell exclaimed with delight, "My God! No one ever cried at me before."[12]

Crawford's memories of Marlon Brando (and later James Dean) detail the inherent charm and inventiveness of the actor who created Stanley Kowalski the year the Actors Studio opened. Crawford related a vivid memory of Brando performing a scene from Robert E. Sherwood's *Reunion in Vienna*, played famously by the Lunts for the Theatre Guild in the thirties. Brando played the exiled Archduke Rudolf Maximilian Von Hapsburg, reduced to driving a cab in the south of France after the fall of the Austro-Hungarian Empire. At a fancy ball where a group of expatriates tried to relive their former splendor, Brando appeared in a rented costume complete with monocle, pencil moustache, and ivory cigarette holder. When he removed a polished boot, he revealed a dirty sock with holes. Crawford was captivated by the charming piece of business that showed how the character had "disguised his poverty for the night."[13]

In contrast to the workmanlike orderliness of Bobby Lewis's approach to teaching, Kazan's vitality and enthusiasm brought "the voltage of a high electric charge" to his classes. Crawford observed Kazan's uncanny ability for drawing truthful performances out of actors who divined some kind of psychological affinity for their roles.[14] His exercises were intended to extend the actor's imagination, to sharpen the senses, develop concentration, and to differentiate between indicating emotions and really experiencing them. He would ask the actors to perform a scene, based on three words ("wine, hair, song," for example). Or, he would offer reproductions of paintings by Toulouse Lautrec and George Grosz and ask the actors to improvise scenes based on what was happening in the paintings.[15]

A great deal has been written about the Actors Studio by the participants, historians, and biographers. Crawford's eye-witness account of the inner workings of the early Studio differs from that of her cohorts. She observed the goings and comings of the remarkable aspirants, the tensions created by the workloads of Kazan and Lewis outside the Studio, and the ever-present danger of turning the workshop into a producing organization.[16]

Crawford herself was guilty of the first breach of protocol. Despite Kazan's frenetic schedule, he and Lewis decided to wind up the Studio's inaugural season with in-house presentations of Anton Chekhov's *The Sea Gull* and Bessie Breuer's *Sundown Beach*, the first (and only) play by the novelist. Set near a Florida psychiatric hospital for convalescing Air Force combat crews, *Sundown Beach* concerned the wives and children waiting for their men and fathers to recover. Kazan cast Breuer's play from his class of unknowns. Crawford thought that the performances of Julie Harris, Martin Balsam, Cloris Leachman, and Steven Hill were worthy of a more extended life and offered to book the show in a summer theater. Lawrence Langner's Westport Country Playhouse in Connecticut agreed to take the low-budget show. Despite the fact that the stage lights went out on opening night, and part of the performance was lit by large flashlights, *Sundown Beach* was well received, and, as Crawford noted with satisfaction, made more money than anything else the Playhouse scheduled that summer. She arranged for the show to travel to Marblehead, Boston, and then, in September, to Broadway's Belasco Theatre.

Crawford blamed Kazan for the ensuing debacle. A few days before the New York opening, he came to the Belasco to rehearse the cast and made the actors "tense and pushing." "He zapped it up and it didn't work anymore," Crawford complained.[17] The play quickly closed.

Not only had Crawford violated the original Studio ban against public productions, she then proceeded to open Pandora's Box, thereby creating a chain of events that shattered the friendship between Kazan and Lewis. From the beginning, she and Kazan had argued with Lewis against turning the Studio into a producing organization. Moreover, Lewis disagreed with them and was bitterly disappointed that his production of *The Sea Gull* had not, unlike *Sundown Beach*, received a public production. Crawford felt that Lewis's unhappiness was justified, even though the Chekhov play required a large cast and multiple sets.

Because of his success staging *Brigadoon*, Crawford asked him to direct the new Lerner-Weill musical. At the outset, he was troubled by Alan Lerner's book, which needed major revisions. He shared the script with Kazan, who advised him to "stay away from the project," unless he could get Lerner to agree to make changes.[18] Convinced that Lerner would not be forthcoming with rewrites, Lewis turned down Crawford's offer. Almost immediately, she turned to Kazan, who told her that he was too busy to handle the production but then changed his mind. Rather than tell Lewis that he was now directing the show, Kazan asked Crawford to communicate his decision to his friend. Reluctantly, she made the call. "I could hear her voice trembling on the telephone," Lewis said. "It was Gadget who was gambling with my friendship, but Cheryl had to be the messenger with bad news."[19]

In his letter of resignation from the Studio, dated June 15, 1948, Lewis blamed Kazan for the miscommunication. "Gadget should have spoken to me when he decided to do the show . . . I would have wished him well and that would have been the last of that." In addition, he was put off by Kazan's self-serving reply. "I think you're the best teacher for young actors in the city today not excluding myself," Kazan wrote. "I think you need Cheryl and me. I think you need the Studio."[20]

Crawford tried to mend the breach between the friends without success. In an effort to explain her mishandling of the *Love Life* matter, she wrote to Lewis: "If I seem to you remiss in friendship and not quite worthy of your trust, it's not through lack of feeling or interest, but those damn human defects I'm still working at, tho' I sometimes think they should have improved more with forty-five years under the belt."[21]

Turning his back on the Studio, Bobby Lewis opened the Robert Lewis

Theatre Workshop, and, for four decades thereafter, gave acting lessons and wrote books on his methods. For her part, Crawford acknowledged that their parting was amicable and blamed the schism on the fact that *The Sea Gull* had not received a public presentation, for which she felt responsible, since she had promoted *Sundown Beach*.[22] Lewis continued to work with Crawford and staged *Regina*, *Paint Your Wagon*, *Reuben Reuben*, and *Mister Johnson* under her producing banner.

In their search for another codirector and teacher, both Kazan and Crawford wanted Strasberg but he was adamant that he did not want a permanent position with the Studio. For three years, they searched for the right person but came up with no candidate who could eventually lead the Studio. In 1951, they finally persuaded Strasberg to become the Studio's artistic director with the two groups of actors consolidated under this guidance. Over the years, he became a father figure for some, and, for others, an alienating influence.

Crawford recalled the story of the encounter between Lee Strasberg and James Dean, the young film actor of *Rebel Without a Cause* and *East of Eden*, who, along with Marlon Brando, came to epitomize the reputed style of the Studio, which involved torn jeans, T-shirts, slouching, mumbling, and scratching. Incensed by the characterization, Crawford complained, "In truth, there was no such style. If a lot of Studio people wore T-shirts and jeans, it was usually out of economic necessity; they were, after all, struggling actors." She elaborated on the erroneous notion of the Studio actor as self-absorbed, inarticulate, and proletarian—the tough, sensitive loners that Marlon Brando and James Dean played in films. "Today, of course, every stratum of society is devoted to jeans, preferably frayed," Crawford observed, "but the fifties were such a conformist period that any emblem of nonconformity, whatever its *raison d'être*, took on an exaggerated importance.[23]

Whereas, Crawford noted, many actors flourished over the years under Strasberg's guidance, a few were harmed when their scenes were poorly received. She regretted that James Dean became one of the lost ones. To prepare his audition piece (an original scene that dealt with an encounter between an intelligent drifter and an aristocratic Southern girl written by actress Chris White), the actor went to Central Park, stopped strangers, and spoke the character's lines to ascertain if he were believable. Dean was admitted to the Studio, but his subsequent scenes were not well received, and he left the Studio expressing great bitterness over the experience.[24]

The peripatetic Marilyn Monroe seemed an unlikely candidate to respond to Strasberg's guidance. Crawford and Monroe knew one another from their Connecticut neighborhood and found themselves seated opposite one another at a dinner party in the apartment of the Theatre Guild's creative adviser, Paul Bigelow, in 1955. During the evening, Crawford had a lengthy discussion with the film star about acting during which Crawford invited her to observe the work at the Studio. Aware that the actress was chronically late for appointments, Crawford picked her up at the Ritz Towers, where she was staying, took her to the Studio, and introduced Marilyn Monroe to Lee Strasberg. Crawford reported that the actress was "enthralled by the work and by Lee" and enrolled in classes at the Studio and also attended Strasberg's private classes that he taught for additional income. She remained a staunch supporter and a frequent contributor to the Studio during her lifetime.[25]

Reflecting upon her work with the Experimental Theatre, which had required original scripts, Crawford urged the development of a playwrights' unit. Her interest was not entirely altruistic. As a producer, she constantly searched for new, groundbreaking scripts and encouraged a cadre of largely unheralded writers for the Studio's new playwriting wing. When she catalogued the most successful of the new writing to reach a larger audience, she included *Camino Real, A Hatful of Rain, End as a Man, The Zoo Story, The Night of the Iguana, Any Wednesday, The Rose Tattoo, Take a Giant Step, The Death of Bessie Smith, Dynamite Tonight, Shadow of a Gunman*, and *The Thirteen Clocks.*

Tensions and disagreements within the Studio were altogether too familiar refrains resonant of her Group Theatre days. Working in league with Kazan and Lewis (and later Strasberg), Crawford experienced the chauvinism that earlier lead to her break with the Group. What was different sixteen years later was the fact that Crawford's creative activities took place *outside* the workshop environment. Moreover, Molly Day Thatcher, Group play-reader, playwright, and married to Kazan, had come onboard as moderator to lead the criticism of first drafts of members' plays to determine if a play in progress was suitable for staging. Women were in the minority in the writer's unit, which included Edward Albee, James Baldwin, William Inge, Arthur Kopit, Arthur Laurents, Norman Mailer, and Lorraine Hansberry—the sole member from the distaff side. No woman was invited into the directors' unit, reflective of the American theater at-large prior to the regional theater movement of the late fifties.

Crawford had long ago suppressed her own ambitions to be a director and was not troubled by the absence of women directors in the Studio. As a commercial producer, she was apolitical, practical, and sanguine. She had teamed up with Margaret Webster, by no means a newcomer, who had a proven Broadway track record with modern and Shakespearean plays. Now, she had at hand Elia Kazan, Robert Lewis, Daniel Mann, Lee Strasberg, and Jack Garfein, the best directors of the day, to stage her commercial plays and musicals. As for herself, Crawford was satisfied to engage in administrative duties in the three-way partnership without the illusion that she was a creative partner. For the most part, she ignored the male egos making proprietary claims on the Studio, until Strasberg's later decision, which she strongly opposed, to take the Studio's newly created production wing to London.

Edward Albee joined the Studio when Molly Thatcher and her associate Michael Wager received a copy of *The Zoo Story* from Albee's agent, Edward Parone, and agreed to give the play a hearing. Director John Stix found the play different from anything he had previously read and agreed to direct. With scripts in hand and a bench for scenery, actors Shepperd Strudwick and Lou Antonio presented Albee's play for the first time in America at the Actors Studio for one performance in the fall of 1959. Mel Gussow described the chaotic discussion following the performance that, in the manner of Strasberg's harsh and longwinded verdicts, often left the playwright wounded and bleeding. As the members started to quarrel with the play, Norman Mailer jumped to his feet and pounded away at the negative criticism for what he viewed as a remarkable play.[26]

In a curious set of circumstances, Crawford did not step forward to produce either *The Zoo Story* or *The Death of Bessie Smith* outside the Studio. The later contretemps over a possible production of the now seminal *Who's Afraid of Virginia Woolf?* lends credence to Crawford's reputed aversion to "dirty" language on stage. With the later successful notoriety of Albee's full-length play, Crawford realized that, when they declined the playwright's offer of *Virginia Woolf*, they lost their last chance to originate another play by Edward Albee.

One of Crawford's sustaining qualities, admired by coworkers and reporters, was her ability to take abominable and devastating failure squarely on the chin.[27] As with the loss of Edward Albee and his award-winning play, Crawford blamed only herself for not recognizing the originality and power of *Who's Afraid of Virginia Woolf?* What was her excuse? "I was scared of its bitterness and brutality," she confessed. "So we passed it up. Of course we made a mistake."[28]

Before the schism, Edward Albee had been instrumental in merging the two groups of playwrights and directors into a single unit. He invited Tennessee Williams to participate, and Williams replied,

> [I]t sounds like a rather formidable unit, but what isn't? I am not scared off. And I certainly do have things I would love to have tried out. My career has turned to a try-out it seems, anyway. I can't think of any better place to have a try-out. Most of my work now, and from now on, I suspect is in the short-long or long-short from, and intensely personal and highly eclectic, and may be unfit for public exposure. But I know from past experience with plays such as the short form of *Camino Real* and *Night of the Iguana*, both of which were explored by the Studio, that the atmosphere there is sympathetically creative and experimental—and it would be of the greatest help to me to have one or two of them tried out as classroom exercises, culminating in the sort of in-group presentation that the Studio provides to nerve-shattered playwrights.
>
> So if you will accept me as a probationary or novitiate sort of a contributor, I will *gladly* contribute.[29]

Never an official member of the Studio, Williams remained informally connected through Elia Kazan's and Cheryl Crawford's commercial interests. Kazan worked on scenes from the early *Ten Blocks on the Camino Real*, which later became the full-length *Camino Real*, and Crawford produced a quartet of his plays on Broadway (*The Rose Tattoo*, *Camino Real*, *Sweet Bird of Youth*, and *Period of Adjustment*), staged by directors and actors associated with the Studio.

Crawford began to feel the financial pressures brought on by the Studio's increasing number of actors, directors, and playwrights accompanied by the familiar clamor for public presentations. Some of her worries were alleviated when a major television network, which produced weekly dramatic programs, approached the Studio to broadcast live programs. Dorothy Willard was instrumental in persuading Kazan and Crawford that a series bearing the imprimatur of the Studio would be an excellent means of gaining support for the workshop. Crawford rejoiced: "In the fall of that year financial support [ten percent of the gross monies paid for the series] came easily for the only time in the Studio's existence."[30]

Tennessee Williams' *Portrait of a Madonna*, with Jessica Tandy as Miss Lucretia Collins and directed by Hume Cronyn, was the first broadcast. The network program received consistently good reviews, won the renowned Peabody Award, and lasted for fifty-six weeks. The series ended in March of 1950, and, despite efforts, was not revived in the following season. Nevertheless, the television exposure and the growing word-of-mouth put pressure on the Studio's leaders to open classes to more professionals and find ways to satisfy the members' demands for public presentations.

Expanding the Dream

In the period between 1948 and 1951, over two thousand actors auditioned for the Studio, including a remarkable number of stage and film stars.[31] In general, applicants were screened first by Studio members, and a smaller number was passed along to the codirectors for final scrutiny. Crawford remarked that she was astonished how many removed their clothes during scenes. "I suspect that they wished to show us how free and uninhibited they were. We certainly witnessed a good number of bare breasts and jock straps."[32]

By 1955, with contributions from friends, members, and fundraising events, the Studio purchased a one-hundred-year-old Greek revival–style church on West Forty-fourth Street between Ninth and Tenth. The building burst with activities from morning until after midnight. Strasberg gave sessions twice a week from eleven A.M. to one P.M., followed by heated discussions. Sometime scene rehearsals went on until three o'clock in the morning. Other instructors were hired for speech, dance, and mime, and Crawford even gave a course on producing.

As time passed, the Actors Studio became the talk of Broadway and Hollywood, and theater people, sponsored by the U.S. State Department, came from all over the world to observe, ask questions, meet and discuss theater with professionals. Crawford was uncomfortable with the presence of journalists, celebrities, and international artists curious to see the inner workings of the Studio. The observers placed additional pressure on the actors, who were expected, in Crawford's lingo, "to put on a show."

Complaining that the purpose of the work was to allow actors to fall on their faces, to experiment, and even fail, Crawford witnessed an unanticipated (and regrettable) scene played out before an audience of film and stage celebrities. Crawford recorded the brawl that ensued between Anne Bancroft and Viveca Lindfors in Strindberg's *The Stronger:*

> Viveca's part called for her to be totally silent; we were to see her reactions to Anne's monologue only from her behavior. But Viveca was not content to remain silent and began to make little noises, which infuriated Anne. A wild fight of screaming and hair-pulling began. It was both frightening and

hilarious. I never knew what the shopworn expression "tempers flew" meant until I saw this. Madeline Sherwood attempted to stop it and was knocked down. Lee yelled, "Keep out of it, Madeline!" As they began to wear out, Lee rose and stopped them. Naturally, this scene caused quite a commotion in the audience.[33]

Crawford blamed the unseemly behavior on the pressures placed on the actors by the presence of celebrities, who often left sessions gossiping about the "ineptitude" of the trial-and-error scene work. "They didn't understand the necessity to fail," she complained.[34]

In a clear sense, Cheryl Crawford was caught in a familiar double-bind. At the same time she raised money for her Broadway productions, she was charged with keeping the Studio solvent. Based on her experiences with the Group Theatre, the A.R.T., and now the Studio, Crawford clearly understood the differences in expectations. Investors in Broadway shows hoped for a return on their investment and those interested in assisting the nonprofit sector were concerned with the mission and in a tax deduction for their contribution. Neither foundations nor wealthy patrons seemed to "find our oyster bed . . . worthy of their altruism," she lamented, "in spite of the many pearls we uncovered in those oysters."[35]

Her explanation for why patrons contributed to buildings (what her friend Harold Clurman called "edifice complexes"), rather than artists, was embedded in her favorite story of two elderly women rocking side by side on the porch of a summer hotel. One was knitting, the other reading. The reader asked the other why she knitted all the time. The answer, "Oh, but if you read you have nothing to show!"

"Money wants something to show," Crawford explained. "I think that is why so many impressive and expensive theatre buildings have been erected to contain very minor achievements."[36]

Crawford was most successful when she explained the Studio's fiscal problems to stage and film celebrities. A few days after speaking with actor-dancer Gene Kelly of *Singin' in the Rain* fame, she received a check for ten thousand dollars. At one time, Marilyn Monroe and Elizabeth Taylor sent checks for ten thousand dollars each. At various times Paul Newman helped financially, and the William Morris Agency was also generous. Nevertheless, it was "never enough," Crawford agonized. "In order to sustain the Studio properly," she explained, "we needed at least sixty thousand dollars a year for salaries, mortgage, building maintenance, and the limited production of new plays." Despite her efforts, "We never got it," she said, adding, "It was my unfortunate task to announce each season that we were practically bankrupt."[37]

One strategy for securing an infusion of money into the Studio's coffers was an annual star-studded benefit with entertainments by such notables as Mary Martin, Laurence Olivier, Sammy Davis Jr., Judy Garland, Marilyn Monroe, Ella Fitzgerald, Mike Nichols, and Elaine May. The most successful (and controversial) benefit, under Crawford's supervision, took place around the New York premiere of Tennessee Williams's first original screenplay, *Baby Doll*, directed by Kazan, and featuring Studio actors Carroll Baker, Eli Wallach, Karl Malden, Mildred Dunnock, Lonny Chapman, and Rip Torn.

Set in a decadent Southern milieu, *Baby Doll* aroused the moral indignation of the Roman Catholic hierarchy. Cardinal Francis Spellman denounced the film from the pulpit of St. Patrick's Cathedral on Fifth Avenue on a Sunday prior to the New York premiere. Reportedly, the Cardinal never saw the film; nevertheless, he warned Catholics against seeing it.

The prescreening controversy, involving the city's religious and political leaders, not only provided publicity for the film but also guaranteed notoriety for the Studio and a wildly successful benefit, which netted forty thousand dollars. Crawford reported that the scandal "brought out a full house," attended by the Rabbi of Temple Israel, the Dean of the Cathedral of St. John the Divine, and the executive director of the national Council of the Churches of Christ, as well as Studio enthusiasts and the curious.[38]

At the start of the new decade, Crawford relentlessly served two masters: her Broadway shows and the nonprofit workshop. Even though the altruistic path was more difficult, she soon learned that the Studio held out personal benefits for a Broadway producer, including a playwright from Mississippi with *The Rose Tattoo* in his typewriter.

10

FOUR BY TENN

Cheryl is a great fighter, she is always there when you need her.
—Tennessee Williams

For ten years, Cheryl Crawford had a loving, rewarding, contentious, and exhausting relationship with Tennessee Williams. During the decade of the fifties when most film and stage artists were contending with the U.S. House Committee on Un-American Activities, she produced four of his plays: *The Rose Tattoo, Camino Real, Sweet Bird of Youth*, and *Period of Adjustment*. She did not produce *Cat on a Hot Tin Roof* or *The Night of the Iguana*, and therein hangs a tale of troubled relations among producers, writers, and agents.

Crawford was nine years older than the playwright. She became aware of the young writer from Mississippi in 1940, when he won a one-hundred-dollar prize in a Group Theatre play contest with a series of four one-act plays, entitled *American Blues*. Although Crawford left the Group the year before Williams received the award, Audrey Wood, by then the playwright's agent, sent a copy of the plays to the producer of *Family Portrait* and the Maplewood Theatre. Impressed with the quality of the writing, Crawford asked to meet the writer, and found herself face to face with a slender young man of "medium height with sandy, slightly curly hair, a sandy moustache, and pale blue eyes." She was unnerved by the fact that he "scarcely seemed to notice" her or other people, but later learned that he "never missed a trick."[1]

Producer and playwright shared much in common. Reluctant to engage in casual conversation, they developed over the years what Crawford called "a comfortable rapport," and displayed a gentle candor in their correspondence. They also shared same-sex preferences that resulted in an unstated bond between them, but, unlike the writer who candidly (and generously) talked about his private life, Crawford was not forthcoming about hers.

Sensitive to the playwright's many contradictions, she wrote, "He is courageous and fearful, suspicious and trusting, generous and acquisitive, sanguine and despairing, impulsive and cautious." Crawford attributed his "endearing cackle" and his explosive laughter as covers for his shyness. Moreover, his sense of humor often "baffled straight-laced people," and the Midwesterner admitted that she was often unable to fathom the things that amused him.[2]

Crawford was working on *The Tempest* in 1945 when *The Glass Menagerie* opened on Broadway. Two years later, when *A Streetcar Named Desire* had its pre-Broadway tryout in New Haven, she was enjoying a sure-fire hit in *Brigadoon*. Curious about the new play, she took the train to New Haven and was overwhelmed by *Streetcar*. Nevertheless, she was seething. Audrey Wood had not given her an opportunity either to read the script or to make an offer to produce it. Determined to avoid another omission of this kind, she argued her position. "I know everyone must be trying to climb on Tenn's bandwagon now," she told the diminutive agent, known for her tailored suits, bright scarves, and expensive hats. She continued,

> But I think it's wrong that a new producer [Irene Mayer Selznick] was handed our best playwright on a golden platter. I hear *Streetcar* was offered to no one else. I wouldn't be angry if it had gone to others who have earned the right. Some of us stuck with the theatre all of our working lives, taken great chances, done the first plays of many authors, taken the failures, kept going.

She ended with, "I want to do his next play, whatever it is. Now, how about it?"[3]

Known to her clients as a patient and able woman, Audrey Wood calmly replied, "No auspices have been set. I think it's a good idea for you two to work together."[4] Nevertheless, in April of 1950, the playwright sent his new script (called *The Eclipse of May 29, 1919*) to Irene Selznick. Dissatisfied with his "shaky" play, he was also conflicted over which woman would be the better producer—Selznick or Crawford. Because of his experience with *Streetcar*, he felt closer to Selznick, admiring her drive and vitality, characterized by Audrey Wood as her intrusive manner and incessant demands.[5] In April, Cheryl Crawford was clearly second choice.

Writing to his agent on the matter, Williams said, "Dear Cheryl, she's as delicate as the play itself, for all her tailored clothes and her square-set jaw, and her clear honest blue eyes, I don't suppose, as a human being, I think any other producer quite measures up to her. After Irene, I suppose she's the one I'd want." He was fearful that Crawford was not "vital or powerful enough to turn not only every stone but also some of the smaller mountains to achieve what she's after!"[6]

Within the month, the matter was settled. Irene Selznick rejected the play as a "ballet or libretto" and produced John Van Druten's fanciful *Bell, Book and Candle* the following November.[7]

Aware of the possibility of losing Williams' play, Crawford campaigned ferociously during trips to Rome and Key West to see the playwright. Before arriving in Key West in early April, Crawford, measuring herself against the gathering forces of Irene Selznick, wrote the playwright that Selznick, as a producer, "has not yet earned her right to such good fortune, and that some of us who have stuck with the theatre all of our working lives . . . deserve the honor of producing Tennessee Williams' plays also."[8]

Unknown to her, she had won by default. The new Tennessee Williams play arrived on her desk in May and was called *The Rose Tattoo*.

Dionysus on Broadway

Crawford was so profoundly pleased to receive the go-ahead from Audrey Wood that she was not put off when she discovered that Irene Selznick had been first choice. Crawford did not agree with the willowy daughter and wife of Hollywood moguls in her assessment of the script, but never thought unkindly of Audrey Wood. In Crawford's opinion, the agent was always thinking of the playwright, who felt that Selznick should have first consideration.[9] Crawford was gracious in the knowledge that she, not Selznick, would produce *The Rose Tattoo*.

Although she did not consider the play a libretto, she realized that it would be difficult to stage. After reading a second draft, she had no doubt that the play would fulfill its promise of being a "serious comedy." The casting of the two leads went smoothly, although the playwright wanted Anna Magnani for the Sicilian widow, Serafina della Rose. Crawford was not deterred by the loss of Magnani, who was unavailable, because the actress spoke "very little English at that time," and had declared she would sign only for a four-month run because of commitments in Italy.[10] (Magnani appeared opposite Burt Lancaster in the film version to magnificent reviews.)

When Crawford turned to Kazan to direct *Rose Tattoo*, she was discouraged by the fact that he was not available. He was preparing to film *Viva Zapata!* for Twentieth Century Fox and working on an uncompleted film script, *The Hook*, with Arthur Miller. Guided by factors of economy and availability, Crawford looked to the Actors Studio to provide both director Daniel Mann (who had directed *Come Back, Little Sheba* that year with distinction) and actors Maureen Stapleton and Eli Wallach, whose work Crawford had observed there. The creative team was fleshed out with set designer Boris Aronson, costume designer Rose Bogdanoff, and composer David Diamond for incidental music.

In early December, *The Rose Tattoo* went into rehearsal. The company departed New York on Christmas Day bound for the Chicago premiere at the Erlanger Theatre four days later. Williams was revising the ending of the script, and the actors were performing at night and working on new dialogue and stage business during the day. All was business-as-usual until flurries of alarm gusted through the theater when the costumes failed to arrive for the final run-through. The designer, who was arriving from New York by train with the costumes, mysteriously took the train back to New York without the depositing the costumes with the company manager. The clothes were never found. "Whether she suffered from amnesia or absentmindedness, we never learned," Crawford reported.[11]

Refusing to be nonplused by the emergency, Crawford turned to Paul Bigelow, trusted friend of both producer and playwright. A "wizard in emergencies," Bigelow "shopped" the complete wardrobe for the show in one day.[12] Their troubles were not over, however. The Chicago critics were baffled by the neurotic mix of Serafina's grief for her late husband, and her passion for the sexually attentive truck driver. As she had done for *The Glass Menagerie*, the doyenne of Chicago critics, Claudia Cassidy, stepped forward with an encouraging review that also pointed to serious lapses, including a lack of "clairvoyant" direction, "mesmeric" acting, or "a luminous finale."[13]

As they worked to "fix" the show, Crawford was scrutinizing the balance sheet on a show capitalized at eighty thousand dollars that had a loss of fifteen thousand dollars in Chicago. When *The Rose Tattoo* moved into Broadway's Martin Beck Theatre, Crawford remained sanguine about the play's earlier reception. From her viewpoint, the purpose of out-of-town tryouts was to look at the play in the presence of an audience, gage their reactions, and decide which elements of dialogue and staging needed to be fixed.

The Rose Tattoo opened in New York on February 3, 1951, with a play-bill note written by the playwright in an effort to off-set objections raised in Chicago to its prurience and lewdness. At the outset, Williams's story of a passionate Sicilian widow (Serafina della Rose), who is pursued romantically by a Sicilian truck driver (Alvaro Mangiacavallo) on the Mississippi Gulf coast, managed to offend "supersensitive" critics and audiences, as Crawford called them, who objected to the onstage display of Dionysian revelry.[14] In defense of his play, Williams wrote, "*The Rose Tattoo* is the Dionysian element in human life, its mystery, its beauty, its significance. . . . Its purest form is probably manifested by children and birds in their rhapsodic moments of flight and play . . . the limitless world of dream. It is the *rosa mystica*."[15]

The New York reviews were largely favorable. Nevertheless, Robert Coleman, writing for the *Daily Mirror*, objected to lewd and sacrilegious episodes, which lead him to conclude that the playwright was going to confuse and antagonize "decent play-goers."[16]

Twenty-six years later, Crawford continued her defense of Williams's celebration of the "inebriate god." She wrote in her memoir: "Our society, nurtured on the Apollonian side . . . accepts the Dionysian only in dreams and fantasies. In the last few years, the Apollonian mantle has rent and the Dionysian has burst out like a streak of lightning. But having been suppressed, it is no longer 'the bare golden flesh of a god' or, as another poet said, 'the fair slim boy who darts along the brake, paling the morning with his silver thigh'; it is ugly and bestial, Yeats's slouching beast. This is evident in many of today's plays and films, which often foretell our social behavior."[17]

Despite her enthusiasm for the play, Crawford was aware that one troublesome scene involved the dropping of an "unmentionable article" (a condom) on stage. She remarked that this incident, and a few other small details, offended the sensibilities of audiences and critics, who also faulted the excessive symbolism of the rose.[18] "It became such an issue." she said, "that I asked Tenn to express his point of view." He responded with what Crawford thought was one of his finest pieces of writing, concluding with,

> Still more undoubtedly its theme [the Dionysian element in human life] overshadows the play. It is the homely light of a kitchen candle burned in praise of a god. I prefer a play to be not a noose but a net with fairly wide meshes. So many of its instants of revelation are wayward flashes, not part of the plan of an author but struck accidentally off, and perhaps these are closest to being a true celebration of the inebriate god.[19]

Cheryl Crawford was not the playwright's muse, but the Congregation-alist-raised, super-sensible producer was his *avocatore*. She knew her Nietzsche, who described in *The Birth of Tragedy* the Apollonian and Dionysian sides of human behavior. Aware that Dionysus slips through Williams's plays, making his creations larger than life, she wrote to Brooks Atkinson asking him to take another look at *The Rose Tattoo*, after the playwright inserted his revisions. "They go in tomorrow," she wrote, "so on some cloudy day when you can't see the murmuration of starlings or an exaltation of larks in the country [she knew Atkinson was a dedicated bird watcher], I hope *The Rose Tattoo* will serve."[20]

Atkinson returned to the Martin Beck and praised Williams as a lyric dramatist, who had opened new horizons for the theater by creating "a lusty comedy" out of the lives of Sicilian villagers living along the Gulf coast.[21]

Crawford still faced audiences repelled by the fury of Serafina's passion and the heavy-handed symbolism of the rose that appeared as a tattoo on the bare chest of her truck driver in imitation of Serafina's dead husband.[22] In the end, the play won over its naysayers with its charm, humor, and simplistic insistence that sexual response is an answer to life's problems.

Crawford found an instant commercial success on her hands in a season that featured *South Pacific, Darkness at Noon, Guys and Dolls, The Country Girl, Call Me Madam*, and *Bell, Book, and Candle*. The relatively uninhibited and joyous paean to the erotic life was given the Antoinette Perry ("Tony") Award for best play, Maureen Stapleton and Eli Wallach were honored for best performances, and Boris Aronson received the prize for set design.

Crawford was in her element. She reported advance sales of $75,000, planned a North American tour, and received a percentage when the play was sold to Paramount Pictures for one hundred thousand dollars. The film deal eventually returned six thousand dollars to her, and off-set her unhappiness over the fact that she had "received no money during the entire two-season run."[23] Moreover, the playwright paid her the compliment of saying that *The Rose Tattoo* had been his "happiest experience in the theatre so far. . . ."[24]

In June, Crawford gave what she called her "yearly do" in her apartment on East Fifty-second Street. She entertained a distinguished roster of guests: Carson McCullers, Lillian Hellman, Joshua Logan, Eli Wallach, Anne Jackson, Frederick Loewe, Daniel Mann, Santha Ratha Rau, and Faubion Bowers, an authority on Far Eastern theater. In a letter to Williams, she described her bacchanal:

> [Faubion Bowers] got high and danced in a somewhat Oriental fashion with crippled Carson, who will never forget it. Even the next day she was saying, "I danced, Cheryl! I danced!" It was high and gay and everyone talked to everyone. Only minor accidents, two cigarette burns on my best rug, one glass broken and one gentleman fell on his face, spilling coffee on afore-mentioned rug, which now considers itself second-hand.[25]

During his work on *The Rose Tattoo*, Williams made frequent visits to Carson McCullers's home in Nyack, New York. After their first meeting in 1946, he nicknamed her "Sister-Woman," gave her a ring that had belonged to his sister Rose, and expressed compassion for the fragile writer, whose instability and addictions mirrored his own. Once Rose Williams, who haunted her brother's consciousness as a tragic victim of a lobotomy in the thirties, was moved into a private, long-term care facility in Ossining, where she resided until her death in 1996, she was located across the Hudson River from Nyack. On occasion, Williams drove his sister to Nyack in the company of Crawford, who witnessed his tenderness toward Rose and the deep friendship between the two writers:

> This was a unique friendship, and I think her [Carson's] special qualities of craziness appealed to him. It isn't going too far to say that he really liked and appreciated and understood and was amused by a crew of eccentrics throughout his life![26]

The Rose Tattoo survived the summer and closed on October 27, 1951, after 306 performances. A month before, the playwright wrote from Copenhagen, where he was attending various Scandinavian openings of the play, to express his gratitude:

> I think you have done a truly amazing job, holding the show together through the summer, keeping it going, and I make a deep bow, my forehead touching the floor, for it means a great deal to me, as you know. You are, when all is said and done, the very best of my various producers and I pray that God is willing to let me give you another play![27]

Cheryl Crawford would produce two musicals (*Flahooley* and *Paint Your Wagon*) before Williams finished *Camino Real*—a "plastic poem on the romantic attitude toward life."[28]

A Prayer for Romantics

In its early form, *Ten Blocks on the Camino Real* had been performed as a series of one-acts at the Actors Studio in the late forties. Kazan found the results exciting and persuaded Williams to develop the script into a full evening for the commercial theater. Moreover, Crawford, enamored with the scenes, wrote immediately to Audrey Wood reminding her that "the least of Tenn's works" must have an audience.[29]

Crawford's legendary economy as a producer entered into the playwright's conversations on her suitability to produce *Camino Real*. He was concerned about her super-caution with expenses. From the time Crawford cut $70,000 in costs from the *Brigadoon* budget by shopping the tartans at Bloomingdale's and Gimbel's, painting cornices on scenery, and substituting muslin for finer cloth, she acquired a reputation for frugality as a producer. Some said that she was expert at combining high aspirations with rock-bottom costs. Those who knew her best remarked that she indulged in "the gambler's typical lavish generosities, followed by incongruous small gestures of economy."[30]

Hoping to temper their concerns, Crawford wrote to Kazan: "I promise not to argue with you about dough. It's true I'm careful, all good producers *should* be, but no one has ever said that any of my productions were "chintzy," at least not to my face."[31] Williams warned Kazan, "... I think she must forget economy ... and give the show a rich production."[32] With the addition of two coproducers, *Camino* was finally capitalized at $125,000—a generous budget in those days for a nonmusical, usually budgeted at sixty thousand dollars.

Before *Camino Real* got underway, the neoconservative politics of the McCarthy period threw the theater and film world into turmoil. Crawford and Williams were not ideologically driven and ignored the political climate. Despite the controversy swirling around Elia Kazan's friendly testimony before HUAC, they wanted him to direct the Broadway production.[33] He had staged Thornton Wilder's *Skin of Our Teeth* with Tallulah Bankhead to great acclaim, and Wilder's play had many similarities to *Camino Real*. With his next Hollywood film (*On the Waterfront*) on hold, Kazan was available.

Earlier, Crawford had received a letter from Williams, posted from Rome, announcing that he had revised the early draft of *Camino Real*.

> This is the one I want you to read. Gadg seemed pleased with the first [draft] and said he wanted to go into rehearsal with it in late October and would see you as soon as he returned to the States for discussion. We would both like you to produce it, but are not sure that you will consider it a good financial risk. It will have to be budgeted very liberally to ensure a full realization of

its plastic values, and of course it is a gamble. We both feel that you would understand it better than anyone else.[34]

With script in hand, Crawford observed, "It certainly was a *gamble:* the material was very unusual and there were no stars."[35]

Kazan called the cosmic fantasy "a prayer for Romantics—a plea for the size and importance of the individual soul."[36] The play, set in an isolated sun-baked plaza, is inhabited by gypsies, pimps, Fascist police, prostitutes, panderers, starving peasants, street cleaners, and legendary romantics (Jacques Casanova, Don Quixote, Lord Byron, and Marguerite "Camille" Gautier) coexisting in a fleabag hotel. Into the plaza walks Kilroy, a former boxer and an American innocent, lost and destitute with a heart as pure as gold. Subjected to humiliation and violence, he cries out near the end: "Had for a button! Stewed, screwed, and tattooed on the Camino Real . . . Did anyone say the deal was rugged?" Finally, the stout-hearted dreamer, Don Quixote, urges Kilroy to come away with him.

"Donde?" Kilroy asks.

"Quién sabe!" Quixote answers.[37]

Crawford described the play as "a dark picture of the world, frequently lightened by macabre comedy."[38] Kazan, on the other hand, read the play as "a love letter to people Williams loved most, the romantics [the outsiders], those innocents who become victims in our business of civilization."[39]

As a Broadway vehicle, *Camino Real* was, indeed, a gamble. It was a dark comedy, a private nightmare that needed twenty-one actors and several coproducers to capitalize the production. By the end of summer, Crawford had negotiated a contract with Audrey Wood and persuaded Ethel Reiner to coproduce, and Walter Chrysler Jr. became an associate producer. Among them, they secured the capital.

In one sense, *Camino Real* was an Actors Studio production with Crawford and Kazan at the helm and sixteen of the thirty-one actors recruited from the Studio, among them Eli Wallach (as Kilroy) and Jo Van Fleet (as Marguerite).[40]

Camino Real presented its earnest producer with several lessons, firstly, that it was difficult "doing business with your friends."[41] She found it awkward to suggest script revisions to the playwright and persuade Kazan of her point of view on artistic matters. She was never satisfied with Lemuel Ayers lugubrious set, which surrounded the plaza with dark, forbidding stone walls and gloomy houses that gave a chilling effect to the fantasy world. The playwright had envisioned the stage setting as having "the haunting loveliness of one of those lonely-looking plazas and colonnades in a Chirico."[42] Nor was Kazan satisfied. He had envisioned the fantastical landscapes of the Mexican primitive artist, Posada, but had not yet learned how to communicate his visual sense to designers.[43]

In a Broadway season with Arthur Miller's *The Crucible* and William Inge's *Picnic*, Williams's surrealistic fantasy opened at the National Theatre on March 19, 1953, to mixed reviews. Atkinson praised the production and performances as "eloquent and rhythmic as a piece of music" but expressed revulsion at the cruelty and decadence of Williams's cosmic fantasy.[44] In general, critics were puzzled by the writing ("a riddle wrapped in an enigma"), offended by its hyperbole ("an enormous jumble of five-cent philosophy"), or revolted by the writer's pessimism ("psychopathic bitterness").[45] Many in the audience were furious and disgusted; others were moved to tears. From her producer's post, Crawford remarked "the going was rough."[46]

On that disastrous night, Williams rose to his feet at the opening-night party and announced that his playwriting days were over.[47] Rejected by Broadway's critics, the group wandered off into the night to go their separate ways. The next day, Crawford steeled herself to see the New York production of *Camino Real* through to its final curtain. She persuaded Audrey Wood that the show "might have a chance to run if we pay no royalties, at least until we see if we can get it out of the woods," and earned the soubriquet "Mother Crawford." Williams wrote to his acerbic friend Maria Britneva (the future Lady Maria St. Just) that Crawford hoped "to scrape along by such economies as lighting the stage by fire-flies and a smokey old kerosene lamp."[48]

With grosses falling below house capacity in the second week, Crawford continued to inform Williams that business was "tremendously encouraging."[49] It was during this struggle to keep the show running that Williams remarked, "Cheryl is a great fighter, she is always there when you need her . . ."[50]

Crawford managed sixty performances in New York, but fewer on the road, where the show closed. Williams blamed her for closing the tour prematurely "because the final week was almost sold out." As Crawford had anticipated, the closing announcement filled the theater and gave false hope to the playwright and cast.[51] Nevertheless, by monitoring the accounts, she knew that there was not enough money to sustain the tour with any security. She had run out of money—and options.

In the wake of *Camino Real*, Crawford became the playwright's confidante. Confiding "embarrassingly personal things" to her "because I think we have a relationship that permits confession and understanding," Williams confessed that he was too shy with Audrey Wood to share his secrets, but comfortable enough with Crawford to seek her help. It is likely that her same-sex lifestyle, as opposed to Audrey Wood's ardent marital relationship with William Liebling, made her the easier woman to share his private thoughts with.[52]

While in Rome, Williams recognized that he was experiencing a serious depression. He wrote to Crawford from his apartment overlooking the Tiber, that he was passing through the "worst nervous crisis of my nervous existence": "I don't understand what is back of these crises, panics. It could simply be a physical thing. Or it could be a physical expression of some deep mental crisis." Then, switching to business, he asked if she had read the new script. "Read it over, please, and let Gadge read it. . . . I want nothing but your usual absolute honesty from you, about this and anything between us, professionally or personally, something one can ask from a very few people one knows in the course of a life-time."[53]

The playwright enclosed with his letter, most likely written in June 1954, the new third act and a new part of the second act of his latest work. When Crawford finally read the completed script of *Cat on a Hot Tin Roof*, she wrote at once: "God! What a volcanic explosion, some of your very best writing and a second act that can lift the roof off the theatre if it doesn't lift the critics' hair off, or toupees, as the case may be."[54]

Still smarting from the critical bashing they received following the opening of *Camino Real* (Walter Kerr called *Camino* "the worst play yet written by the best playwright of his generation"), Crawford was overly cautious. She admonished in a letter that *Cat on a Hot Tin Roof* was "too damned important for haste and inconsidered action."[55] What concerned her most was the lack of anyone "to root for": "All the people seem monstrous except Big Daddy and I don't think an audience can take such an unrelieved attack. In *Streetcar* they had their cathartic in good Greek fashion through Blanche."[56]

Despite Crawford's urging against haste for the ostensible reason that she did not trust the play to attract a summer audience, Kazan and Williams were eager to go into production in the late spring. Kazan had a previous arrangement to stage Robert Anderson's new play, *Tea and Sympathy*, in the fall and needed to move up the opening of *Cat*. Crawford needed a delay for her own projects. She was juggling *Trouble in Tahiti* by Leonard Bernstein and preparing to produce *The Honeys* by Roald Dahl. Since she was unable to convince her erstwhile collaborators to wait, she was unavailable to produce *Cat*, and Audrey Wood negotiated with the Playwrights Company to handle Williams's new play. Nevertheless, Crawford's early thoughts on the script ("there's no one to root for") were taken to heart. Kazan worked with Williams to get Big Daddy into the last act and also to change the ending into a more hopeful scene. In the heat of the New York summer, the play was an enormous success and won a Pulitzer Prize.

"So much for my sense of season, and alas for me," Crawford said with profound regret.[57]

Bird on the Wing

Two years passed before Crawford received word of a new Tennessee Williams play being performed ("as discretely as possible") in Coral Gables, Florida, at the small Studio M Playhouse. The playwright cabled her to see the play because "you are still my favorite producer by ten country miles. . . ."[58]

In mid-April of 1956, she traveled to Florida to see the first performance of *Sweet Bird of Youth*, and immediately wrote her ritual letter to Audrey Wood. "After my error on *Cat on a Hot Tin Roof*, I wanted to get a bid in fast," she said. She reprised her history with the playwright:

> To review the past, I did keep *Tattoo* going two seasons and served it well, I think, though not to any financial advantage to myself. I worked like hell, long and hard, to get the money for *Camino*, which I think few producers would have touched, and while I am not as proud of the production as I would like to be, I think I gave it every publicity chance, expense-wise and getting the Guild subscription. You can understand why this made me fearful of not giving such an important play as *Cat* the best break, which seemed to me would have been a fall rather than a late spring production. Unluckily for me, I had a faint heart at the wrong time, which cost me an awful lot of sleeping pills.
>
> Then, when you returned from the Coast and told me Tenn and Gadg felt they must go ahead for a late spring opening, you also told me that Tenn had asked you to tell me that I would have first chance at his next play. I guess you know how that made me feel.
>
> When I heard he was planning on *Orpheus Descending*, I called you to tell you I was interested, and you explained that it was a special set-up involving Anna [Magnani] and Marlon [Brando] and a corporate holding. So I bowed.

> But I want desperately to be involved with *Sweet Bird,* and I believe I can bring something of value to the production. If the trouble is fitting me into a tax relief corporate set-up, I can be hired. Not by Hollywood or TV but by The Sweet Bird of Youth, Incorporated.[59]

When it was settled that Crawford had the play, she "began to sleep nights."[60]

While she waited for Williams's script, she had a run of bad luck with a series of undistinguished plays that were not saved by strong casts. She produced Roald Dahl's *The Honeys* with Jessica Tandy and Hume Cronyn, Marc Blitzstein's musical *Reuben, Reuben* with Eddie Albert, Norman Rosten's *Mr. Johnson* with Earle Hyman, John Patrick's *Good as Gold* with Roddy MacDowell, Speed Lamkin's *Comes the Day* with Judith Anderson, Sean O'Casey's *The Shadow of a Gunman* with Susan Strasberg, Norman Corwin's *The Rivalry* with Richard Boone, and N. Richard Nash's *Girls of Summer* with Shelley Winters, Pat Hingle, and George Peppard. She was not consoled by Williams's sanguine comment on the string of failures: "But that's how it goes, rough as a cob sometimes, and sometimes smooth as silk."[61]

Although both producer and playwright kept working, they were at a juncture where both needed an artistically and commercially successful production as a matter of survival. Crawford was blunt about her condition: "I was hanging on by my teeth, which were loosening under the strain."[62]

During the hiatus, they corresponded regularly, and Williams and Frank Merlo visited "Eastham," where the playwright worked every day after breakfast writing on a yellow pad at her dining room table. "It was his life," Crawford said. "I doubt if there was never a day he didn't write."[63]

When the new script of *Sweet Bird* arrived, Crawford began preparations for the Broadway production. Writing to Tenn in early August of 1958, she focused on money and casting.

> I'm running Broadway now—'count of you. Every day people come in, call up, friends, strangers, all begging me to take their checks for *Sweet Bird*—any amount. It's like a continuous scene from *Volpone* on the cupidity of man. Fun tho! I never had it happen before. Remember how we sweated over *Camino?*
>
> I've made a good deal on Newman—fair, not killing. The only thing I don't like is that Warner Bros. say they will release him for only nine months from rehearsal date. Wrote Gadg about that. Maybe he can do something with

Warner's because of his relationship. I also told Gadg I didn't think Geraldine [Page] was right for the Princess Kosmonopolis. She's too young! . . . [Crawford would shortly change her mind when she heard Page read the part.]

I'm seeing Jack Small of the Shubert office tomorrow about the Barrymore. I've already been offered the [Martin] Beck for March. It can gross $47,176 now, which is something to think about if Paul plays only seven months here.[64]

Kazan's commitments and Newman's availability delayed the opening of *Sweet Bird* until March. In a season with *A Raisin in the Sun*, *Gypsy*, *The Sound of Music*, and *The Miracle Worker*, Williams's play opened with a stellar cast helmed by Paul Newman, Geraldine Page, Sidney Blackmer, Madeleine Sherwood, and Rip Torn. The reviews were glowing: "brilliantly staged and acted," Williams's "finest drama," "blockbuster," "enormously exciting," "sure-fire hit," "beautifully" directed, "luminous" settings, Williams's "best." Walter Kerr responded to the excitement of the "noise of passion, of creative energy, of exploration and adventure," and John Chapman paused to acknowledge that *Sweet Bird* was "produced with great effect by Cheryl Crawford."[65]

Even the weekly and monthly critics, dubious about the play's inconsistencies and decadent subject matter, and Kazan's "mannered" direction, did not stem the tide of the *succès de scandale* that ran for 383 performances.[66] Throughout, Crawford exulted: "At last Tenn and I had the larger-than-life hit we had wanted. I reveled in it. We *were* 'running' Broadway, and it was wonderful."[67]

Miscalculations

Williams dedicated the published version of *Sweet Bird* to his producer, but Crawford's exaltations over their success were short-lived. The playwright was working simultaneously on two plays: *Period of Adjustment* and *The Night of the Iguana*. The former, an upbeat comedy about the marriages of two middle-class couples living in Southern suburbia, was given an early try-out at the Coconut Grove Playhouse in Miami.[68] Unable to attend the Miami preview, Crawford got a copy of the script and found the characters "endearing and pitiful," and the play itself, written in the idiom of rather ordinary American life, "delightful."[69] She signed on as producer and soon found that her appreciation of the casting differed from the playwright's.

Pleased with the Miami cast, headed by Barbara Baxley, the playwright rejected Crawford's idea that the "funny and touching story of a delicate time in the marriages of two young couples" would be enhanced by casting young actors to make the characters' problems more sympathetic. (When the dust settled over Broadway, she would revisit her earlier suggestion.) Fresh from Hollywood's *Butch Cassidy and the Sundance Kid* and *The Sting*, George Roy Hill, whose first Broadway direction was the Pulitzer Prize winning *Look Homeward, Angel*, directed Barbara Baxley, James Daly, Robert Webber, and Helen Martin as the foursome in a comedy that defied Williams's familiar landscape of repressed Southern belles, blackmailing gigolos, and corrupt politicians—and ended happily.

After the opening of *Period of Adjustment*, Williams hand wrote a note, which she treasured for the remainder of her days.

Dearest Cheryl:

My coffee has not come up from the elegantly dilatory room-service of this establishment, and I have exhausted its stationery on piddling rewrites—but I must say a word to you of congratulation for last night and *all* the nights when I have observed your dedication (and gallantry) in the best uses of the theatre and to say how very much I love you for it.

Sometimes it is a tattered ensign that we may seem to be flying—but to fly it because it still has our devotion, the purest part of us, is a thing in you that I want to salute with my heart this early morning, late in my life.

Forgive the rhetoric, love, when I come back I hope to visit you—

Love, ever,
Tennessee[70]

Despite their mutual satisfaction with the production and the sale of the play to a film company, the critics were not as responsive as Crawford had hoped. Audiences did not flock to the theater. Crawford diagnosed the problem in an interview with Donald Spoto: "The problem was, to put it bluntly, that the original cast was too old. The audience didn't really care very much about the problems and the arguments of couples who, because they weren't young onstage, couldn't make credible the cries and complaints and nervousness natural for young married couples."[71]

Williams was unhappy with the play's reception and with the mutual decision of his agent and producer to close the show. Reluctantly, Crawford explained that she and Audrey Wood had made a joint decision:

Audrey was at the meeting when we looked over the financial situation, found that we had no advance, that only about 25 mail orders a day were coming in even after the very extensive two weeks of T.V. advertising. The closing was

a *mutual* decision. I assumed she had written or phoned you about it. . . .
We can break even for the next two weeks on $11,000 to $11,500 a week. We
will probably lose quite a lot this week as so far the closing announcement
has not worked. But *we are playing,* and I did not do anything arbitrarily.

You seemed to indicate on the phone that you thought you had lost your
investment in the play. At present there is enough money to repay all investors entirely. Leaving the investment aside, you have made $105,000 from
the author's share of the first movie payment plus $60,000 due from the next
payment plus about $7,000 from the gross on profitable weeks plus $30,000
on weekly royalties. This totals $202,000 minus $20,200, which represents
the 10% of your earnings to MCA. [Wood and her husband had sold their
Liebling-Wood agency and transferred their offices, along with their lists of
playwrights and authors, to Music Corporation of America in 1954.]

The show itself has so far made around $6,000 in profits, but we will prob-
ably lose that this week. I haven't made anything so far. Not a complaint, just
facts. This week on five performances we have taken in $6,806.

Distressed by the apparent misunderstanding, Crawford ended with a
subtle plea for understanding and friendship: "You and I have faced too
much together over too many years not to understand each other now."[72]

What Crawford did not foresee was the extent of Williams's descent
into his "Stoned Age," as he called the sixties, when his world collapsed
around him.[73] Under the influence of drugs and alcohol, now addictions
that exacerbated his paranoia, he rejected the two professionals (Cheryl
Crawford and Audrey Wood) who were the most loving, loyal, and supportive of his talent.

In a Dark Wood

Cheryl Crawford was among the first of his close associates to be ejected
from the playwright's professional life. What she called a breakdown of
communication, others referred to as a subtle transformation in Williams's attitude toward friends and associates. The result for Crawford
was the loss of *The Night of the Iguana* followed by an alienation of affection from her friend of more than ten years.

In 1960, the Actors Studio presented an early draft of *Iguana*, directed
by Frank Corsaro, which the playwright attended. Unaware of the tec-
tonic changes in her longtime friend, Crawford shared her thoughts with
him. "Remember you said last Sunday that you wish people would level
with you," she wrote. "You said it quite insistently. I'm not sure I believe
you. But I'm going to pretend I do because I think in 'Iguana' you can
have your finest play to date and a play, stealing movie slogans, I would

be proud to present. I don't think it is all there yet. Put on as is, it would appeal to people sensitive and aware enough to dig it. The majority, I think, would be intrigued and baffled."[74]

As she had done after reading *Cat on a Hot Tin Roof*, which should have been a warning, she proceeded to analyze omissions of plot and the audience's reactions.

> In the first half (Acts One and Two) some simple plot situation is needed. Perhaps it should be developing Shannon's desire to return to the church. I want an audience during the intermission to be saying "What's going to happen next?" "*What* is he (or she) going to do?" They weren't. They were saying, "interesting," "isn't that actor, what's his name, good?" You often speak of having no plot in "Period of Adjustment. "You're wrong. People will rush back to their seats to find out what is going to happen. They didn't at "Iguana." They strolled. That's dangerous. But if Shannon's struggle is stronger, if the whole letter writing scene is heightened, the carryover of interest and curiosity between Acts Two and Three may be greater.

She ended on an impassioned note: "I wish I had words of fire or iron to put my first point to you with greater impact. The audience simply does not know who or what to follow by the end of Act Two. Consequently, they were not identifying and not caring." Her final sentence is a curious projection of things to come: "This is all for now. Are you still speaking?"[75]

Crawford did not hear from the playwright for a year. Rumor and confusion surrounded the subject of who would produce the new Tennessee Williams play with the Liebling-Wood Agency, with Two Rivers Enterprise (Williams's own corporation) and independent producer Charles Bowden contending for the prize. Distrusting theatrical rumor mills, Crawford tried once more to secure the project for herself. In a poignant letter, she wrote, "Every night before dinner I look at the phone and think I will call you—and don't. And every day I think I will write you—and can't. So I think of you, Ten [*sic*], but my heart is still sore with the realization that you and I will probably never be associated again. It makes my life in the theatre, which is my whole life, seem empty of purpose." She reflected on the fact that Audrey Wood also wanted to produce *Iguana*. Setting herself apart from the agent, she argued, "Perhaps I'm all muddled, but I think of it as the principle. I've taken a chance on more plays by new authors than any other producer except the now-leaking Theatre Guild. So once in a while I look forward to leaping where there is a net."[76]

Although she resented Audrey Wood for "wanting her taste" of producing, she was unaware that the relationship between the playwright and his agent had begun to unravel as early as *Cat on a Hot Tin Roof* and would reach an irreversible turning point during the failed 1971 production of *Out Cry* in Chicago. Backstage in Chicago's Ivanhoe Theatre, Williams turned on his agent of thirty years and accused her of wanting him "finished and dead." As she exited the theater, she heard him say, "That bitch! I'm through with her!"[77]

An early version of *The Night of the Iguana* with an Actors Studio cast played at the Coconut Grove Playhouse in Miami in August 1960. In a letter, written in January, assuring Crawford that *Iguana* would be his last play, Williams claimed, however disingenuously, that he never thought she wanted to produce *Iguana*.[78]

> I thought that, being a truly kind person, you wanted to encourage me by seeming to want it, just that, and when I got your notes, I realized I couldn't please you with it and still please myself. This play is a dramatic poem of the most intensely personal nature and Bowden for some unknown reason, seemed to want it like that . . .

In an effort to soften the blow, he closed on a personal note: "We've done four plays together and none of them are failures in the true sense. I hope and trust and pray that one of the ones I am holding in reserve will be a right one for you, since working with you has always been a deeply human as well as a professional satisfaction to me. . . . Why do you offer to take another beating now? I love you for it, but don't think it makes sense for you." He closed with, "I hope you are out of your dark room. I'm still in mine and not at all sure it isn't going to get darker before it gets brighter again."[79]

Crawford knew that their association was over. Resigned to her loss, she confided, "So I did not produce *Night of the Iguana*; as I had foreseen our professional relationship had come to a close." Sometimes, she had tried to comfort the playwright in his insecurities about his writing by reminding him that the "great Euripides wrote ninety-two plays, but received only four prizes."[80] Now she regretted that she had not been of more comfort to him. She felt that they had both lost their way in Dante's "dark wood, where the straight way was lost."

Tennessee Williams died in 1983, a month before his seventy-second birthday, in his favorite New York hotel, the Elysée on East Fifty-fourth

Street. When Crawford was told of his death, she wept for the passing of her troubled friend, perhaps recalling Williams's words written for the close of *Sweet Bird of Youth*. "I don't ask for your pity," Chance Wayne says, "but just for your understanding—not even that—no. Just for your recognition of me in you, and the enemy, time, in us all."[81]

Part Three

A Tattered Ensign, 1962–1986

11

WHO'S MINDING THE STORE?

Now that an Actors Studio Theatre had become a reality, where—and what—were its goals, its ideals, its vision?

—Foster Hirsch

The year was 1962, and Cheryl Crawford was sixty years old. With the Tennessee Williams decade behind her, her immediate future lay with plans to initiate a theater under the auspices of the Actors Studio. Foster Hirsch suggested that the idea of a producing theater had been in the air since the founding of the Studio in the fall of 1947.[1] The possibility to test training in production was steadfastly woven into the fabric of the Studio's history. Although Crawford and Kazan largely resisted the impulse for sixteen years until, under Strasberg's indecisive leadership, they gradually succumbed to pressure for public presentations and agreed to the creation of the Actors Studio Theatre.

Answered Prayers

It is not without irony that the Actors Studio Theatre, as it was called to forge its identity with the Studio, became Crawford's last hope to create a nonprofit theater to showcase the work of an ensemble of actors. Against the backdrop of the failed Group Theatre and the American Repertory Theatre, Crawford, as executive administrator, and Lee Strasberg, as artistic director, announced the formation of the Actors Studio Theatre in June of 1962. Operating under the Studio's tax-exempt charter, the theater answered several prayers. First, the Studio members were eager for public presentations of their work. Strasberg also wanted a public venue to showcase the Studio's training, and devised the idea of a revolving company in which one actor would replace another, so that productions could be maintained by the presence of a strong constellation of actors.

Elia Kazan was uncertain that the Studio needed a theater. When faced with a *fait accompli*, he argued for a small nonprofit one in the manner of the British Clubs or the Off Broadway theaters.

All too aware that the Group's efforts to create a public venue had floundered on the lack of new plays, Crawford looked to the playwrights' unit to fill the vacuum. In addition, the climate had changed for nonprofits in New York City in the late fifties. The Rockefeller and Ford foundations had come onto the cultural scene, along with the city's sponsorship of Lincoln Center as a future cultural complex north of Broadway. The Lincoln Center developers visualized homes for music, opera, dance, and drama and approached the Actors Studio to occupy the theater that was planned for the new complex. The Studio's directors rejoiced at the idea of having a home for a resident company. Eager to be part of the project with visions of new American plays and modern American classics, they supplied documents of intent and attended meetings for the next five years.[2]

Early in the discussions, an unbreachable divide opened up between Rockefeller's advisers, who envisioned a classical theater on the European model, and the Studio's mandate to produce American plays to showcase their theatricalized style of realism in acting.[3] Kazan articulated the Studio's vision in a six-page letter, written to John D. Rockefeller III, in which he outlined the worthiness of a trained company of actors in a repertoire based upon contemporary American classics of the last forty years.[4] Strasberg made stubborn declarations that he would brook no interference from other authorities, and Crawford found herself in a familiar situation caught between Kazan and Strasberg with a future theater at risk. The Foundation people were soon put off by their "authoritarian manner" and discussions came to a halt in 1957.[5]

The Lincoln Center developers turned two new theaters over to codirectors Robert Whitehead and Elia Kazan, effectively dashing the hope that the Studio would be part of the new project. Accused of betraying the Studio, Kazan explained that he hoped to involve the Studio at a later time, but he was never able to do so.[6]

Later, Kazan claimed that he offered Lincoln Center's smaller theater (now the Mitzi Newhouse) that was part of the Vivian Beaumont Theater building to Strasberg and the Studio for experimental productions, but Strasberg never responded to his invitation. Moreover, when Kazan approached several of the Studio members to join the new repertory company, the actors, feeling betrayed, turned him down. Their hopes had been very high, and, according to Crawford, they were furious in their disappointment.[7]

To avoid the appearance of a conflict of interest and also dodge the lingering fury over his new role in the Lincoln Center project, Kazan resigned from the Studio's directorate. His letter was written to Crawford, his long-time collaborator, and followed up with a telegram to the members: "To all: I resigned as director only. That was necessary. But I'm still with you and for any and all efforts you make. I'm sure whatever you do will bring credit to our years of work and to Lee's teaching. Signed, The First Member.[8]

And, so, the Studio continued on its solitary way, minus a key founder, and without a permanent space to house its producing wing.

Four times in the Studio's sixteen-year history, prior to 1963, the Studio produced a play for an outside audience. The first was Bessie Breuer's *Sundown Beach*, and *End as a Man* was the second. At a party in 1952, Jack Garfein, then a young Studio director, met playwright Calder Willingham, who talked about his new play about a Southern military school. Garfein convinced him to let the Studio work on the script with actors Ben Gazzara and James Dean.

When *End as a Man* was staged, it was the first time outsiders were allowed to see work at the Studio. It was so well received that Garfein was able (for five thousand dollars) to transfer the production Off Broadway to the Theatre de Lys with a mention of the Studio's name in the playbill, reluctantly granted by its leaders. The response for the Off Broadway production was so strong that the producers decided to move the show to a Broadway house, where it received mixed reviews and had a modest run.

The third public production, again staged in the Studio for outsiders, was *A Hatful of Rain*. Michael Gazzo brought an idea for improvisation to his fellow actors about a veteran who is a drug addict and tries to conceal it from his wife. The give and take among the writer, director, and actors evolved into a quintessential Studio piece in fifties-style naturalism: a problem drama with raw language and intense ensemble acting. The five performances in the Studio were followed by a Broadway opening in 1955 with an outside producer credited with the 358 performances.

With Crawford and Strasberg as minority voices, the Studio was moving steadily toward a production company. As members endeavored to turn projects into full-blown productions, Crawford and Kazan, the two most knowledgeable about commercial venues, were not available to offer creative ideas or practical guidance. During the fifties, Crawford produced fourteen straight plays on Broadway along with *Flahooley* and *Paint Your Wagon*.

Entr'acte

Paint Your Wagon marked the dissolution of Crawford's "professional marriage" to Lerner and Loewe. Reunited as a team, the composer and lyricist came to Eastham shortly after *Flahooley*, developed by the creators of *Finian's Rainbow*, closed to mixed reviews. The "boys," as she called them, lifted her out of her Broadway doldrums with a show about the gold rush to California, where the mining camps were full of lusty men without women until a stagecoach arrives with a group of finely dressed women, characterized as "no better than they should be."[9] She was delighted to have the winning *Brigadoon* team together again around her piano, composing "I Talk to the Trees" and "I Call the Wind Maria."

Despite Crawford's euphoria, the show was soon beset with problems, firstly, an unwieldy book. Moreover, the creative team with Robert Lewis, Agnes de Mille, Oliver Smith, and costume designers Motley proved fractious. Lerner and Loewe added to the disarray by holding production meetings without their producer. Crawford raised hell with them but was further mystified when suddenly the creators, without warning, abandoned their director, whose suggestions on book changes they disagreed with. When they demanded that Crawford find another director, she turned to the Studio's Daniel Mann, who had staged *The Rose Tattoo*. Crawford admitted that she was bewildered by the shenanigans. "Perhaps Alan wished to show his power by dangling people," she surmised.[10]

Meanwhile, Lerner and Loewe traveled to the West Coast where, again without consulting their producer, they chose two performers for the leads—Olga San Juan and James Barton. (Crawford had wanted Walter Huston, who sang "September Song" in *Knickerbocker Holiday*; he had expressed interest but died before the show was ready.) Crawford had never seen the two West Coast actors but knew that James Barton had been a vaudeville headliner famous for his "drunk" routine.

The show was clobbered by the Philadelphia critics. Once they progressed to Boston with cuts and rewrites, James Barton, who played the chief prospector, proceeded to expand his routine in Act One, in which he brings home a new bride, whom he has just purchased, and proceeds to entertain the audience with his famous vaudeville turn. The scene was supposed to run no more than nine minutes, but, by the time the show reached Boston, Barton had stretched it to twenty. Facing a disastrous first act, an angry Frederick Loewe walked into a nearby bar holding two large water glasses. As Agnes de Mille and coproducer Bea Lawrence looked on, he instructed the bartender to "fill both of these to the top."

"Where are you going with all that liquor?" the women inquired. Loewe glared at them and replied in an ominous tone, "I'm going to talk to Barton right after the curtain." Not to be denied another drunken scene, the women followed the composer backstage and stood outside Barton's dressing room to overhear Loewe say, "Drink this down, Barton, you're going to need it!"

In the women's account, cheerfully relayed to Cheryl Crawford, "Fritz said loudly and firmly, 'I mean what I'm telling you; if your drunk routine ever goes beyond nine minutes again, I am going to get a gun and I'm going to kill you. I'm a fine shot and you'd better believe what I say. That's all. Good night.'"[11]

Paint Your Wagon arrived in New York, capitalized to Crawford's satisfaction and with two show-stopping dances created by Agnes de Mille: the arrival of the prostitutes introduced by a chorus of miners singing "There's a Coach Comin' In," and a knock-out can-can number in the Palace bar.

Despite the sound and fury prior to the Broadway opening, Crawford was optimistic. The reviews were mostly favorable. Atkinson called the show "a bountiful and exultant musical jamboree." Nevertheless, Walter Kerr queried the uncertain tone of Barton's performance, varying from the tenderness of his song about his first love, "I Still See Elisa," to the broad comedy of his vaudeville routine.[12]

Paint Your Wagon was burdened with excessive operating expenses. There were sixty-four actors, singers, and dancers plus understudies. The size of the cast was not the foremost factor, but the size of the profit ($6,000 a week) was. Crawford was bombarded with complaints from investors, who also had money in *The King and I*, which claimed a weekly profit of $10,200 to $10,500. Crawford was unable to remedy the costs. "To make even $7,000 a week," she complained, "we would have to cut two characters and five musicians and minimize our advertising budget." When approached, Lerner and Loewe refused to make concessions, and, although she "wanted to get the hell out," Crawford stayed with the show through its nearly three hundred performances.[13]

Even though her relationship with Lerner and Loewe had been shaky from the moment they cut her out of the production meetings, she received an opening-night note from Lerner thanking her for her friendship and assistance and asking, "What do I do next?" Her answer: "*Pygmalion* as a musical for Mary Martin." Nevertheless, the enthusiasm of the musical team for Shaw's comedy was tepid. They didn't think they could convert the play into a musical and Martin didn't think she could play Eliza Doolittle, the Cockney flower girl. "So I dropped the idea," Crawford mused, only to learn a few years later that Lerner and Loewe had reincarnated Shaw's play as *My Fair Lady*—with another producer. Reading the announcement in *Variety*, Crawford concluded, "Our professional marriage was over."[14]

Fits and Starts

Throughout her Broadway misadventures, Crawford continued to monitor the Studio's operations. By 1958, the members were putting considerable pressure on their leaders to arrange an increasing number of public productions. "The issue became a turning point in the Studio's history," Crawford recalled.[15] Responding to the demands, the codirectors arrived at a solution. They accommodated the profit versus nonprofit arguments by choosing a large-scale production of Archibald MacLeish's *J. B.*, to be directed by Kazan in a Broadway theater, and a series of smaller-scale productions in an Off Broadway house.

Kazan hesitated about *J.B.*, thereby allowing producer Alfred de Liagre Jr. to option the play. Crawford's chagrin over de Liagre's refusal to accept the Studio's offer to coproduce the play with him was compounded by Kazan's decision to direct the play without the Studio. *J.B.* won the Pulitzer Prize for drama, and Kazan received kudos for the sheer theatricality of his staging.[16] The Studio was left with the *The Shadow of a Gunman* by Sean O'Casey play set in the backwaters of the Irish Republican rebellion, which, as a commercial production, had the potential to threaten the Studio's tax-exempt charter.

Crawford found a solution among her many contacts in the commercial theater. She enlisted Joel Schenker, president of Webb and Knapp Construction Company, to form a partnership (Crawschenk Theatre Corporation) to present plays by the Actors Studio in the six-hundred seat Bijou Theatre on Forty-fifth Street. Schenker raised one hundred and fifty thousand dollars to produce three plays, beginning with *The Shadow of a Gunman*, and, with Crawford guiding the negotiations, agreed to give the Studio twenty percent of the profits.[17]

Crawford worked out the deal without having seen a rehearsal. When she went to a run-through, she was "shocked" by how "dull, lifeless, and totally unrepresentative of our work" the production had become. She called in Strasberg to try to overcome this "disaster" for the Studio's reputation.

Garfein objected and offered to buy out the production. Crawford refused and threatened to close the show unless the director allowed Strasberg to work with the actors. When the show opened, Walter Kerr complained that "the celebrated Actors Studio has given only a shadow of a performance."[18]

Crawford was in a quandary. Why did a successful workshop production not play well in a commercial venue? Was it the difference in scale, or in casting technique? Was it the freedom of the workshop environment versus the constraints of the commercial theater? She was distressed that she had no answers, and, more importantly, no new plays wherewith to launch the Actors Studio Theatre.

The new playwrights and directors combined unit offered interesting possibilities by the 1957–58 season. The writers were eager to put on inexpensive productions in the Studio with minimum sets and props, and with small sums paid to the participants to cover expenses. Crawford wrote grants to the Ford Foundation and to the Rockefeller Brothers Fund. She was turned down by Ford, but an official from the Rockefeller Fund came to see the work and awarded a play-development grant of $56,400. Two plays developed under the grant became part of the Actors Studio Theatre's first season.

It has been argued that the AST grew out of the disappointment of the members over being excluded from the Lincoln Center project. Crawford confirmed that resentment made the actors more determined to start a theater to "show them" their worth.[19] They enlisted the help of Roger Stevens, who volunteered to speak to the Ford Foundation and also to private individuals to raise financing. When the AST was announced in the summer of 1962, it was made clear that the producing organization would be a branch of the Studio, functioning under its tax-exempt umbrella, and using exclusively Studio actors and directors.

During a trip to New York, notable British actor Laurence Olivier praised the Studio's newly minted production wing. "The Actors Studio has, without question, made Herculean efforts to meet the creative needs of the American actor," he wrote. "As a privileged witness to some of their work, I can say without reservation that I think this should be extended, if it is possible, so that after much careful and exploratory nursing it could well become the logical center for the creation of a true ensemble in the U.S."[20]

The AST was organized around another threesome: Strasberg, Crawford, and Roger Stevens. Crawford was named AST's executive producer to handle business affairs and production management, Strasberg artistic director with final say on the choice of plays, and Roger Stevens general administrator. Martha Coigney, then secretary of the Studio between 1956 and 1959, and later director of the U. S. Center of the International Theatre Institute (ITI), described their executive producer as a hand-maiden, slogging along through the daily business of the Studio while counting pennies and turning off lights.[21]

Crawford credited Roger Stevens with persuading W. McNeil Lowry and the Ford Foundation to put up a matching grant of two hundred fifty thousand dollars for the AST. A production board of eleven members was formed, with Paul Newman, Edward Albee, Anne Bancroft, Frank Corsaro, and Michael Wager, to review policies and financial support and recommend changes. The next step was to find appropriate plays for the Studio's naturalistic style. At this point, Crawford and her erstwhile associates made a fatal blunder. They passed on Edward Albee's *Who's Afraid of Virginia Woolf?* and the playwright severed all future ties with the Studio.[22]

Crawford acknowledged their "mistake," but the lost opportunity to produce the best American play since *Death of a Salesman* and *A Streetcar Named Desire* was far greater than a mistake. "Not doing *Virginia Woolf*," Michael Wager prophesized, "was the beginning of the end."[23]

Not one to linger over "what might have been," Crawford turned her energies to acquiring Eugene O'Neill's *Strange Interlude* for AST's inaugural production. She knew Carlotta O'Neill, the playwright's wife, and approached her for the rights, only to learn that O'Neill's plays had been promised to Lincoln Center, but an "authorized" production of *Desire Under the Elms* was planned by José Quintero and Ted Mann for the Circle in the Square. Not to be deterred, Rip Torn, appearing in *Desire Under the Elms*, campaigned successfully to persuade Quintero to ask Mrs. O'Neill's permission to allow the AST to stage *Strange Interlude* with José Quintero directing.

Strange Interlude opened at the Hudson Theatre in March of 1963 with an extraordinary cast: Geraldine Page, Pat Hingle, Ben Gazzara, William Prince, Betty Field, Franchot Tone, Jane Fonda, and Richard Thomas. O'Neill's sprawling psychiatric canvas, with Nina Leeds as one of the great neurotics of modern drama, was a solid choice—a major American play by a great playwright. The nine-act extravaganza of Freudian naiveté, interior monologues, and weighty subjects of sexual ambivalence had to be played with a dinner interval.

Crawford recalled that the play was well received by critics and audiences. Howard Taubman wrote that with the "brilliant" revival, "the Actors Studio has taken a step forward and it may turn out to be "a giant step forward for the good of the theater in America."[24] The ever-cautious Crawford leased the Hudson Theatre for only three months, reasoning that "it was usually not in demand." The owners now wanted a large increase to extend the rental lease. The decision to move the show to the Martin Beck Theatre expended most of the profit in the transfer and spoiled the triumph. Crawford complained, "That was the unhappy result of not having a permanent home."[25]

Despite the accolades and popular success, *Strange Interlude* was seen as a breach of faith with the Studio family. Quintero was a non-Studio director, and Franchot Tone and Betty Field were non-Studio actors. In defense, Strasberg pointed out the shortage of older actors among the members. In truth, the lines of creative authority were ill defined among the executive producer, the artistic director, and the production board, and the Studio protocols were often overwhelmed by a tendency to accommodate the convenient and commercially viable.[26] Then, too, the Studio's leaders were frequently engaged elsewhere, or indecisive. Crawford was producing Ketti Frings's *The Long Dream, Kukla, Burr and Ollie*, and *Period of Adjustment*; Roger Stevens, as newly appointed president of the John F. Kennedy Center for the Performing Arts, had his hands full planning the national cultural center in Washington, D.C.; and Lee Strasberg had long ago revealed himself as an indecisive artistic director, when it came to defining and implementing artistic choices.

AST produced six plays in its first (and final) season: O'Neill's *Strange Interlude*, June Havoc's *Marathon 33*, Arnold Weinstein and Bill Bolcom's *Dynamite Tonight*, James Costigan's *Baby Want a Kiss*, James Baldwin's *Blues for Mr. Charlie*, and Anton Chekhov's *The Three Sisters*.

With the exception of *Baby Want a Kiss*, each production brought a new set of problems for the ill-defined theater. *Marathon 33*, June Havoc's Depression era *tour de force* set in a marathon dance contest, was to have opened in an unused ballroom, the Riviera Terrace on Broadway in the fifties, that could operate under a cabaret license, allowing the sale of liquor and food. Renovation plans called for an adaptable open space that could be converted into a thrust stage or a central platform with audiences on three or four sides. Planning for the space was halted when Columbia University, the building's owner, sold the property.[27]

Crawford reeled from the double loss of the environmental space for Havoc's dance marathon, and an advance sale of nearly a quarter of a million dollars from theater parties that evaporated in the three months it took to find another theater. She eventually secured the ANTA Playhouse as an imperfect home for *Marathon 33*, according to June Havoc's reminiscences (aptly titled *Early Havoc*). Even with the construction of a thrust forestage and the use of entrances and exits through the aisles, the formal proscenium arrangement distanced audiences from the sweaty, desperate couples dancing for their next meal, the carnival barkers urging them on, and the raw cheers of onstage spectators washing over their favorite contestants.

Confusion over a suitable space for the show (environmental versus proscenium), choice of director, and Strasberg's well-made revisions imposed a weak storyline upon Havoc's loosely arranged story with vaudevillian turns. Praised for the "theatrical flair and gusto" of the Depression era marathon, the production received four Tony nominations, and Havoc received the award for best director.[28] Thereafter, Crawford expressed only admiration for *Marathon 33*: "I don't care what anybody else says about it—it was one of my favorite productions."[29]

Of the four remaining productions in AST's inaugural season, *Dynamite Tonight*, an antiwar comic opera with libretto by Arnold Weinstein and music by Bill Bolcom in the style of Brecht and Weill, was presented Off Broadway. It closed after one performance. An insider's view concluded that the improvisations, which had charmed them in the Studio, "suffered an inexplicable sea change" when moved with cast changes from the Studio's workshop space.[30] Even though there were a number of enthusiastic reviews, once Howard Taubman panned the play ("the Actors Studio Theater [gave] its judgment of what is viable on the stage as a thoroughly black eye"), the AST board closed the show.[31]

Crawford was greatly relieved, when, within a month, James Costigan's *Baby Want a Kiss*, with Paul Newman, Joanne Woodward, and a sheepdog named Barney, made a considerable amount of money. Crawford crowed that the "funny, sexy [play] with something to say about people," had only one set, three characters (playing at Equity minimum), and audiences who wanted to see the stars playing "two smug film stars," more so than the comedy itself.[32]

The show received unanimously unfavorable reviews ("eventless," "muggy," "irritating hodge-podge") but played to sold-out houses for four months.[33] Crawford observed with great satisfaction that the "illustrious names and their minimum salaries made us a considerable amount of money."[34]

Crawford spent 1964 tirelessly overseeing the final productions of the Actors Studio Theatre. The previous year, she and Richard Halliday had produced the musical *Jennie* with Mary Martin, and Crawford's only obligation was to maintain the show during its run. Four days following the opening of *Baby Want a Kiss*, the fourth play in the AST series, James Baldwin's *Blues for Mr. Charlie*, premiered amid a storm of controversy.

Crawford described Baldwin's play about race relations in the American South as "vigorous social comment."[35] Kazan had given his assistant on *J. B.* and *Sweet Bird of Youth* the idea for writing a play based on the Emmett Till case. Kazan expected to stage Baldwin's new play at Lincoln Center, but the writer gave the work to the Actors Studio, ostensibly because there were no blacks on the Lincoln Center board. Baldwin later revealed a deeper motive when he informed Kazan that he regarded him as a father figure and felt compelled to free himself of the paternal influence.[36] In the interim, Rip Torn, a member of the production board, aggressively pursued the young writer in an effort to secure the script for the Studio, promising the playwright that his script would be staged exactly as he had written it.

At the height of the Civil Rights movement, the Studio had in its possession an incendiary new play about racial prejudice. ("Mr. Charlie" was the phrase used for the ubiquitous white oppressor.) Richard Henry, the young black man played by Al Freeman Jr., returns from the North determined to taunt the redneck Southerner into killing him in order to incite his people. The AST production board was divided over the merits and wisdom of producing the play. Once the decision was made, Frank Corsaro, who was to direct, withdrew when Baldwin refused to soften his polemic against the white race. Burgess Meredith stepped in as director and immediately faced objections to the "raw language." Crawford tried to blue-pencil some of Baldwin's expletives but was voted down.[37]

Blues for Mr. Charlie revealed the weakness of the AST's administrative structure that contributed to, in Crawford's view, the theater's demise. Since the play was five hours long, and "not really in shape to produce on Broadway," the production board voted to stage it as a workshop production. Strasberg concurred, but on his way to catch a plane to California, he changed his mind and telephoned from the airport to announce that the play should be given a full-scale production. "This decision was final," Crawford recollected, "and it is an example of the kind of administration that became our downfall." "We never planned," she added, "to give the artistic director the power to overrule the Board; it simply happened."[38]

When Crawford enumerated the number of mistakes that flowed from Strasberg's impetuous telephone call, she began with Baldwin's script. "It should have been done in workshop for three to four months," she reflected. With the confidence of hindsight, Crawford concluded, "given time to experiment I am sure a much finer play would have evolved."[39] She also faulted the production board for rescinding its authority in the face of Strasberg's decree. In the time required to condense the play (and the number of characters), Crawford found it difficult to set a date for an opening and build up an advance sale. Determined to make it possible for a subway audience to come to the theater and convinced that the incendiary play would not attract "the carriage trade," she set the top ticket price at four dollars and eighty cents.

Rehearsals were fraught with displays of temper. Crawford described a scene in which the playwright—dissatisfied with rehearsals and blaming the director and the leading actor, who disagreed with one another on how to play the white man who shoots the young black man—climbed to the top of an A-frame ladder left on the bare stage, and, with the entire company present, unloaded his rage with a long diatribe on the ineptitude of the Studio's work and the incompetence of Lee Strasberg.

As a witness to the extraordinary scene, Crawford remembered that all of them, including Strasberg, looked up, silently waiting for him to tire." Finally, Baldwin left his perch and the theater before Strasberg could answer him.[40]

When the play opened at the ANTA Playhouse on April 23, 1964, critics expressed reservations about the play's sprawling structure and stereotypical Southern whites. Nevertheless, the "relevance and authenticity" of Baldwin's "shout of protest" and the "fierce energy and passion" of the performances of Al Freeman Jr., Diana Sands, Pat Hingle, and Rip Torn offset the criticisms of the awkward and overblown writing, and the simplistic characterization of Southern whites. Reflecting upon the earlier ardor of the Group Theatre, Howard Taubman wrote that Baldwin's play "resembles *Waiting for Lefty* of three decades ago." It was a play "with fires of fury in its belly, tears of anguish in its eyes and a roar of protest in its throat." [41]

Once the show opened, Crawford's work was cut out for her. The five-hour play with twenty-seven actors and low ticket prices "lost money every week" for four months.[42]

Baldwin began a campaign to keep the play running though the summer by taking out large ads in newspapers with imposing names (Roy Wilkins, the executive director of the NAACP, and the daughters of Nelson Rockefeller were signatories) appealing for attendance. Nevertheless, the playhouse had been booked for another production in the fall. Even Crawford's best efforts could not raise the eight thousand dollars to move the show to another theater. She cabled Baldwin, who was in Beirut at the time, that they had to close the show. He cabled back, vehemently protesting that whatever it cost to move "the most underproduced show in recent Broadway history" a few blocks, was not too much. He was convinced that the show "had proved it had an audience." Rejecting Crawford's carefully reasoned arguments, he threatened to take the Studio to court.[43]

To her relief, Crawford reported that nothing happened when the show closed. "The erupting volcano was a smokepot."[44]

Finale

AST's final production was dedicated to Marilyn Monroe, whose death in 1962 cast a pall over the Studio. Crawford possessed the happiest of photographs of herself driving a wind-blown Marilyn and a neighborhood child in her roadster down Norwalk streets.

In August of 1962, Crawford had been spending a holiday on Cape Cod. One morning she drove into Cotuit to get a newspaper and was stunned when she glimpsed the headline announcing the actress's death. "I sat in the car alone for a long time," she recalled in understated grief. [45]

Around that time, Crawford was negotiating with poet Randall Jarrell to use his new version of *The Three Sisters* for AST's final production. For years, Strasberg had longed to direct Chekhov's play. He believed that the Moscow Art Theatre production, which he had seen in 1924, "did not fully reflect Chekhov's vision." In his view, the play required more simplicity and emotion without the obvious or sentimental.[46]

Strasberg's cast was comprised of Kim Stanley as Masha, Geraldine Page as Olga, and Shirley Knight as Irina. The sisters were supported by Barbara Baxley as the sister-in-law Natasha, Kevin McCarthy as Vershinin, and Luther Adler as Chebutykin. Strasberg had not had a directing success on Broadway since the Group's *Men in White* in 1934, and the pressure was intense. With the challenge of the play that had shaped Stanislavski's ideas about inner technique, and the American director unsure of his abilities, the "stage seemed to be set for a disaster," Foster Hirsch observed.[47]

When the reviews appeared in June, Crawford and Strasberg were pleased with the responses of the major critics. Howard Taubman raved that the company, under Strasberg's direction, was "doing the best work of its youthful career." Others remarked on Kim Stanley's "deeply affecting" performance, and the AST's "stunning achievement."[48] Jerry Tallmer, writing for the *New York Post*, put AST's accomplishment in perspective: The Actors Studio "talks a good deal about truth," he wrote. "Last night at the Morosco Theatre it nailed for our lifetime the right to do so and Lee Strasberg proved to a world waiting twenty years that he could direct a play—if it's the right play—with all the creative truth and strength a human being can command."[49]

The Three Sisters ran for three months and closed in early October. Despite the kudos, the AST had no money and no prospects for subsidy. Foster Hirsch called *The Three Sisters* the theater's "last stand," and Crawford, in agreement, despaired as she contemplated the end of another dream.[50]

Dire Predictions

Just as the Studio's production company was "about to be shoveled under," as Crawford aptly put its near-burial, they received a letter from British producer Peter Daubeny inviting the AST to appear at the World Theatre Festival at the Aldwych Theatre in London. The festival organizer called the Studio "a cultural oasis absolutely unique in the annuals of world theatre." [51] Daubeny wanted *Blues for Mr. Charlie* and *The Three Sisters*. As the only AST board member with experience transferring shows to London's West End, Crawford was not enthusiastic about the invitation. She was acutely aware that there were no funds for a second season (the Ford Foundation had declined to renew its grant), and she was confronted with a production board that wanted to gamble on a well-received London engagement to renew foundation interest in the AST. She was a gambler, but she knew that without resources and the original casts, the gamble was absurd.

As she listened to their reasons for taking the plays to London, Crawford calculated that fifty or sixty thousand dollars would have to be raised (and quickly). She also knew that the two shows would have to be recast because a number of original actors were unavailable. Despite Crawford's warnings, the production board voted to accept Daubeny's invitation. Effectively silenced, she was thrust into a frenzy of appeals for money.

When her request to the U.S. State Department for assistance was denied, she turned to Paul Newman, and, together, they talked a top official of Pan American Airways into contributing free round-trip flights to London for the company and movables, including sets, costumes, and furniture. Crawford credited the film star with raising the additional fifty-five thousand dollars from several Hollywood studios, and for making a personal contribution to the fund. Raising the money and recasting took time and cut into rehearsals for the replacements. Nan Martin replaced Geraldine Page, who had married Rip Torn and was pregnant; Shirley Knight refused to work with Lee Strasberg again in her lifetime and was replaced by Sandy Dennis; Kim Stanley refused to play with Kevin McCarthy and insisted on George C. Scott as Vershinin. Crawford thought that Scott was "completely wrong for the dreamy, sentimental Vershinin," and Strasberg agreed, but neither wanted to argue with the volatile actress.[52]

The original cast for *Blues for Mr. Charlie* did not fare much better. In an effort to protect Baldwin's script, Rip Torn argued with the cuts and changes devised for the English censor, and Strasberg and Crawford fired him from the London-bound production. Ralph Waite took over his part. At the time, Diana Sands was in the Broadway success of *The Owl and the Pussycat* and could, or would not, leave the show.

In effect, the recasting cut into the heart of the two productions. Analyzing the results of the changes, Crawford reasoned: "A new actor, however, excellent, cannot come into an established company without tearing the existing fabric; the entire company had to re-rehearse sufficiently to accommodate the changes. Otherwise the result is expedience, not art."[53] Her warning that the existing fabric of both shows was now tattered proved prophetic—expedience trumped art at the Aldwych.

There was little opportunity to repair the tatters during rehearsals in London because no rehearsal space was available. They scouted the city and turned up lofts, armories, tennis courts, and cramped rooms. Before the shows even opened, Crawford declared the situation "a godawful disaster."[54]

When Kazan learned of the crisis with rehearsal space, he blamed Crawford as executive administrator for failing to make facilities available to the company in advance of their arrival. He conjectured that she had been demoralized by the decision to take the shows to London. "She'd had no part in making decisions," he said in her defense, "but [had] been ordered by Lee to carry out those he'd already made."[55] The lingering bitterness between Kazan and Strasberg over the Lincoln Center affair often flowed around and over Cheryl Crawford, who continued to work with both men in separate arenas.

Expedience Trumps Art

Blues for Mr. Charlie was the first disaster, but not the last. Crawford attributed the production's lack of effectiveness on the complex and subtle lighting that was nonexistent on the Aldwych stage. They had not had enough time or the equipment to light the stage properly, and the play was performed in ghostly, gloomy half-light. During the second act, two members of the British National Party began shouting, "Filth!" and "Why don't you go back to Africa?" The cast, remaining in character, answered the hecklers: "Ain't you people had no education?"[56] The critics panned the show, calling it "old-fashioned without having the richness of a tradition," and, "a straggling, overloaded propaganda tract with little fire in it."[57]

In a press conference the next day, Strasberg infuriated Cheryl Crawford, James Baldwin, Burgess Meredith, and the actors by apologizing for the shortcomings of the play and the production. Crawford listened for a few moments, then abruptly left the theater in disgust. Nevertheless, the hostile reception for James Baldwin's play was a milder version of the critical outrage that greeted *The Three Sisters*.

The *Mr. Charlie* cast, playing in unencumbered space where lighting was paramount, had not been troubled by the raked stage at the Aldwych. When the heavy sets for *The Three Sisters* were set up on the raked stage with an eighteen-foot apron, the actors had little time to adjust to the space, the new lighting plot, and to each other. The ensemble achieved at the Morosco was nonexistent at the Aldwych.

Crawford, whom Daubeny called a woman of "vitalizing energy and immense charm," had not seen any of the rehearsals in London.[58] On opening night, she sat in the Aldwych in a state bordering on shock. "They were all fucked up in London," she later told Foster Hirsch. "So many things went wrong. The lighting was so dark you could hardly see some of the actors. There were miscast substitutes. The raked stage seemed to throw people off. The tempos were all wrong. I was upset, and I criticized Strasberg for saying actors could be substituted—not those substitutes, at any rate."[59] In turn, Strasberg placed the blame on a performance that fell apart for a multitude of reasons, including the absence of the original company and uncontrolled technical problems.

Crawford's version of the disastrous opening spared no one. First, she observed that the actors could not seem to get organized backstage in the unfamiliar theater, and delayed the start of the show. "When they finally did start," she reported, "they gave an unbelievable, self-indulgent performance." The play took almost four hours because of the pauses during the scenes and between the acts, and some of the audience departed into the Strand. When Sandy Dennis as Irina came on toward the end and gave her line, "Oh, it's been a terrible evening," the audience laughed. At the curtain call, shouts and boos from the gallery terrified the cast.[60]

The harsh reviews spelled the end of the Actors Studio Theatre. Writing for the *Observer*, Penelope Gilliatt, long an admirer of the Studio's work, expressed her disappointment: "The admirable World Theatre Season's last dismal task has been to mount the suicide of the Actors Studio—the whole endeavour is absurd and agonizing, like playing the harpsichord in boxing gloves, like filling the Spanish riding school with hippopotami." Other reviews were not as colorful as Gilliatt's, but the overall result was a "humiliating, lacerating blow" to the reputation of the Studio and to the existence of the AST.[61]

In retrospect, Peter Daubeny explained that British audiences had been expecting a "jewel-like perfection" from the Actors Studio. Rightly or wrongly, they had credited the AST with being a "permanent repertory company providing the creative inspiration for all American theatre," and, instead, experienced "an under-rehearsed and poorly assembled company."[62]

A Dream Exploded

Following the London debacle, Crawford was too sick-at-heart to return to New York immediately. She stayed in her room at the Savoy to give herself time to assess why and how the theater had failed. Flailing away at the "severe and painful" miscalculations that brought the AST to an end, she took comfort in the fact that, for better or worse, they had produced six plays (two classics and four new American authors) for a total cost of $462,500. "Remarkably little money for such productions," she said.[63] Nevertheless, she could no longer ignore W. McNeil Lowry, then head of the Ford Foundation, who asked a penetrating question when he declined to continue the Foundation's support for a second season. "Who's minding the store?" he had asked. Crawford now answered with the wisdom of hindsight: "Everyone and thus no one, was minding the store."[64]

As she took stock of events contributing to the failure of the theater, she admitted that the administrative structure had never been clear. There had been three directors with different assignments, a business manager with little authority, and a production board with voting powers. In practice, decision-making did not obey the rules of the administrative structure.

Lee Strasberg's image as father figure and head of the Studio "emotionally overwhelmed the executive organization." As a result, instead of functioning as an executive, Crawford found herself in an uncomfortably familiar situation as a mere vehicle for carrying out decisions made by the artistic director and the production board.[65]

Crawford also blamed her preoccupations with other projects. She had had several productions of her own that season, including *Andorra*, *Mother Courage and Her Children*, and *Jennie*. Moreover, as Strasberg took on the artistic leadership of the AST, he seesawed between caution and the assertion of authority with little innate ability to delegate responsibility. In the end, Crawford blamed only herself. "I had somehow fizzled," she said. "Dazzled, as always, by Lee's brilliant theories, I did not assert enough of the expertise my long practical experience had given me."[66]

With characteristic bluntness, Kazan analyzed his friend's shortcomings in the circumstances: "She didn't challenge him [Strasberg]; she surrendered everywhere."[67]

Crawford knew from experience that Strasberg's great gifts were teaching and inspirational guidance, not administration and management. He had dithered about approving *Strange Interlude*, and the company had had to trick their "reluctant dragon," as he was called, by getting him to agree *post facto* to the O'Neill play, if they could get the rights. Strasberg thought the rights were irrevocably tied up by the new theater at Lincoln Center until it was announced that the Actors Studio Theatre would produce the play with Quintero directing.

With Strasberg's customary inability to act decisively as an administrator coupled with his ambivalence when confronted with artistic decisions, the Studio side-stepped three important new American plays. They failed to produce *A Hatful of Rain*, *The Night of the Iguana*, and *Who's Afraid of Virginia Woolf?* All three plays would have added money to the Studio's depleted coffers and enhanced the reputation of the Actors Studio, as fertile ground for new American playwriting.

For a brief moment, Ely Landau, then a television producer, offered a financial reprieve. He agreed to film in Electronovision the first of a series of twelve productions over a three-year period. Landau agreed to pay all costs with each production receiving a fifty thousand dollar advance against a fifty-fifty sharing of the profits. Crawford rejoiced in the unexpected windfall that would also subsidize future productions.

The televised version of *The Three Sisters*, the first in the series taped in 1965, was done quickly to minimize expenses with member-director Paul Bogart (of *All in the Family* and *Golden Girls* fame) more or less replicating Strasberg's original staging. Bogart returned from Hollywood to find the cast of *The Three Sisters* (post–New York and London productions) "combustible." The cast and director were tired of one another—and with Chekhov—and Crawford, occupied with other projects, was not very visible.[68] The notable performances of Kim Stanley's Masha, Geraldine Page's Olga, and replacements Shelley Winters (as Natasha) and Sandy Dennis (as Irina) were captured on tape, but, like many filmed stage performances, it was not a success and remains the only record of an AST production.

Crawford's hope for subsidy from sales to television networks vanished. Despite her disappointment, she wrote to Paul Bogart thanking him for his good work in a difficult situation.[69]

The most painful part of Crawford's after-the-fact deliberations was the knowledge that this was the fourth time she had engaged in the creation of an idealistic theater—and failed. Haunted by memories of the Group Theatre, the American Repertory Theatre, and the Experimental Theatre, she walked away from the AST in the knowledge that she had done her best, even though she had been overwhelmed, again, by the shortage of money and by her own inability to utilize her considerable management skills in the face of inspirational personalities. This time, she was confronting the most painful disappointment of her life. "When I had failed before," she remonstrated with herself, "I had at least failed with honor. That is one thing. It is quite another to fail ignobly. What was lost was so valuable, and the way it was lost so unworthy."[70]

Cheryl Crawford and Lee Strasberg, who had worked together since 1928, were never close again after the disaster in London. As the "keeper of the flame" for sixteen years, Crawford resigned her executive position with the Studio and returned only a few times to the old church on Forty-fourth Street, where the Studio still exists today as a testament to the vision and energy of its founders—Elia Kazan, Robert Lewis, and Cheryl Crawford.

12

DREAMS DEFERRED

*The theatre, which is perpetually struggling for survival, is continually in
need of her kind of spirit to replenish its vitality.*
—Tennessee Williams

Just as writing was Tennessee Williams's life, so producing was Cheryl
Crawford's. Following the collapse of the Actors Studio Theatre,
Crawford was thrust once again into the world of the independent
producer. From 1962 to 1972, she produced seven Broadway shows,
with varying success, along with four Off Broadway productions that
provided spiritual uplift but were financial question marks. In general,
she made a comfortable percentage on the sale of film rights that com-
pensated for the loss of income on the theatrical properties.

As a producer, Crawford was a legend of economy. She was economical
in the extreme with show expenses and parsimonious when it came to
accepting producer's fees for herself. She was one of the last producers
to take a percentage of the weekly gross. In hindsight, she called it "a
foolish gesture."[1] In those days, backers received all of the profits from a
variety of sources (film rights, foreign, stock, and amateur rights) until
their full investment was returned, and, only then, was there a fifty-fifty
division of profits between investors and producers. Nevertheless, she
would not have exchanged the financially precarious theater business for
her father's real estate empire in Akron, or for a stolid executive position
in New York City. In her chosen profession, she teased her dreams of a
"hit" show for another twenty years.

Mistakes and Errors

Over the years, Crawford's guarded choices resulted in a number of regrettable mistakes. As Janet Flanner said of her propensity to take risks,

"She is not as good a gambler as she thinks she is, but she is an enduring gambler."[2] Looking back on the plays that she either missed or turned down, she named *Death of a Salesman, The Member of the Wedding, Cat on a Hot Tin Roof, The Threepenny Opera*, and *The Diary of Anne Frank*. She failed to accommodate the extra workload when *Cat on a Hot Tin Roof* became available, and she famously declined Kazan's offer of *Death of a Salesman*, saying, "Who would want to see a play about an unhappy traveling salesman?"[3] After reading *The Member of the Wedding*, she explained to Carson McCullers: "no one doubts your writing ability. And your dialogue here is charming. But the play's story is so slight, so small. I doubt a Broadway audience would be interested in a tomboy full of fantasies."[4] Two years later, Crawford regretted her twin stupidities, as the two plays racked up record audiences and McCullers's fragile play ran for 501 performances, credited to luminous acting by Julie Harris, Ethel Waters, and Brandon de Wilde.

A new English version of the Brecht-Weill *Threepenny Opera* was Marc Blitzstein's long-dreamed-of project that Crawford encouraged to the extent that she drove him to Kurt Weill's home in New City, where Weill listened to Blizstein's idiomatic lyrics. Weill approved of the new setting (New York in the 1870s during the days of gangsterism in the notorious Five Points) and gave Blitzstein the rights to translate the work. During the development phase, Crawford lost confidence in the musical's appeal to the general public and withdrew from the project. In truth, Kurt Weill died suddenly in April of 1950, and, despite his contentious feelings toward her lack of taste and judgment about musicals, Crawford was deeply affected and found that she was unable to work surrounded by his music.[5] She masked her pain with tired excuses of "cold feet" and "loss of self-confidence." Blitzstein's version languished for several years, found new producers, and, with Lotte Lenya as Jenny Diver, opened Off Broadway, and ran for years.

The Diary of Anne Frank served to remind Crawford that one person's error is another's fortune.[6] Novelist Meyer Levin brought her *The Diary of Anne Frank*, which he wanted to adapt for the stage. She persuaded Otto Frank, Anne's father, who was in New York, to award her the rights to adapt the book and promised Levin that he could develop the script. Their agreement, according to Crawford, gave the playwright permission to show his script to other producers, but, if it was not accepted, then the rights to the dramatization reverted to her. Levin's script was not optioned, and, in November 1952, she approached Carson McCullers, then living in France, to start a fresh adaptation.[7] Levin challenged their arrangement. By April, Crawford, weary of all the complications surrounding *Anne Frank*, withdrew from the project only to have Kermit Bloomgarden pick up the rights and persuade Frances Goodrich and Albert Hackett to adapt the *Diary*, and their success is stage history.

Claiming that he was not "morally bound" by his contract with Otto Frank, Meyer Levin took all parties to court (Otto Frank, Cheryl Crawford, and Kermit Bloomgarden), citing damages in the amount of $200,000. Crawford was nonplused. Unlike Bloomgarden, she lost her advance, endured Levin's anger, and enjoyed none of the pleasures of having a hit. "My rewards were legal fees," she complained, "and several days in a courtroom when I could have been more pleasantly employed."[8]

She counted *West Side Story* among the soaring blunders in a career rich in highs and lows. Leonard Bernstein came to her office n 1956 to tell her that he and Stephen Sondheim were writing the score and lyrics for a musical based on *Romeo and Juliet*, with book by Arthur Laurents. The advance was more than she felt able to afford at the time, and she asked Roger Stevens to coproduce. She remained enthusiastic until a backers' audition in April of the following year, during which none of the well-dressed potential investors opened his checkbook. Knowing that the production had been dismissed by other producers as too operatic with too many onstage deaths and that it would cost more money than any show she had produced, she was in a quandary.

After agonizing over the mammoth costs and casting hurdles, she faced the creative team in her office and informed them of her decision to withdraw. Conflicting testimonies muddy the waters of what happened next. Harsh words were exchanged, and Crawford was called "an immoral woman."[9] She referred to the dust-up as "a miserable meeting," in which she relinquished a project that had all the elements of success with the exception of three hundred thousand dollars. As they proceeded with *West Side Story* without her, the participants remained perplexed. Why did Cheryl Crawford abandon the show without even trying to assemble a team of coproducers?[10]

Unknown to her detractors, who concluded she was losing her edge as a commercial producer, Crawford had received a subpoena from HUAC and was horrified to be dragged into Cold War politics. She felt vulnerable, dispirited, and betrayed by her government. Not knowing what her legal expenses would be, she had no stomach for the super-expensive show about rival street gangs.

Incidental Politics

Crawford was unable to imagine that she would become mired in Cold War politics. Living a carefully guarded private life, her public existence was defined by her deals on Broadway and *pro bono* work for nonprofit groups struggling with a different kind of idealism. In her Congregationalist ethos, work and talent superseded politics. Nevertheless, she had read the headlines about subpoenas that swept actors, directors, screenwriters, and friends from her Group Theatre days before HUAC during the "Red scare" of the early fifties. She had never imagined that the McCarthyites would be interested in her.

Crawford took no pleasure in the subpoena that arrived in 1957, requiring her to appear before the committee. She had ignored (or forgotten) the photograph published in the conservative *Sign* together with an article questioning the publicity that the *New York Times* gave to people in the entertainment industry with "front" records. Among those theatrical personalities cited as having "red paint on their escutcheons" were Broadway notables Margaret Webster, Tennessee Williams, Elmer Rice, Burgess Meredith, Woollcott Gibbs, Herman Shumlin, and Cheryl Crawford.[11]

Somehow, the "fronter" label had not stuck. Among her friends and acquaintances, she was known as an idealist and reformer, but not as a "Red" or socialist. She had compassion for the oppressed, the mistreated, and the unfortunate. She served on civic and cultural committees to improve the rights of minorities and had been a conspicuous fighter for the presence of African-American actors on Broadway's stages.

As a potential congressional witness, she turned to her attorney William Fitelson, who obtained a list of her political activities that had attracted the attention of the FBI and HUAC. She was on record as a sponsor and/or signatory to letters for four "front" groups, and as a faculty member of the New Theatre League's training school, run by a suspect group of union workers. Her name had appeared in an advertisement sponsored by the Committee for the First Amendment protesting HUAC and on a telegram of greetings to the testimonial dinner for the Hollywood Ten, sponsored by the Freedom from Fear Committee. On record as signatory to a letter on behalf of Paul Robeson to *Nation* magazine regarding the 1949 Peekskill riots, she also sponsored the Committee for Equal Justice for Mrs. Recy Taylor, a victim of gang rape in rural Alabama, and the Committee to End Jim Crow in Baseball. Concluding the list of "front" groups was the National Council of American-Soviet Friendship. She and Harold Clurman were speakers on Soviet theater at the first conference of the NCASF.

As she reviewed the "petty and ridiculous" list in Fitelson's office, she was troubled by the summons to appear before the committee. "I hate angry voices," she asserted. "I had never been browbeaten, and I did not know how I would react if I were."[12] Like most potential witnesses holding a subpoena, she spent nights roiling questions in her mind: What did I know? What would they ask? What would I answer? Who did I know who might be subversive?

When he read Crawford's memoir, Kazan thought there was something disingenuous about her claim of ignorance about a cell of communists and sympathizers in the Group Theatre. He was astonished that she had no suspicion of the cell's weekly meetings in the Belasco Theatre during the run of Odets's *Gold Eagle Guy* in 1934.[13]

Even during his work on *The House of Connolly*, Paul Green recognized that some Group members were taken with communist ideology, and felt "closer to Joseph Stalin than to Thomas Jefferson."[14]

Despite Elia Kazan and Paul Green to the contrary, Crawford insisted that politics had always been incidental to her life. Crawford's nose-to-the-grindstone apolitical record was reinforced by the silence of the theater community, who neither mentioned her politics nor her sexuality.[15]

Then, without explanation, she received a telegram indefinitely postponing the hearing. Once she was "let off the hook," her relief was inexpressible. When she regained her equilibrium, she insisted, "The fact is I didn't know much."[16]

Staying Afloat

The next twenty-eight years of producing were often financially "too close to the bone" for comfort. With the exceptions of *Sweet Bird of Youth*, *Brecht on Brecht*, and *Yentl*, Crawford complained that she worked sixteen hours a day on productions with important directors and stellar casts, but critics were often dismissive of the results. She tried to persuade Clifford Odets, Thornton Wilder, and Paul Green to write scripts for her to produce but failed after many drinks and ideas for plays tossed out by Odets without results and enticing letters exchanged with an ever elusive Thornton Wilder.

During her twenty-year pursuit of Wilder, they developed an enduring friendship and a correspondence that she treasured until his death in 1975. During the writer's travels, he wrote to her about his work and plays he was seeing. In turn, she sent him novels hoping that one would interest him as a potential play and, on one occasion, included her producer's bedtime prayer:

Now I lay me down to sleep
I pray you Lord my soul to keep
You let me do a play by Thorn
And I'll thank you for being born.

At one point, when he was working on a version of Euripides' *The Alcestiad*, Wilder jokingly signed himself "Euripides." Crawford hastened to reply: "You may call yourself anything, darling, but remember Euripides, if he is your model, wrote ninety-two plays—so you'd better hurry. Wouldn't it be nice to have that many to split among your admirers?[17]

Only Paul Green responded to her pleas, by sending scripts about the Revolutionary War and Jamestown settlers intended for his outdoor pageants. Crawford wrote gentle rejection letters, ending with, "See your agent."[18] Evident in their fifty years of correspondence (Green died in 1981), Crawford never shut the door on a relationship with a writer but persistently inquired about new material and encouraged development of new work.

Crawford admitted that her lack of persuasion, string of failures ("Sometimes the opening-night flowers lasted longer the play," she carped.), and minor successes began to take their toll on her physical and mental well-being.[19] She compared herself to Humpty Dumpty, whom three successive osteopaths were unable to put back together. She took refuge in her "restorative retreat," Eastham, where she could salve her wounds beyond the reach of Broadway's mavens, and commune with the squirrels, woodchucks, and fireflies, who lived less complicated lives.

A portrait of comfortable domesticity at Eastham with her partner, Ruth Norman, emerged from friends who visited from New York, and, weather permitting, swam in the pool in the rear of the house and stayed for dinner. With light brown hair, sturdy frame, radiant smile, and a comfortable "American" presence, Ruth Norman, who favored combinations of clothing in blues and whites, immediately put guests at ease. Described as a "great appreciator," she was a quiet person who laughed easily. She deferred to Crawford during conversations and took charge only when she turned her capable hands to preparing dinner for their guests. Crawford, known for her one-dish meals, dutifully assisted by setting the table and preparing salads under Norman's watchful eye.

Norman was a friend and associate of celebrated chef and food writer James Beard and coauthored several cookbooks (*Cook Until Done* with George Bradshaw and *Art of Fine Cooking* with James Beard). The two chefs often cooked together for Eastham guests, selecting vegetables grown in the garden and producing simple, elegant meals served on various combinations of china that were never repeated. If *The Fantasticks* composer Harvey Schmidt and lyricist Tom Jones were among the guests, they were asked to play numbers on the grand piano in the living room from the show they were working on at the time, or, in lieu of new work,

Schmidt played romantic show tunes , during which Crawford became nostalgic and teary-eyed.[20] Crawford-the-romantic often sat in the curve of the grand piano that Lerner, Loewe, and Kurt Weill had once played in rehearsals, while Schmidt, pleased to be part of that illustrious musical succession, played her favorite songs, and, in a "rich, deep baritone" she would often sing "Bye, Bye Blackbird," or "Try to Remember."[21]

From time to time, conversations continued around the breakfast table with guests who stayed overnight. Crawford's droll observations often surprised her friends. Returning from a morning walk with her poodle, Ami, she explained that she had been mulling something over in her head: "Who can you think of, in the theater or in films, man or woman, who has sex appeal?" The question startled her breakfast guests, because it was apparent that Crawford thought there were very few people in that category. Speaking in her laconic style without intonation, she named Ina Claire, Alla Nazimova, and Marlon Brando. Then, considering her choices, she added the names of Vivien Leigh, Laurence Olivier, and Clark Gable. "But there were damn few," she concluded.[22]

For the moment, Eastham was the cherished place where the private woman could safely retreat from the commercial world of Broadway and the gathering naysayers. Despite the fact she received an honorary doctorate in literature from Smith College, was inducted into the Theatre Hall of Fame, and was awarded Brandeis University's Medal of Achievement for Distinguished Contributions to American Theatre Arts—all of which she described as "an exhilarating run of luck"—she had accumulated too many failures in the early sixties, and her Connecticut home had become a liability.[23]

She walked from room to room looking at her "treasures," many left over from Broadway flops rather than long runs, which usually left draperies and furnishings too beat-up to rescue. Taking stock of her mementos (a wing chair from *What Every Woman Knows*, the piano from *Brigadoon*, a coffee table from *The Perfect Marriage*, and a bookcase from *The Closing Door*), she would raise the price of the property. Finally, she borrowed money in the hope that the next production would save her home.

This was most likely the time that Ruth Norman and friends, also chefs, made the decision to fulfill their fantasy of opening a restaurant in Westport, some twenty minutes from Eastham. They enlisted composer Harvey Schmidt, also a painter, to design a logo and menu cover for *Bon Appétit*. Somewhat later, Norman invested in a house nearby where she could rest after long hours of managing the restaurant. She treated the Westport property as a convenience and maintained the home she shared with Crawford in New York City as a permanent residence and the houses they shared in Norwalk (and later in Bridgehampton, Long Island) as country retreats.

During the frenetic sixties, Crawford searched for new material in London, Rome, and Berlin and returned from Europe with Max Frisch's *Andorra* ("a savage parable on anti-Semitism") and Brecht's *Mother Courage and Her Children* (a "diamond hard" voyage through a brutal landscape).[24] Neither production translated into enthusiasm from American audiences. In contrast, she discovered George Tabori's *Brecht on Brecht* at the Theatre de Lys in the same year she produced *Sweet Bird of Youth*. The results were two gigantic hits. She took over Tabori's show with the original cast of Lotte Lenya, Anne Jackson, Viveca Lindfors, George Voskovec, and Michael Wager for a celebrated run of 424 performances.

To explain her persistent rejection of middle-class security in favor of the producer's high-risk life, she devised a fable featuring a woodchuck and a squirrel:

> One woodchuck lived in a deep, comfortable hole, coming out only to eat. A frisky squirrel played near his home. I would watch them, fancying the squirrel asking the woodchuck, "How can you lead so dull a life? Why don't you come out more often?"
>
> The woodchuck would reply, "Yes, it's dull but it's safe. At least I'm alive. To which, in my mind, the squirrel shot back, "How would you know?"[25]

For a lifetime, Crawford exchanged the middle-class values of her family rooted in Ohio for the excitement of Manhattan and Broadway. Unlike the woodchuck, she turned down the opportunity for job security with the Shakespeare Festival Theatre in Connecticut for the frantic insecurities of the commercial theater. However, nothing prepared her for the shock of betrayal by a trusted confidant that resulted in the irreparable loss of Eastham.

Misplaced Trust

Richard Chandler, a young man from Peoria, Illinois, entered her life by way of a letter sent to her office. She did not reply to his request for a job, but he turned up unannounced one day in 1957. He assured her he would work for nothing until he proved himself useful.

Chandler was tall and handsome with curly brown hair and blue eyes. He was well-educated and an excellent typist to boot. The sudden appearance of a friendly helper with Ivy League manners raised no alarm bells. "This sort of thing happens all the time in the theatre," Crawford rationalized. "Its glamour attracts people, particularly affluent ones, who are willing to do anything just to be part of it."[26]

Crawford surmised that Chandler was affluent based on the stories he spun about his Midwestern roots that included a wealthy aunt with homes in London, Majorca, and Paris whose fortune he was to inherit. To prove his *bona fides*, he showed her a photograph from an old issue of *Time* magazine and pointed to a tastefully dressed woman, identified as his "aunt," in a group of women surrounding society hostess Elsa Maxwell. Crawford's concerns were assuaged by her knowledge of Elsa Maxwell and the Elisabeth Marbury-Elsie de Wolfe social circle.

Marbury and de Wolfe were well-known theatrical legends. Marbury pioneered as the first theatrical agent to represent American and European authors and instituted the modern royalty system, and de Wolfe, a stylish performer in theatricals notable for her back flip over a loveseat in full-skirted regalia, became an arbiter of fashion on Broadway. Meanwhile the women sustained a "Boston marriage," while excelling outside conventional theatrical roles in the first quarter of the twentieth century. Their wealth and their social and theatrical connections, through Marbury's theatrical agency and de Wolfe's successful interior-decorating career, made the two successful women models of unconventional accomplishment.[27]

Crawford would not have known Marbury, who died in 1933, but, in her circle of New York patrons and investors, she could easily have encountered Elsie de Wolfe, who lived until 1950. She certainly knew of the doyenne of high society (the "hostess with the mostest"), Elsa Maxwell, who was rumored to be part of the de Wolfe circle. As Robert Lewis said of Crawford's social connections, "she was not one of us," referring to Elia Kazan and other theater buddies. Drawing upon Crawford's "lesbianship" as a talking-point, Lewis told Mel Gussow in an Actors Studio interview: "The rest of us didn't pal around with those girls—they were society girls. I won't say we were exactly poor, but we were not on that level. We were very much more on the level of the artistic world, not the society world."[28]

Richard Chandler's appearance in Crawford's life was at once calculated and fortuitous. The mysterious helper, who had a real aunt, just not the one of Elsa Maxwell's acquaintance, appeared at a time when Crawford's mother had died two years earlier, Ruth Norman was engaged with her new restaurant, and Crawford felt an acute sense of insecurity in her own work. She was haunted by the HUAC subpoena and the five flops in a row on Broadway and hard-pressed to believe in her prowess as a producer. And she was physically tired. She had a minimal office staff to implement the day-to-day work of an independent producer and to address the demands of the Actors Studio. At a low point financially and emotionally, Crawford readily accepted the young man. "Free help was not to be scoffed at," she assured herself.[29] Whatever Chandler's true intentions, his relative's presumed connection with society and wealth, along with his ingratiating manners, convinced Crawford that he was trustworthy.

Chandler proved so helpful that she paid him a small salary and expressed concern that she was unable to offer him more money. Ingratiating himself as an energetic helper and trusted confidant, he wrote flattering notes that he deposited on her desk. In one note he vowed, "I want to work with you as long as I can, and I want to fight on your side as long as I am able. I don't know what the future will whisper to me, but I know that no matter where I am or what I am doing, you will always be my chief."[30]

During the Chandler years, Crawford's father died, she produced few winners, and the office coffers were constantly lean. Shortly before *Period of Adjustment* opened, she produced *The Long Dream*, adapted by Ketti Frings from a novel by Richard Wright. The drama about race relations in a Southern town was found wanting by the critics, and Crawford faulted herself for not recognizing the lifelessness of the dramatization.

Failure followed failure, and by 1966 the outlook was grim. At a time when she needed a winner, she chose the "Zen-Buddhist-Hebrew" musical *Chu Chem* to produce. Occidental actors join a troupe of Chinese performers to enact a story about the title character and his family, who journey to China to study traces of Jews who lived there in previous centuries. One Philadelphia critic gleefully dubbed Crawford's eccentric choice as "*The King and Oy.*" Yet, Crawford had not been altogether wrong-headed. The musical was the inspiration of *Man of La Mancha* composer, Mitch Leigh, and featured Menasha Skulnik and Molly Picon, popular stars from the Yiddish theater and Broadway.

While the casting was inspired, the fault lay backstage. The composer had promised Molly Picon a song that he had not written by the time the show opened in Philadelphia. The Yiddish theater star refused to leave her dressing room until the song was delivered. No song was produced and Picon remained closeted in her dressing room. As word leaked out that the star was not appearing, box office business declined and long lines for ticket refunds stretched around the block.[31]

Chandler chose this low point in his employer's life to present her with a play of his own. *The Freaking Out of Stephanie Blake* was a comedy about an Ohio spinster who comes to New York to embark on a European trip, only to find her beloved niece involved with hippies in Greenwich Village. Crawford agreed to produce Chandler's comedy and turned to Jean Arthur, whose last Broadway show was *Peter Pan*, seventeen years earlier. Although Arthur had a reputation for being unreliable (her withdrawal from *Born Yesterday* made her replacement, Judy Holliday, a Broadway star), she assured Crawford that her unprofessional behavior was a thing of the past. Crawford soon learned differently.

As *Stephanie Blake* moved toward opening night, there were replacements and delays. There were reports in the press that the set designer and the director withdrew over artistic differences with the playwright. Crawford next hired designers Ben Edwards and Jean Rosenthal and director Michael Kahn and sat back to enjoy full houses with audiences eager to see the film star of *Mr. Smith Goes to Washington, Foreign Affair,* and *Shane.* Sitting on the aisle in the last row for the third preview, Crawford watched in astonishment as Jean Arthur came on stage, removed her hat, got on her knees, and told the audience that she couldn't go on because of illness. Before the actress finished her speech of contrition, Crawford was on her feet shouting, "You will go on. You will play the play!"[32]

The stunned actress finished the performance, left the theater, and called her doctor, who told the producer that Arthur was "suffering from exhaustion" and unable to continue in the production. Crawford announced in the *New York Times* that she had been unable to talk with Miss Arthur and sent her a telegram: "Your failure to appear at rehearsal this afternoon and at performances tonight and tomorrow will necessitate the closing of the play . . . with an estimated loss of $250,000."[33]

Crawford cancelled the show and lamented, "So much for *Stephanie Blake,* on which I lost more money than I care to think about."[34]

Crawford was more troubled over the sizable loss of money than by Chandler's disputes with the designer and director. Shortly after the *Stephanie Blake* fiasco, Chandler volunteered that his wealthy aunt had passed away and his lawyer in Peoria was coming East to transfer a hundred thousand dollars from the legacy to Crawford. She would have an annuity for life. This information had a calculated effect. "I was touched that Richard wanted to make me comfortable," she remarked.[35]

With no forewarning of things to come, they produced their first and final production together in 1969—the musical *Celebration.* Although she had not produced *The Fantasticks,* she admired the youthful team of

Tom Jones and Harvey Schmidt and asked them to write a musical for her to produce and invited them to Eastham to dine with her and Ruth Norman. Thus began a friendship that lasted throughout Crawford's remaining years.[36]

Crawford introduced her new protégées, who began their collaboration as students at the University of Texas, Austin, to other theater people, who offered commissions that interrupted their work on Crawford's show. The "boys," as she called them, created two productions for producer David Merrick (*110 in the Shade* and *I Do! I Do!*) before finalizing *Celebration* in their Portfolio Studio in a converted brownstone on West Forty-seventh Street. Throughout the developmental process of the fable, depicting the battle between Winter and Summer, Crawford was encouraging, helpful, and remarkably quiet and never intruded on their creative process.[37]

Crawford's delight in the experimental Off Broadway–style musical was dampened by the critics. First performed in the Portfolio space, the show went directly to Broadway's Ambassador Theatre. Critics, recalling *The Fantasticks*, found the new musical lacked its simplicity, uplift, and stage magic. Nevertheless, the reviews for the "fairy tale for adults," which had a respectable run, were a minor set-back in comparison to the bizarre happenings that followed at the hands of Richard Chandler.

Bizarre Incidents

While they were producing *Celebration*, Crawford and Chandler discussed how he would use his inherited wealth and agreed upon a plan to fund needy playwrights and poets. Seated at her desk one afternoon, Crawford suddenly felt a sharp crack on her head. "It stunned me, and my head bled badly," she recalled.[38] Chandler explained to the doctor, who stitched the wound, that the sharp edge of the *One Touch of Venus* poster had fallen and hit the producer. Crawford was skeptical about how the poster could have fallen with such force, but she accepted his explanation and put the matter aside.

Chandler's lawyer from Peoria was twice anticipated and twice failed to arrive. On the second occasion, she and Chandler waited until late afternoon in a nearby restaurant (most likely Sardi's). Suddenly, Crawford felt ill and could scarcely move. She asked him to take her to her apartment and call a doctor. "While I went to bed, Richard called, or so he claimed, but was unable to get an answer," she remembered later. "Fortunately, my maid was there and I sent her out to get medicine, since Richard said he felt ill too."[39]

A longtime friend dropped by, and the bedraggled Crawford joked that she felt as though she had been given a "Mickey Finn," an old speakeasy term for a drink that's been drugged. What transpired later convinced her that her drink had been spiked, and had her maid not been in the apartment, the outcome might have been worse than a severe headache.

A few weeks after the incident in the restaurant, she arrived at her office to find a handwritten note. "Would she forgive him?" Chandler wrote, adding that he was leaving New York forever. Crawford was puzzled and called the lawyer in Peoria, only to be stunned by the truth. The attorney had not been to New York in many years; there was no legacy for Richard Chandler; and the aunt's Peoria "mansion" was a lower-middle-class dwelling. Then, the other shoe dropped.

For some time, Chandler had been in charge of her office accounts and personal finances. On the day of his disappearance, she found a bank statement in the office mail containing forged checks made out to him. It took many weary days to reconstruct her finances. Operating a small-time Ponzi scheme, Chandler manipulated the accounts by closing out one office account only to open another; he forged her name on checks written on the second account and paid money to himself. When there were insufficient funds from the shows to keep his scheme going, he disappeared. Reviewing the carnage, she lashed out in disappointment, anger, and grief. "I had fed the mouth that bit me," she fumed. "How could I have been so vulnerable?"[40]

She filed charges with the Manhattan district attorney. Meanwhile, Chandler returned to New York, was arrested for embezzlement, and appeared in court. Crawford did not demand his incarceration, and he was ordered to report weekly to a probation officer and return his future earnings to her until his debt was cleared. Crawford did not attend the court proceeding and never saw Richard Chandler again.

When she wrote her memoir ten years later, the Chandler episode was still fresh in her mind. She faulted herself for not recognizing the con game, even though it was no "ordinary" con job. His wealthy aunt had been a fiction, and, much to her chagrin, she now recognized herself as that aunt. During the twelve years she unwittingly supported him, he had lived in a duplex garden apartment filled with books, recordings, and paintings. He had also taken trips abroad at her expense to promote himself as a producer. Completely shattered by Chandler's betrayal more so than by any previous miscalculation on a production that had failed, she confessed, "Trust had always been a strength to me, not a weakness. I was more vulnerable, wide open, than I realized.[41]

Chandler's embezzlement now endangered Eastham. As she contemplated the necessity to sell her home, now a liability, fate intervened. Late in the evening of February 5, 1969, just fifteen days after the opening of *Celebration*, she received a frantic telephone call. "Eastham is burning!" she heard in disbelief.[42] She telephoned Ruth Norman in Westport, who dashed to Eastham and, assisted by neighbors, managed to save a few smoke-filled books and some pieces of charred furniture. The next day, Crawford hired a driver to take her to Norwalk. As she stared at the blackened skeleton of her beloved retreat, her mind was filled with thoughts that she had no home, no refuge, and no explanation of the origin of the fire. Nor did the firemen, police, and insurance agents ever determine the fire's origins.

Somewhere in the recesses of her mind, she recalled that trouble usually came in threes. Richard Chandler had been responsible for two, if not three, of her recent calamities: the falling poster, the embezzlement, and now the suspicious fire that destroyed her sanctuary. What she knew for a certainty was that *betrayal* was harder to endure than the destruction of her beloved home.[43]

Cold Comfort

For a year following the fire, Crawford found it difficult to continue her well-established routines. She and Ruth Norman lived in their Manhattan apartment, and the restaurateur commuted by train to Westport. From time to time when they wanted to escape the city, they rented a place in the Hamptons. Crawford remained depressed over the loss of her treasures and bereft of ambition and ideas for the next project. She recognized that her depression was rather like Edna Ferber's prescription for drowning—"not bad once you stop struggling."[44]

Then, playwright Elinor Jones (known to friends as "Ellie" and married at the time to Tom Jones) brought her a script that lifted her spirits. *Colette* was Jones's first play, based on *Earthly Paradise*, a collection of Collette's writings. Crawford found it irresistible. The playwright's first impression of Cheryl Crawford was of "an energy of mind in a stiff little body." "She turns her head with difficulty," she recalled, "but when she talks of something that excites her, her blue eyes light up, her cheeks get very red, and her fingers start dancing."[45]

The rejuvenated producer gave the writer an immediate answer: she would produce the play, if Zoe Caldwell, an "ideal Colette," would agree to do the role.[46] Caldwell was not completely sold on the material, sending producer and writer to extract new scenes from Colette's writings. One scene about a woman's attraction to a handsome young man betrayed Crawford's raw emotional connection to the material. In these conferences, Crawford reiterated that "passion" was the key to writing for the theater. Her advice to the writer: "Be brave, don't be dull, and take risks."[47]

Zoe Caldwell liked the new script, and Crawford set the production in motion. Harvey Schmidt and Tom Jones provided original music and lyrics (Schmidt played the on-stage piano), and Gerald Freedman, another Ohioan and associate from *West Side Story*, directed. Then, Crawford made an eccentric choice. She chose the Ellen Stewart Theatre, an Off-Off Broadway house on East Fourth Street in lower Manhattan with 250 seats. She considered its interior ambience ideal for Colette's story. In the seventies, the choice of a theater in an out-of-the-way location for New York theatergoers was a considerable risk.

When *Colette* opened, risk vanished in the flurry of ecstatic reviews. Gerald Freedman described the street in front of the theater crowded with limos and taxis carrying the hoi polloi of Broadway to the Lower East Side while neighbors looked on from tenement windows.[48] The euphoria over the "sellout business" lasted three months. Caldwell had a previous engagement, and Crawford was unable to find a replacement (leading actresses were reluctant to follow Caldwell's much-lauded performance) to imbue the show with the same excitement as Zoe Caldwell's performance. The hit show closed after 101 performances, and Crawford was "on the ropes, again."[49]

During the run of *Colette*, Crawford was increasingly described as small and fragile. During her convalescence from a mastectomy, she discovered a bright side to the Eastham tragedy. The house and furniture had been heavily insured and the five and one-half acres were worth more in 1970 more than the original cost of the property and house. When the insurance claim was settled and the property sold, she had "a healthy sum" safely deposited in a new bank account. Should she save the money for her old age or find another refuge? The refuge won. She had been spending weekends with various friends in their country places and did not want to spend the remainder of her years as a weekend guest.

During one of these weekends, she was in Bridgehampton, Long Island, where she saw for sale a reconstructed stable refinished in early American detail with low ceilings and wide floor boards, large windows and glass doors overlooking a pond, and space for a small garden and flagstone terrace. Crawford was enchanted. "Overnight, I bought it," she announced. The house and landscape proved an unending delight, with rolling breakers close by and geese cackling at dawn in the nearby pond. She awoke to be reminded of the sounds of ladies on matinee days.

While the pastoral scene enchanted her, she had no intention of abandoning New York City, which poet Marianne Moore praised for its "accessibility to experience."[50] For Crawford, that accessibility had been the glittering backdrop to her fifty years in the theater and a window to her future.

The Last Hurrah

After *Colette*, Crawford produced four shows before encountering an unexpected doorway that thrust her into the dying light of her favorite poem by Dylan Thomas. She ended her thirty-seven year Broadway career with the triumphant *Yentl*, based on Isaac Bashevis Singer's stories. Before closing on a high note, she explored the potential of Off Broadway with new writers Romulus Linney and Dolores Sutton, who had something to say about the Vietnam War and the love entanglements of an accomplished older woman with a famous writer. *The Love Suicide at Schofield Barracks* cemented a friendship between Linney and his producer. "Our play was not a hit," he said of his convoluted story of a suicide pact between a U.S. Army general and his wife to stop the Vietnam War, "but our friendship was and remained so until her death."[51]

Dolores Sutton's adaptation of Thomas Wolfe's posthumous novel *The Web and the Rock* did not fare a great deal better in the critical eye. Set as a memory play, the love story between a young Southern writer and a Broadway stage designer twenty years his senior appealed to its producer on many levels. Critics called it "a quietly rewarding evening."[52]

Stage and opera designer Peter Wexler, hired to create the setting, provided one of the late portraits of Cheryl Crawford. With an eye for detail, he called the legendary force in the theater "a petite lady who looked put together and unkempt at the same time." He explained, "The coat she wore was a good cut, but the cloth was not quite right, and, as women of her generation, she wore a small hat at all times."[53]

Like so many who encounter legendary people in their waning years, Wexler was very much aware that he was working with two legends: producer Cheryl Crawford and director José Ferrer. The designer volunteered that he was unable with "Miss Crawford to get beyond the legend," but Dolores Sutton, who lived several blocks from her producer, recalled a small, fragile-looking woman who distanced herself from the "mess" that the show became with its series of leading men and its unnerved actress-writer.[54]

With a combined total of eighteen performances for two Off Broadway shows, Crawford's office accounts were depleted. In order to keep eating, as she bluntly put her situation, she agreed to teach a course called "First Script to First Night" in Hunter College's theater department. She and Harold Clurman, also on the faculty, held a legendary meeting at Roosevelt House on East Sixty-fifth Street, during which they shared their Group Theatre experiences with graduate students. As in their Group days, Crawford deferred to the loquacious Clurman to wrap up the session with a peroration on his dream of theater.[55]

Crawford also taught briefly at the New York branch of the Lee Strasberg Theater Institute, where she talked about the Group, the Russian theater, and the Actors Studio, but she was not inspired, found the sessions tiring, and finally admitted that she did not enjoy teaching.[56] Speaking in the persona of her fabled woodchuck, she said, "[Teaching] may be safe, but it is not as exciting as finding a play, working with an author, choosing a director, designers, and a company of actors. And well, yes, reading rapturous reviews, however infrequent."[57]

Rapturous reviews were in her future when she went to the Chelsea Theater Center in Brooklyn to see a bittersweet play, *Yentl the Yeshiva Boy*, about a girl too intelligent and independent to accept the traditional restrictions of orthodoxy imposed on Jewish women. She disguises herself as a boy and enrolls in a Yeshiva. Love entanglements follow in a situation far more complicated than Shakespeare's *Twelfth Night*. Once Yentl discovered that, by wearing men's clothing, not only has she deceived others but herself as well, the play became about love that transcends categories and goes beyond gender.[58]

By Crawford's own admission, the play touched a personal chord deep within her. It is likely that she identified with Singer's unorthodox heroine who stepped beyond gender taboos imposed by a rigid society in order to redefine herself in the modern world. The play's issues illuminated Crawford's own life story of unconventional relationships, misrepresentations, pretense, and constant negotiations between society's expectations and individual desire for fulfillment in love and career. Robert Kalfin, the play's director and artistic head of the Chelsea Theater Center, clarified the source of Crawford's infatuation with the play when he wrote:

> [*Yentl*] pointed up the tragedy of living in a world that doesn't let an individual pursue his work or love freely, and it illuminated the experience of anyone who ever misrepresented a significant aspect of what he thought to be himself only to find as much reality in the pretense as in what it hid.[59]

Crawford moved quickly to offer the Chelsea a Broadway contract, so-licited Moe Septee to coproduce, shortened the title to *Yentl*, and brought the play into the Eugene O'Neill Theatre with the original Yentl, actress Tovah Feldshuh.

Yentl costume designer Carrie F. Robbins recalled an incident that captured "Crawford-as-producer" in a crisis moment. Crawford was confronted with a seemingly insolvable problem created by the leading actress refusing the director's staging in a critical scene. Robert Kalfin wanted Feldshuh to turn toward the audience during the revelatory scene in which Yentl showed her breasts to her love-interest to convince him that she was a woman. The actress decided the audience should not see her breasts, but Kalfin understood the character's painful act of personal exposure as the dramatic high point of a play about societal definitions of gender that destroy lives.[60] Crawford picked up the telephone and dialed the designer for a solution.

When Carrie Robbins answered the telephone, she heard Crawford announcing that she was on a speaker phone in her office surrounded by lawyers. The producer asked if the designer could invent something which would both cover Miss Feldshuh's breasts, so the actress would feel completely "opaque'd" (Robbins's word for "covered"), and, at the same time, when she faced downstage, the audience would be convinced that Yentl's chest appeared uncovered. Robbins replied that she would "come up with something."

"I didn't explain, and she didn't ask," Robbins recalled. Trusting the designer's ability to find a solution, Crawford said, "Fine, now we can finish Tovah's contract." As evidence of her frustration and relief, Craw-ford did not attempt to negotiate costs for the design solution. Robbins adapted technology (latex casting) in use at the time in the film industry. She used plaster-of-Paris to make a mold of the actress' chest; once dry and sanded, she poured a thin layer of liquid latex into the mold and cast copies of both left and right breasts; thus, carefully tinted for color, the actress was able to use the latex breasts to cover her own.[61]

When the show opened on Broadway, the actress turned full-front and showed her faux chest to her study-partner and the audience. All legalities (religious and contractual) were met, and the show gave Cheryl Crawford a final Broadway hit of 223 performances.

As she reflected upon *Yentl*, the costume designer offered a variation on the Crawford legend. She pronounced Cheryl Crawford "the Henry Kissinger of producing" to describe her ability to take an untenable posi-tion between two resolutely opposing parties (in this instance, the director and the leading actress), and find a solution agreeable to both sides that allowed the show to move forward to a successful opening night.[62]

Crawford was embraced by the Chelsea Theater Center and invited to become a member of its board of directors. Reflecting upon the new group, she said, "You might think that by now I would look on adventurous and innovative people with a jaundiced eye, but, as ever, I cannot resist."[63]

In the two years following *Yentl*, as Crawford was reconstructing her life and career for her autobiography, Ruth Norman, suffering from heart disease, died in a hospital on Long Island eight months before the book was published. Despite her pain and grief over her partner's irreversible illness and death, she went through the motion of writing, but her personal narrative was drained not only of a sense of self, but of the presence of her companion of some thirty years. Ruth Norman is mentioned only three times: as one among the several friends who encouraged her to buy Eastham; as the friend who planted vegetables in the garden and cooked with frequent visitor James Beard; and, again, as the friend she called in Westport when she learned that Eastham was burning.

A book reviewer regretted that Crawford's prose was lifeless and dull, even numbing and muted, and queried whether or not she enjoyed writing about herself. The truth of the matter is that Crawford's immersion in her grief precluded introspection and public expression of feeling, and she had a habit of following through on projects despite her reluctance, in this instance, to engage the emotional waters below the surface of her sixty-year career, where women who were not actresses were practically unheard of, and her lesbianism was something unspoken.[64]

In her late seventies, a frail Cheryl Crawford produced two musicals and two straight plays: a musical revue, *The Housewives' Cantata*, a good-natured satire on women who endure the men who use, abuse, bore, and ignore them in the name of married love; a popular touring production of James Kirkwood's *Legends* with Carol Channing and Mary Martin; a two-hander *Do You Turn Somersaults?* with Mary Martin and Anthony Quayle; and a final dramatic play, *So Long on Lonely Street*, written by Atlanta-based Sandra Deer.

Those who worked with Crawford during the waning days of her career offered warm and amusing insights into her Grant Wood–like severity, relieved by neon-blue eyes, a warm smile, and unfailing appreciation for pretty chorus girls.[65]

To celebrate the new decade, the Chelsea Theater Center organized a "Tribute to Cheryl Crawford" and dedicated the Cheryl Crawford Theatre in the Chelsea's Westside Theatre on West Forty-third Street, flanked by the Harold Clurman Theater and Strasberg's Actors Studio. Amused to be positioned once again between her two Old Testament Prophets, she jested, paraphrasing the time-honored joke, "But mine is biggest with 200 seats."[66]

The tribute on the evening of December 15, 1980, brought together a "Who's Who" of the American stage recalling amusing stories of their producer and pointing up highpoints of their work with her: Barbara Baxley, Agnes de Mille, Anne Jackson, Elia Kazan, James Kirkwood, Mary Martin, Maureen Stapleton, Eli Wallach, and Tennessee Williams. The dedication in the playbill was fulsome with praise. "It is most fitting and exciting that we pay tribute this evening to this woman whose contribution to the American theatre not only shines from the past, but will glisten in the future as well."[67]

When she turned to the Alliance Theatre in Atlanta five years later, she was ahead of her peers, who now looked routinely to regional theaters for Broadway vehicles. After reading a review of *So Long on Lonely Street*, she traveled to Atlanta to see the new comedy about a Southern family, a funeral, and around-the-coffin revelations. She found it "beautifully constructed and the characters totally believable."[68]

During her absence because of a medical crisis, general manager and coproducer Paul B. Berkowsky supervised the production. She had wanted to present the Alliance production with its original cast, reasoning that "sometimes plays that work well in regional theatres are redirected and recast for New York—and destroyed."[69] Nevertheless, she was not on hand to take a leadership role in critical decisions, especially about the New York market. With bruised face and one arm in a cast as a result of the unfortunate accident on the front steps of New Dramatists as she was on her way to auditions for understudies, she blamed herself afterward for approving an inept advertising campaign that depicted on posters and playbills a dour scene of a sofa, surrounded by darkness, and lit by a single street lamp with the legend "Lonely Street" on the street sign.

As battered as she was, she insisted that the playwright accept her mink coat, now too large for her "shrinking" frame, to wear to the Boston opening. Just as the director and leading actor, Kent Stephens and Ray Dooley, regretted Crawford's absence from rehearsals, so, too, the company felt the loss of their legendary producer.[70]

When the production came to New York, the *Times* critic objected to the stereotypical characters, contrived plot twists, and prosaic dialogue, and the play lasted fifty-three performances at the Jack Lawrence Theatre on Forty-eighth Street.[71]

In private, Crawford tried to assuage the playwright's distress, saying from her perspective of sixty years in the business, "It's not the end of the world. You live to fight another day."[72] Nevertheless, Crawford's "fighting" days were curtailed as a result of complications from her fall. Over the summer months, as a result of the fall, she experienced paralysis and an inability to speak and, in early October, died in a New York hospital.

Teasing Dreams

On one occasion in her Bridgehampton cottage, Crawford asked weekend visitors, "Do you have dreams?" and proceeded to answer her question. "I do, but they're so banal. I wish my dreams were more dramatic," and added, "The only interesting dream I ever have is that I'm flying. I fly all around and go anywhere I want."[73]

Crawford's personal library contained many books by Sigmund Freud on psychoanalysis. When she relayed her dreams of flying to Elinor Jones around the breakfast table in Bridgehampton, she had worked out, to her satisfaction, their message: the recurring dream images were her lifelong wish for high-flying achievement coupled with her present-day anxiety that perhaps her flying days were over. The dream recurrences in later years teased her twin anxieties: her loss with age of sexuality and potency for work. She understood the flying dreams as remnants of childhood expressions of freedom translated into latter-day anxieties that the physical body no longer permitted the freedoms and pleasures of mobility. Erotic desire and career pleasures were both grounded by the passage of time.

When the conversation on dreams took place in 1978, significant endings had occurred in Crawford's life. Ruth Norman had been dead for almost a year; her autobiography had been in print for the same amount of time; and she had produced her final show on Broadway. She would work ("at flying") another nine years, but the title of her book, *One Naked Individual*, revealed to close friends the vulnerability she felt in mind and body.

She anticipated objections to the title of her memoir and was not surprised to receive a handwritten letter from close friend Thornton Wilder begging her to change the book's title. She had sent him a draft of the manuscript with questions about several of his plays, and, after addressing her questions, he expressed his concerns: "Thirty years ago the word [naked] might claim a certain challenge and courage, but now its resonances are merely tawdry." "You are a doer, a builder, a maker," he continued, "why should you use so subjective a title? . . . It was a hard life's work and you will tell us so, but you were creative and effective. We must get that into the title."[74]

With her friend's words of caution in mind, she explained in a prefatory note that the title emerged from her childhood experiences. In the process of skipping a grade in Akron's elementary school, she missed learning the "Pledge of Allegiance." To avoid showing her ignorance, she rose with the other children, raised her right hand, and repeated what she thought they were saying: "I pledge allegiance to the flag of the United States of America and to the Republic for which it stands, one naked individual, with liberty and justice for all."[75]

She treasured the spoonerism throughout her career, finding that "one naked individual" perfectly described her sense of self in the face of the formidable world in which she had lived her professional life. "Out on the barricades I was finite and vulnerable, and I had only myself to depend on. Alone against the world, one instinctively grabs for armor. What I discovered was that the reality of being one naked individual was, when I accepted it, a superior armor."[76]

POSTSCRIPT

I recognize in her a mariner steering for the pole star.

—*Clifford Odets*

heryl Crawford's story is one of improbable dreams fulfilled. In contrast to playwrights and actors, *producers* are not creators in the true sense of those who invent and embody stories, situations, and people who then live on in theatrical literature and world stages—Porgy and Bess, Princess Kosmonopolis, Chance Wayne, Regina Giddens, Serafina della Rosa, and Big Daddy, for example. Producers, on the other hand, play many parts: negotiator, employer, dispute-manager, advocate, second-guesser, gambler, salesman, banker, truth-teller, guru, critic, psychiatrist, peacemaker, den mother, and many, many more. Taken altogether, the theatrical producer's career is not for the faint-hearted.

Crawford often remarked that a producer had to have "guts," because disasters happened every day—the leading lady walks out in previews, a show closes after two performances, investors renege on promises, and so on. Crawford insisted with a gambler's stoicism that "success and failure are in the lap of the gods anyway."[1]

Often asked by would-be candidates how they might become producers, Crawford readily described the unpredictable, risk-laden life of the theatrical producer, as she knew it. "If they cannot be induced to engage in a more sensible profession," she advised her petitioners, "if they are not deterred by the failure of their best efforts or by panic over how to pay the rent and eat; if they are able to endure, without recriminations, scrubby betrayals by neurotic talents; if they can accept the power of those Cyclops critics; if they can persuade wealthy widows and smart moneymen who see no profit in their cherished dream to invest anyway; and if they have an overwhelming desire to entertain, to instruct, and to enjoy an unpredictable life doing so, then I have only one piece of advice to offer—Try."[2]

For over sixty years, Cheryl Crawford had been a self-effacing impresario, parsimonious with words and public displays of feeling. She prided herself on rarely displaying artistic temperament, except in the instance of Jean Arthur's decamping from the ill-fated play. ("I very seldom get angry—about once every two or three years," she boasted.[3]) The gravity of her poker-face, called "a Grant Wood–like severity," was belied by her blue eyes, which lighted up, followed by a droll smile, when a kindness or witticism pleased her.[4] For the most part, her public self was dour and guarded by the lack of facial expression described as "dead-faced." Foster Hirsch found her seeming impassivity as "a form of self-protection, and no doubt a formidable weapon."[5] For some, she was the heroine of the American theater of her day; for others, she lacked personal charm and magnetism but achieved improbable success through hard work, judgment, and taste.

As an independent producer, she avoided the avant-garde, the politically or artistically radical. She refused to risk investors' money on material that had no commercial gloss. Her work represented the essentially conservative tastes of a cultivated Broadway theatergoer of her generation. She produced well-crafted comedies, intense domestic dramas, and innovative musicals written by the best composers and lyricists of her day—George and Ira Gershwin, Kurt Weill, Alan Jay Lerner, Frederick Loewe, Marc Blitzstein—and staged them with the best directors available, namely, Elia Kazan, Robert Lewis, and Daniel Mann. The musical was her nod to stylized material. She was warned that *Brigadoon* wouldn't work because it was a "fantasy," but she trusted the material and moved ahead. Nevertheless, most of her work falls into the category of American realism with clear story-lines, recognizable people, and entertaining circumstances of social significance.

Although she said in an interview in 1986 that she no longer went to the theater on a regular basis, she participated in *Legends* as one of five producers who raised one million dollars to sponsor a national tour of James Kirkwood's comedy starring Mary Martin and Carol Channing. This was her last hurrah in a producing career unsurpassed for longevity and sterling quality. Even in her final days, in true Crawford fashion, she had other irons in the fire. She confessed to reading four or five scripts a week, although she was no longer a regular theatergoer. She also talked about doing a play inspired by a newly published biography about radical labor organizer and founding member of the American Communist Party Mother (Ella Reeve) Bloor, whom she had met in the thirties.[6] She also talked about producing Elia Kazan's new work-in-progress, called *The Chain*. With Lee Strasberg's death, Kazan returned intermittently to the Actors Studio and worked on an earlier acting exercise, a play-within-a-play that merged the Oresteia story with the modern tragedies of Hiroshima and Nagasaki. Crawford announced that she would produce Kazan's new play, which she called *Cutting the Chain*, "as soon as I raise the money."[7]

Further along in development was a musical revue about the American Civil War in the style of Joan Littlewood's *Oh, What a Lovely War*, using material and songs from the period. The theme of *Hoorah, Boys, Hoorah*, dealing with brothers fighting brothers within an American context, appealed to her. She told friends that she had enlisted a writer for the musical and boasted that she had a grant from the National Endowment for the Arts to complete the project. Nonetheless, she was alarmed about the show's sizeable budget, namely the projected operating expenses, and told Foster Hirsch that "the numbers didn't make any sense to her."[8]

In a career of many, many years, there were, naturally, regrets. She named five in her autobiography that still troubled her fifty years later. First, her *inability* to recognize some distinguished plays, like *Death of a Salesman*, that she passed along to other producers. Second, she viewed the collapse of the Actors Studio Theatre as a wasted opportunity for actors, directors, and playwrights. She told Foster Hirsch twenty years after the demise of the AST that she felt the Studio had not been ready to take on a producing theater. "I felt we weren't ready for it. And I disputed [Strasberg's] theory that actors would be given a four-month contract and then would be replaced by someone equally good." "Also, Lee Strasberg," she concluded, "wasn't a good producer or administrator."[9] Finally, on a less serious note, she regretted that she was never asked to have her caricature drawn to adorn the walls of Sardi's, where she had eaten ("when I could afford it") since 1932.[10]

It must have offered some satisfaction that the launch party for her memoir was held upstairs at Sardi's. In a Q-and-A session, she offered an opinion as to why there were few women theatrical producers. "Maybe women are smarter than men," she joked; then she added in a more serious tone, "It's hard, demanding work. You have to be totally involved."[11]

By implication, the total involvement of the female producer's life *sans* complications of husband, housewifery, children, and other distractions was how she had lived her life. She neglected to say that she had also lived the majority of her adult years in the company of another professional woman of remarkable culinary and career skills and reputation.

Finally, Cheryl Crawford never flagged in her devotion to the city that had been her "accessibility to experience" from the moment she stepped off the train that brought her from Smith College to Grand Central Station. From there, she proceeded to the entrance of the Theatre Guild and a profession that occupied her for six decades. In her Eastside apartment overlooking the city, she reminisced,

> Frequently I stand at my sixteenth floor window gazing out over the lighted, thrusting skyscrapers, thinking that here anything is possible. From the windows I was once able to see the East River with the Fifty-ninth Street Bridge, glamorous at night with vari-colored lights. And on the west I was able to see the spires of St. Patrick's with the sun setting behind the Hudson . . . But over the years about fifty skyscrapers have obscured the views. Fortunately they are far enough removed to serve as a glittering theatre backdrop. I guess after fifty years the theatre is never far from my mind."[12]

This was the Manhattan she loved. The forty blocks of Broadway where she made her bones, as the gamblers say; and the iconic New Dramatists, home of playwrights, where she met with an accident and subsequently died from complications as a result of her injuries on October 7, 1986.

The next day and thereafter, the obituaries failed to surprise. They reprised Crawford's half-century in the theater, her one hundred or more productions, and praised her autobiography as a candid account of her life in the theater. For the obituary writers, the Crawford legacy was twofold. The early themes stressed a personality of "fortitude, indomitability, and persistence against all odds." Her "tough-minded commercial pragmatism" was another variation on the theme.[13]

When interviewed as a leading businesswoman for a citywide publication, Crawford reinforced this view. Of her intrepid progress through the Broadway theater, she told a reporter, "Sometime I think a producer is a person who is absolutely unable to do anything else, who has a strong interest in all the arts but the talent for none of them, and enough business sense to know that sometimes you must dare to go to the edge of disaster to achieve what you desire . . . But, above all, the most important thing is to keep going."[14]

The obituary writers listed the positions Crawford held with the The-atre Guild, the Group Theatre, the American Repertory Theatre, ANTA, and the Actors Studio and stressed that her contributions to the theater had not been *artistic*, though she always wanted them to be. She came to use "creative collaborator" to identify her various efforts with play-wrights, investors, casting choices, and determining the "right look for a show."[15] Leslie Bennetts, writing for the *New York Times*, explained, "She was good at raising money, settling disputes, getting in a co-producer, the thousand and one things a producer has to do."[16]

The overlooked themes were Crawford's devotion to socially relevant plays, her unusual occupation as a woman on the business-end of the commercial theater, and the idealism that swept her up in the creation of the Group Theatre, the American Repertory Theatre, and the Actors Studio. She told one reporter in 1964: "If I have any mission in the theater it is . . . to be associated with a group of people who have common aims and common methods of work."[17]

Her undaunted belief that a serious work of art could also be a com-mercial success was also missing from these latter-day reflections, along with mention of her joyful embrace of composers and their creations for the musical stage. When asked about her favorite musical, she always named *Brigadoon*. "Looking back, the best time I ever had as a producer was on the morning after *Brigadoon* opened," she said. "It was the only time in my life I ever had a show all the critics loved."[18] Her playfulness, generosity, shyness, candor, tongue-in-cheek wit, and gambling instincts honed at an early age were also missing from the life-sketches. When a *Brigadoon* investor wanted the ending changed at the last minute, she burst out with, "Over my dead body!" And, it would have been, if the investor's forty thousand dollars had been withdrawn from the show at that late date.[19]

On an August afternoon, some twenty years after the obituaries and tributes had been written, I found myself sifting through newspaper clippings, filed among Crawford's papers in the New York Public Library for the Performing Arts, searching one final time for cogent remarks she had made to journalists, cohorts, and friends. The most interesting were not Crawford's comments on theater (mostly all on producing) but the personal sketches describing her appearance, her speech, her manner-isms. When she spoke of actors and authors, one writer commented, she sounded "like a schoolmarm bringing order into a world of precocity."[20] The writer added that Crawford characteristically spoke "with economy in the flat, low-keyed tones of the Midwesterner and occasionally her speech is dotted with homey phrases—grist to the mill, another kettle of fish, the real McCoy."[21] Earlier on, another wrote, "Along with a masculine mind she has close-cropped light brown hair, a soap and water face, small thrifty-looking hands and a very firm handclasp. In fact, Miss Crawford is very firm in a quiet, unobtrusive way."[22]

The source of Cheryl Crawford's courage and street-smarts, even though she looked like "a misplaced home economics teacher," can be summed up as an unusual combination of thrift, idealism, and hard-driving, no-nonsense persistence, or, as she often phrased it, "work, work, work."[23] The theater was her first love for over sixty years, and the intimate details of her private life remain as elusive (and protected by the passage of time) as she wanted them to be.

This is an appropriate place to take leave of Cheryl Crawford, with her insular private life confounded by a clear and open record of public achievement against the odds of gender, ready capital, and the whims of investors, critics, and theatergoers. In her aim for accomplishment on America's stages, she was as determined and steadfast as Clifford Odets's enduring image of her as *a mariner steering for the pole star.*[24]

ABBREVIATIONS

NOTES

SELECTED BIBLIOGRAPHY

INDEX

ABBREVIATIONS

ANTA American National Theatre and Academy
A.R.T. American Repertory Theatre
AST Actors Studio Theatre
HRHRC Harry Ransom Humanities Research Center,
University of Texas at Austin
HUAC U.S. House Committee on Un-American Activities
LC Manuscript Division, Library of Congress, Washington, D. C.
MAT Moscow Art Theatre
NYPL New York Public Library for the Performing
Arts at Lincoln Center
PG-SHC Paul Green Papers, Southern Historical Collection, Wilson
Library, University of North Carolina at Chapel Hill
UOHL Special Collections, University of Houston Libraries, Texas
WLRC The Weill-Lenya Research Center, Kurt Weill
Foundation for Music, New York

NOTES

1. Three Brothers and a Sister

1. Cheryl Crawford, *One Naked Individual: My Fifty Years in the Theatre* (Indianapolis: Bobbs-Merrill Company, 1977), 9.
2. Crawford, 6.
3. Crawford, 9.
4. Crawford, 9.
5. Author conversation with Elinor Jones, March 15, 2005.
6. Crawford, 13.
7. From the unpublished journal of Elinor Jones, dated July 1982.
8. From the unpublished journal of Elinor Jones, dated July 1982.
9. Crawford, 10.
10. Crawford, 6.
11. Janet Flanner, "Profiles: A Woman in the House," *The New Yorker* 24 (May 8, 1948): 44.
12. From the unpublished journal of Elinor Jones, July 1982.
13. Crawford, 13.
14. Crawford, 13.
15. Crawford, 11.
16. From the unpublished journal of Elinor Jones, July 1982.
17. Jay Plum, "Cheryl Crawford: One Not So Naked Individual," in *Passing Performances: Queer Readings of Leading Players in American Theater History*, ed. Robert A. Schanke and Kim Marra (Ann Arbor: University of Michigan Press, 1998), 239–61.
18. Crawford, 8.
19. Plum, 242–45.
20. Crawford, 13.
21. Crawford, 10.
22. Crawford, 14.
23. Crawford, 14.
24. Quoted in the unpublished journal of Elinor Jones, July 1982.

2. Signs of a Calling

1. Lillian Faderman, *Odd Girls and Twilight Lovers: A History of Lesbian Life in Twentieth-Century America* (New York: Penguin Books, 1991), 11–36.
2. Crawford, 15.
3. Crawford, 15.
4. Crawford, 17.
5. Crawford, 17.
6. Crawford, 17.

7. Florence Ramon, "Cheryl's Chock Full of Swell Stage Ideas," *Morning Telegraph*, N. Y., May 30, 1941, in clippings file, Cheryl Crawford Papers, Billy Rose Theatre Collection, NYPL.
8. Crawford, 19.
9. Crawford, 20.
10. Arthur and Barbara Gelb, *O'Neill* (New York: Harper and Brothers, 1962), 543. *Desire Under the Elms* opened at the Greenwich Village Theatre on November 1, 1924, and transferred to Broadway in January.
11. Crawford, 21.
12. Crawford, 22.
13. Crawford, 22.
14. Crawford, 23.
15. Crawford, 23.
16. Crawford, 23.
17. Crawford, 24.
18. Plum, 246. See also *American Sexual Politics: Sex, Gender, and Race since the Civil War*, ed. John C. Fout and Maura Shaw Tantillo (Chicago: University of Chicago Press, 1993).
19. Faderman, 5.
20. Crawford, ix.
21. Christopher Lehmann-Haupt, "Books of the Times," *New York Times*, April 26, 1977, 37.
22. Crawford, 27.
23. Crawford, 24.
24. Quoted in Crawford, 25.
25. Quoted in Crawford, 25.
26. Newspaper clipping, dated June 12, 1925, in the Smith College Archives.
27. Quoted in Crawford, 26.

3. The Producer's Apprentice

1. Crawford, 27.
2. Quoted in Crawford, 29.
3. Crawford, 28.
4. Crawford, 29.
5. Quoted in Crawford, 29.
6. Crawford, 29.
7. See Theresa Helburn, *A Wayward Quest: The Autobiography* (Boston, Little, Brown and Company, 1960).
8. *New York Times*, August 19, 1959.
9. Crawford, 29.
10. Crawford, 31.
11. Crawford, 31.
12. Helburn, 178.
13. Quoted in Crawford, 32.
14. Crawford, 33.
15. Crawford, 41.
16. See Morgan Y. Himelstein, *Drama Was a Weapon—The Left Wing Theatre in New York, 1929–1941* (New Brunswick, New Jersey: Rutgers University Press, 1963), 128.

17. *New York Times*, January 27, 1931.

18. Crawford, 34.

19. Crawford, 37, 40. See also Margot Peters, *Design for Living: Alfred Lunt and Lynn Fontanne: A Biography* (New York: Alfred A. Knopf, 2003), 99.

20. Crawford, 35. Also see Jared Brown, *The Fabulous Lunts: A Biography of Alfred Lunt and Lynn Fontanne* (New York: Atheneum, 1986), 148.

21. Crawford, 38.

22. Roy S. Waldau, *The Vintage Years of the Theatre Guild 1928–1939* (Cleveland, Ohio: Press of Case Western Reserve University, 1972), 31.

23. Crawford, 37–38.

24. See Faderman, 67–72. Also Crawford, 39.

25. Crawford, 40.

26. Crawford, 40.

27. Flanner, 37.

28. Crawford, 42–43.

29. Quoted in Flanner, 27.

30. *New York Times*, April 28, 1929.

31. Crawford, 38.

32. Crawford, 39.

33. Crawford, 45–46.

34. Helburn, 218–19.

35. Crawford, 52.

36. Helen Krich Chinoy, "REUNION: A Self Portrait of the Group Theatre," *Educational Theatre Journal* 28.4 (December 1976): 490. Also Crawford, 51.

37. Harold Clurman, *The Fervent Years: The Group Theatre and the Thirties*, rpt. (New York: Da Capo, Press, 1983), 15, 27–28.

38. Clurman, *Fervent Years*, 66.

39. Crawford, 45.

40. Quoted in Crawford, 49.

41. Crawford, 49.

42. Lawrence Langner, *The Magic Curtain: The Story of a Life in Two Fields* (New York: E. P. Dutton and Company, Inc., 1951), 250–51. The founding members of the Theatre Guild, seated around the table with Cheryl Crawford, were Theresa Helburn, manager and playwright; Lawrence Langner, patent lawyer, producer, and playwright; Maurice Wertheim, investment banker; Lee Simonson, scene designer; Philip Moeller, director and playwright; and Helen Westley, actress.

43. Letter from Theresa Helburn to Paul Green, March 17, 1931, PG-SHC.

44. Letter from Theresa Helburn to Paul Green, May 8, 1931, PG-SHC.

45. Letter from Paul Green to Theresa Helburn, May 10, 1931, PG-SHC; also see Laurence G. Avery, ed., *A Southern Life: Letters of Paul Green 1916–1981* (Chapel Hill: University of North Carolina Press, 1994), 185–86.

46. Helburn, 224.

47. Letter from Paul Green to Cheryl Crawford, April 22, 1975, PG-SHC.

48. Flanner, 38.

49. Paul Green described his stay with the Group in "With the Group Theatre—A Remembrance," in Paul Green, *Plough and Furrow: Some Essays and Papers on Life in the Theatre* (New York: Samuel French, 1953), 42–56. Also see Clurman, *Fervent Years*, 36–50.

50. Chinoy, 492.

51. Avery, 680.

52. See Paul Green, *The House of Connelly and Other Plays* (New York: Samuel French, 1931), 119; also see Avery, 187, n. 1.

53. Letter from Paul Green to Cheryl Crawford, April 22, 1975, PG-SHC. See also Avery, 680–82.

54. Chinoy, 492.

55. Chinoy, 493.

56. Helburn, 180.

57. Quoted in Waldau, 132.

58. Crawford, 50.

59. Crawford, 51.

60. Crawford, 27.

61. Helburn, "Behind the Scenes with the Executive Director," in Walter Prichard Eaton, *The Theatre Guild: The First Ten Years* (New York: Brentano's, 1991; rpt. St. Clair Shores, Michigan: Scholarly Press, 1971), 147.

62. Crawford, 51.

4. Raising the Roof

1. Crawford, 63.

2. Foster Hirsch, *The Boys from Syracuse: The Shuberts' Theatrical Empire* (Carbondale: Southern Illinois University Press, 1998); rpt. New York: Cooper Square Press, 2003), 208.

3. Hirsch, *Boys from Syracuse*, 134; Crawford, 58–59.

4. Hirsch, *Boys from Syracuse*, 134.

5. Hirsch, *Boys from Syracuse*, 208.

6. Entries in Crawford's diary, dated December 27, 1932, and January 17, 1933. See also Crawford, 60.

7. Flanner, 37–38. Also see Plum, 251.

8. Clurman, *Fervent Years*, 51.

9. Crawford, 60–61.

10. Flanner, 38.

11. Entry in Crawford's diary, dated June 26, 1933. See Crawford, 63.

12. Crawford, 61; also Flanner, 43.

13. Crawford, 62. See also John Wilson, *The Dorothy Patten Story: From Chattanooga To Broadway* (Chattanooga, Tenn.: Roy McDonald Publisher, 1986), 50.

14. Wilson, 69–71.

15. Clurman, *Fervent Years*, 104.

16. Crawford, 62. Also see Cindy Adams, *Lee Strasberg: The Imperfect Genius of the Actors Studio* (Garden City, NY: Doubleday and Company, 1980), 150–51.

17. Crawford, 57–58.

18. Crawford, 62.

19. Chinoy, 494.

20. Crawford, 65.

21. Chinoy, 494.

22. *New York Herald Tribune*, September 27, 1933.

23. Quoted in Chinoy, 494; also Crawford, 65.

24. Crawford, 61.

25. Crawford, 68.

26. Letter from Cheryl Crawford to Clifford Odets, March 18, 1957, Cheryl Crawford Collection, Special Collections, UOHL.

27. Crawford, 255.

28. Crawford, 70.

29. *New York Times*, March 27, 1935. Also see Alfred Kazin, *Starting Out in the Thirties* (Boston: Little, Brown, and Company, 1965).

30. Samuel G. Freedman, "Four Decades Later, Group Theater Reassembles," *New York Times*, December 13, 1983, C17.

31. Richard Schickel, *Elia Kazan: A Biography* (New York: HarperCollins Publishers, 2005), 7.

32. Gerald Weales, *Odets The Playwright* (New York: Methuen, Inc., 1985), 59.

33. Clifford Odets, *Six Plays of Clifford Odets* (New York: Grove Press, Inc., 1979), 31.

34. Crawford, 71.

35. Harold Clurman's account of who initiated the trip to the Soviet Union contradicted Crawford's. He said that she decided to "join him" on the trip, rather than the reverse. See *Fervent Years*, 159.

36. Crawford, 75. Sergei Eisenstein would fall into disfavor with the Stalinists and die an outcast in 1948; Gordon Craig lived until 1966.

37. Crawford, 77.

38. Crawford, 79.

39. Crawford, 79.

40. Crawford, 89.

41. Crawford, 85.

42. Crawford, 89.

43. Clurman, *Fervent Years*, 183–85. A new Actors' Committee, comprised of Stella Adler, Roman Bohnen, Morris Carnovsky, and Elia Kazan, was elected by the members to work in tandem with the leadership.

44. Crawford, 91–93.

45. Crawford, 90

46. Robert Lewis confirmed that Crawford introduced Kurt Weill to Paul Green, Oral History Interview with Peggy Meyer Sherry, dated May 29, 1991, series 60, WLRC. Nevertheless, when Clurman wrote his book on the Group Theatre, he took credit for initiating the Weill-Green collaboration on the new musical. In his version, he handed Crawford the project to develop with composer and playwright. See *Fervent Years*, 183–84.

47. Letter from Paul Green to Cheryl Crawford, April 22, 1975, PG-SHC.

48. See Brooks Atkinson, *New York Times*, November 20, 1936, 26.

49. Letter from Paul Green to Elizabeth Lay Green, June 18, 1936, PG-SHC. Also in Avery, 258.

50. Crawford, 94.

51. Quoted in Crawford, 96. Crawford and Clurman differ on the amount of Whitney's investment. See Crawford, 95; and Clurman, *Fervent Years*, 188.

52. Undated presentation letter from Kurt Weill to Cheryl Crawford, undated, in Cheryl Crawford Collection, Special Collections, UOHL. Rpt. with the permission of the Kurt Weill Foundation for Music, New York.

53. *New York Times*, November 20, 1936.

54. Crawford, 97.

55. Wilson, 55.
56. Clurman, *Fervent Years*, 195; also Crawford, 97.
57. Crawford, 98.
58. *New York Times*, January 9, 1937.
59. Crawford, 98.
60. Crawford, 99.
61. Letter from Kurt Weill to Cheryl Crawford, March 5, 1937, in Cheryl Crawford Collection, Special Collections, UOHL.
62. Crawford, 100.
63. Clurman, *Fervent Years*, 204.
64. Crawford, 100.
65. Quoted in Foster Hirsch, "Still Savvy after All These Years," *American Theatre* 3 (March 1986): 14.

5. Dizzy Spells

1. Crawford, 101.
2. Adams, 113.
3. Crawford, 101.
4. Crawford, 103.
5. *New York Times*, March 25, 1938.
6. *New York Times*, March 25, 1938.
7. Crawford, 104.
8. Unmarked clippings file, dated 1940–1949, in Cheryl Crawford Papers, Billy Rose Theatre Collection, NYPL. Also see Crawford, 104.
9. Letter from Margaret Webster to May Whitty, September 9, 1939, LC.
10. Crawford, 106.
11. Crawford, 106–7.
12. Margaret Webster, *Don't Put Your Daughter on the Stage* (New York: Alfred A. Knopf, 1972), 37.
13. Plum, 248–49.
14. Crawford, 104.
15. Webster, *Daughter*, 39; also Crawford, 107.
16. Webster, *Daughter*, 40.
17. *New York Times*, March 19, 1939.
18. Crawford, 107.
19. Crawford, 107–8.
20. Milly S. Barranger, *Margaret Webster: A Life in the Theater* (Ann Arbor: University of Michigan Press, 2004), 99–100.
21. Crawford, 108–9.
22. Crawford, 109.
23. Quoted in Crawford, 109–10.
24. Crawford, 109.
25. Crawford, 110.
26. Crawford, 111.
27. Crawford, 111.
28. John Ferris, "Maplewood Summer Theater Is Success," in unmarked clippings file, dated 1940–1949, Cheryl Crawford Papers, Billy Rose Theatre Collection, NYPL.
29. Flanner, 43.

30. Crawford, 112.
31. Wilson, 64.
32. Ferris, "Maplewood Summer Theater Is Success," in unmarked clippings file, dated 1940–1949, Cheryl Crawford Papers, Billy Rose Theatre Collection, NYPL.
33. Crawford, 114.
34. Crawford, 115.
35. Crawford, 115.
36. *Cheryl Crawford Speaking on the Past 50 Years in the American Theatre*, NYPL.
37. Crawford, 115.

6. No Wooden Nickels

1. Florence Ramon, "Cheryl's Chock Full of Swell Stage Ideas, *Morning Telegraph*, N.Y., May 30, 1941, in unmarked clippings file, dated 1940–1949, in Cheryl Crawford Papers, Billy Rose Theatre Collection, NYPL.
2. *Morning Telegraph*, N. Y., May 30, 1941; *New York Herald Tribune*, February 1, 1942; *About Town* (May 9, 1942): 13; in unmarked clippings file, dated 1940–1949, in Cheryl Crawford Papers, Billy Rose Theatre Collection, NYPL.
3. *New York Herald Tribune*, February 1, 1943.
4. Crawford, 121.
5. Crawford, 117.
6. Crawford, 118.
7. Crawford, 118.
8. Crawford, 118.
9. Crawford, 119.
10. Crawford, 120.
11. Crawford, 119–20.
12. Foster Hirsch, *Kurt Weill on Stage: From Berlin to Broadway* (New York: Alfred A. Knopf, 2002), 211.
13. Crawford, 120.
14. Crawford, 120.
15. Crawford 121.
16. Crawford, 121.
17. Crawford, 121.
18. Crawford, 123; also Hirsch, *Kurt Weill*, 212.
19. Crawford, 123.
20. Quoted in, Crawford, 124; also Hirsch, *Kurt Weill*, 215.
21. Quoted in Crawford, 125.
22. Mary Martin, *My Heart Belongs* (New York: William Morrow and Company, 1976; rpt. New York: Quill, 1984), 108.
23. Martin, 108; also Hirsch, *Kurt Weill*, 216.
24. Schickel, 110.
25. Crawford, 127.
26. Elia Kazan, *A Life* (New York: Alfred A. Knopf, 1988), 223.
27. Martin, 112–13. Also Letter from Mary Martin to Cheryl Crawford, April 30, 1974, in Cheryl Crawford Collection, Special Collections, UOHL.
28. Quoted in Crawford, 128. See also Letter from Mary Martin to Cheryl Crawford, April 30, 1974, in Cheryl Crawford Collection, Special Collections, UOHL.
29. Martin, 113.

30. Crawford, 128.

31. Quoted in Crawford, 129.

32. Quoted in Schickel, 111.

33. Quoted in Schickel, 111.

34. *New York Times*, October 17, 1943, II, 1.

35. Kazan, 234–35.

36. Crawford, 125.

37. Kazan, 235.

38. See *The Cambridge Companion to the Musical*, ed. William A. Everett and Paul R. Laird (New York: Cambridge University Press, 2002), 171, 199.

39. Crawford, 126.

40. Martin, 109.

41. Martin, 110; also Crawford, 126–27.

42. Crawford, 127.

43. Crawford, 130.

44. Crawford, 135; also Hirsch, *Kurt Weill*, 288.

45. Crawford, 138; also Hirsch, *Kurt Weill*, 288.

46. Crawford, 136; also Hirsch, *Kurt Weill*, 229.

47. Crawford, 136.

48. Robert Saffron, "Cheryl Crawford Reaches Goal," *New York World Telegram*, n. d.; and Grace Turner, "She Knows What We Like," *New York Herald Tribune*, May 24, 1942, in unmarked clippings file, dated 1940–1949, in Cheryl Crawford Papers, Billy Rose Theatre Collection, NYPL.

49. Crawford, 137.

50. *New York Times*, October 8, 1943; *New York Newspaper PM*, October 8, 1943; *New York Daily News*, October 8, 1943; *New York Journal-American*, October 8, 1943.

51. *New York World-Telegram*, October 8, 1943.

52. *New York Sun*, October 8, 1943.

53. Martin, 108.

54. Stacy Wolf, "Mary Martin: Washin' That Man Right Outta Her Hair," *Passing Performances: Queer Readings of Leading Players in American Theater History*, ed. Robert A. Schanke and Kim Marra (Ann Arbor: University of Michigan Press, 1998), 283.

55. Kazan, 235.

56. Wolf, 288, 299.

57. Author telephone conversation with Anne Jackson, October 29, 2007.

58. Letter from Romulus Linney to Author, October 26, 2007.

59. Arthur Laurents, *Original Story By: A Memoir of Broadway and Hollywood* (New York: Applause Theatre Books, 2000), 325.

60. Letters from Kurt Weill to Cheryl Crawford, November 27, 1943, and January 20, 1944, series 40, WLRC. Also Author telephone conversation with Foster Hirsch, February 23, 2009.

61. Crawford, 143.

62. Letter from John Wildberg to Cheryl Crawford, January 25, 1943, in Cheryl Crawford Collection, Special Collections, UOHL.

63. Crawford, 143.

64. Letter from John Wildberg to Cheryl Crawford, September 30, 1942, Cheryl Crawford Collection, Special Collections, UOHL.

65. Letter from Cheryl Crawford to John Wildberg, August 24, 1943, in Cheryl Crawford Collection, Special Collections, UOHL.
66. Letter from John Wildberg to Cheryl Crawford, June 22, 1943, in Cheryl Crawford Collection, Special Collections, UOHL.
67. Cheryl Crawford and John J. Wildberg revised partnership agreement, dated January 29, 1944, Cheryl Crawford Collection, Special Collections, UOHL.
68. Crawford, 140. See also Letter from Mary Martin to Cheryl Crawford, April 30, 1974, in Cheryl Crawford Collection, Special Collections, UOHL.
69. Crawford, 141.
70. Flanner, 34.
71. Flanner, 42–43; also Crawford, 145.

7. Producers in Skirts

1. "Cheryl Crawford Upsets Apple Cart," *New York Journal-American*, February 28, 1942, in unmarked clippings file, dated 1940–1949, in Cheryl Crawford Papers, Billy Rose Theatre Collection, NYPL.
2. Crawford, 146.
3. Virginia Spencer Carr, *The Lonely Hunter: A Biography of Carson McCullers* (New York: Carroll and Graf Publishers, Inc., 1975), 226.
4. Carr, 226.
5. Sherill Tippins, *February House* (New York: Houghton Mifflin Company, 2006), 33–61.
6. Donald Spoto interview with Cheryl Crawford, January 18, 1984; quoted in Donald Spoto, *The Kindness of Strangers: The Life of Tennessee Williams* (Boston: Little, Brown and Company, 1985), 173.
7. Carr, 305.
8. Carr, 306. Carson McCullers died in 1967.
9. Crawford, 146. Brooks Atkinson called *The Perfect Marriage* "gloomily cynical," *New York Times*, October 2, 1944.
10. Webster, *Daughter on the Stage*, 119.
11. Crawford, 147.
12. Webster, *Daughter on the Stage*, 196.
13. Cheryl Crawford, "Such Stuff As Dreams Are Made Of," *The Tempest Souvenir Program* (January 1945): 11.
14. Crawford, *Tempest Souvenir Program*, 11.
15. Crawford, 148.
16. Webster, *Daughter on the Stage*, 121.
17. Crawford, 148–49.
18. Webster, *Daughter on the Stage*, 122.
19. Crawford, 150.
20. Crawford, 152.
21. Crawford, 150.
22. Mary Anderson, "Kudos of 3 Hits Go to Two Women Producers," *New York World Telegram*, February 11, 1944, in unmarked clippings file, Cheryl Crawford Papers, Billy Rose Theatre Collection, NYPL. The two producers were Cheryl Crawford (for *One Touch of Venus*) and Margaret Webster (for *Othello* and *The Cherry Orchard*).
23. Plum, 24.

24. Robert A. Schanke, *Shattered Applause: The Lives of Eva Le Gallienne* (Carbondale: Southern Illinois University Press, 1992), 172.
25. Barbara Heggie, "We: A Margaret Webster Profile," *The New Yorker* May 20, 1944: 32–43.
26. Flanner, 34–39.
27. Helen Sheehy, *Eva Le Gallienne: A Biography* (New York: Alfred A. Knopf, 1983), 26, 54, 228. Also see *Milwaukee News*, January 9, 1934.
28. Webster, *Daughter on the Stage*, 151.
29. Eva Le Gallienne, *With a Quiet Heart: An Autobiography* (New York: Viking Press, 1953), 243.
30. Crawford, 151.
31. Margaret Webster, Eva Le Gallienne, and Cheryl Crawford, *Plan for the American Repertory Theatre*, 1945, 3–13, LC.
32. Webster, *Daughter on the Stage*, 152–53.
33. *Plan for the American Repertory Theatre*, 13, LC.
34. Sheehy, 285.
35. Crawford, 152.
36. Quoted in Sheehy, 283.
37. Letter from Margaret Webster to Cheryl Crawford, August 11, 1945, UOHL.
38. Le Gallienne, *With a Quiet Heart*, 248; also Webster, *Daughter on the Stage*, 154.
39. Eli Wallach, *The Good, the Bad, and Me: In my Anecdotage* (New York: Harcourt, Inc., 2005), 101.
40. Sheehy, 281.
41. Crawford, 152.
42. Quoted in Sheehy, 283.
43. Crawford, 152. Also Webster, *Daughter on the Stage*, 154.
44. Webster, *Daughter on the Stage*, 154, 157.
45. Sheehy, 287.
46. Webster, *Daughter on the Stage*, 157.
47. Crawford, 150.
48. Crawford, 151.
49. Crawford, 151. See also Eva Le Gallienne, *At 33* (New York: Longmans, Green, and Company, 1934), 251–52.
50. Schanke, 175.
51. Le Gallienne, *With a Quiet Heart*, 260.
52. Grace Turner, "She Knows What We Like," *New York Herald Tribune*, May 24, 1942, 39, in unmarked clippings file, 1940–1949, Cheryl Crawford Papers, Billy Rose Theatre Collection, NYPL.
53. Ann X. Smith, "The Theater—A Tough Job: Cheryl Crawford Explodes Legends about Producers," *The Sunday Star-Ledger*, April 25, 1948, 39, in unmarked clippings file, 1940–1949, Cheryl Crawford Papers, Billy Rose Theatre Collection, NYPL.
54. Norris Houghton, "It's a Woman's World," *Theatre Arts* 31 (January 1947): 31–34.
55. *Plan for the American Repertory Theatre*, 9, LC.
56. Ward Morehouse, *The Sun*, November 7, 1946; Howard Barnes, *New York Herald Tribune*, November 7, 1946; Robert Garland, *New York Journal-American*, November 7, 1946.

57. John Chapman, *New York Daily News*, November 13, 1946; George Jean Nathan, *Theatre Book of the Year, 1947–1948* (New York: Alfred A. Knopf, 1948), 275; Mary T. McCarthy, *Theatre Chronicles, 1937–1962* (New York: Farrar, Straus and Giroux, 1963), 93.
58. Crawford, 154.
59. Howard Barnes, *New York Herald Tribune*, November 13, 1946.
60. Crawford, 155.
61. Quoted in Sheehy, 291.
62. Crawford, 155.
63. Crawford, 154.
64. Brooks Atkinson, *New York Times*, February 23, 1947.
65. Crawford, 156.
66. Brooks Atkinson, *New York Times*, April 7 and 13, 1947.
67. Crawford, 155.
68. Letter from Cheryl Crawford to Margaret Webster, July 4, 1946, LC.
69. Letter from Cheryl Crawford to Eva Le Gallienne and Margaret Webster, June 10, 1947, Eva Le Gallienne Papers, LC.
70. Author conversation with Anne Jackson, October 29, 2007; also email from Tom Jones to Author, dated January 19, 2009.
71. Quoted in Crawford, 155–56.
72. Webster, *Daughter on the Stage*, 170; also Barranger, *Margaret Webster*, 174.
73. Webster, *Daughter on the Stage*, 169–70.
74. Crawford, 156.

8. Musical Adventures

1. "Miss Crawford a Success in a Tough Career," *Philadelphia Inquirer*, March 2, 1947, in unmarked clippings file, 1940–1949, Cheryl Crawford Papers, Billy Rose Theatre Collection, NYPL.
2. Crawford, 163.
3. Crawford, 164.
4. Crawford, 164.
5. Descriptions of Ruth Norman and the apartment overlooking the East River provided by Tom Jones in email to Author, January 19, 2009, and a memorandum from Harvey Schmidt to Author, January 15, 2009.
6. Janet Flanner (1892–1978) and Natalia Danesi Murray (1902–1994) sustained an intimate friendship that lasted for Flanner's lifetime.
7. Esther Newton, *Cherry Grove, Fire Island: Sixty Years in America's First Gay and Lesbian Town* (Boston: Beacon Press, 1993), 15–41.
8. Newton, 75.
9. Newton, 88.
10. Crawford, 164.
11. Crawford, 164.
12. Crawford, 165.
13. Crawford, 165.
14. Crawford, 166–67.
15. Brooks Atkinson, *New York Times*, March 14 and 23, 1947; Robert Garland, *New York Journal-American*, March 14, 1947; Richard Watts, Jr., *New York Post*, March 14, 1947.

16. Crawford, 167.

17. Crawford. 167.

18. *New York Journal-American*, March 14, 1947.

19. Crawford, 167.

20. Crawford, 168; also Foster Hirsch, *A Method to Their Madness: The History of the Actors Studio* (New York: W. W. Norton and Company, 1984).

21. Crawford, 169. See also Letter from Tennessee Williams to Cheryl Crawford, June 26, 1950, in *The Selected Letters of Tennessee Williams, 1945–1957*, ed. Albert J. Devlin and Nancy M. Tischler, vol. 2 (New York: New Directions Publishing, 2004), 328.

22. Crawford, 169.

23. Crawford, 170.

24. Hirsch, *Kurt Weill*, 289.

25. Brooks Atkinson, *New York Times*, October 8, 1948; *New York Star*, October 10, 1948; *New York Post*, October 8, 1948.

26. George Freedley, *New York Telegraph*, October 9, 1948.

27. Hirsch, *Kurt Weill*, 293.

28. Lucinda Ballard, interview with Peggy Meyer Sherry, October 1, 1991, Lehman Engel Papers, Gilmore Music Library, Yale University, New Haven.

29. Quoted in Michael Kidd, interview with Peggy Meyer Sherry, October 1, 1991, Lehman Engel Papers, Gilmore Music Library, Yale University, New Haven.

30. Quoted in Michael Kidd, interview with Peggy Meyer Sherry, October 1, 1991, Lehman Engel Papers, Gilmore Music Library, Yale University, New Haven.

31. Crawford, 171.

32. Crawford, 171.

33. Letter from Tennessee Williams to Cheryl Crawford, June 16, 1950, in Cheryl Crawford Papers, Billy Rose Theatre Collection, NYPL.

34. Letter from Tennessee Williams to Irene Mayer Selznick, April 10, 1950, in *Selected Letters of Tennessee Williams*, vol. 2, 305.

35. Crawford, 171.

36. *The Times* (London), April 16, 1949.

37. Crawford, 172.

38. Cheryl Crawford, interview with Lehman Engel, February 25, 1978, in Lehman Engel Papers, Gilmore Music Library, Yale University, New Haven.

39. Crawford, 172.

40. Quoted in William Wright, *Lillian Hellman: The Image, The Woman* (New York: Simon and Schuster, 1986), 230–31.

41. Wright, 231.

42. Crawford, 172.

43. Crawford, 173.

44. *New York Times*, November 1, 1949; *Daily Mirror*, November 1, 1949; *Daily News*, November 1, 1949.

45. Letter from John Martin to Cheryl Crawford, December 19, 1949, in Crawford, 173–74.

46. Crawford, 157.

47. Crawford, 157.

48. *New York Times*, December 8, 1947.

49. *New York Times*, December 8, 1947.

50. *New York Journal-American*, January 29. 1951; *Daily News*, January 29, 1951.

51. Letter from Cheryl Crawford to Paul Green, February 13, 1951, PG-SHC.

52. Letter from Paul Green to Cheryl Crawford, January 20, 1951, PG-SHC.

53. Crawford, 161.

54. "Cheryl Crawford," *Current Biography 1945* (New York: H. W. Wilson Company, 1945), 122.

55. Crawford, 161–62.

9. The Oyster Bed

1. See Foster Hirsh, "Arthur Penn's Open Door," *American Theatre* 15 (January 1998): 24–26, 28.

2. Quoted in Crawford, 216.

3. Quoted in Crawford, 216.

4. Robert Lewis, *Slings and Arrows: Theater in My Life* (New York: Stein and Day Publishers, 1984), 181–96.

5. Kazan, 302.

6. Mel Gussow, "First Things First: An Interview with Robert Lewis (1909–1997), *American Theatre* 15 (January 1998): 27.

7. Lewis, 182.

8. Crawford, 217.

9. Lewis, 183.

10. Crawford, 217.

11. Crawford, 218.

12. Quoted in Crawford, 218.

13. Crawford, 218.

14. Crawford, 219.

15. Described in Crawford, 219.

16. See Crawford, 216–42; also Foster Hirsch, *A Method to Their Madness: A History of the Actors Studio* (New York: W. W. Norton and Company, 1984), 123–24; David Garfield, *The Actors Studio: A Players Place* (New York: Macmillan, 1980; rpt. New York: Collier Books, 1984), 69–70; and Wallach, 124–25.

17. *Cheryl Crawford Speaking on the Past 50 Years in the American Theatre*, NYPL.

18. Lewis, 188.

19. Lewis, 188.

20. Quoted in Lewis, 189.

21. Quoted in Lewis, 189.

22. Crawford, 220.

23. Crawford, 222.

24. Crawford, 222.

25. Crawford, 223–24; also *Cheryl Crawford Speaking on the Past Fifty Years in the American Theatre*, NYPL.

26. Mel Gussow, *Edward Albee: A Singular Journey: A Biography* (New York: Simon and Schuster, 1999), 120.

27. Rex Reed, *Daily News*, June 12, 1977.

28. Quoted in Gussow, *Edward Albee*, 166.

29. Crawford, 225.

30. Crawford, 220. See also Garfield, 72–73.

31. Among the stage and film stars were Paul Newman, Anthony Franciosa, Ben Gazzara, Walter Matthau, Pat Hingle, Rod Steiger, Cliff Robertson, Sidney Poitier, Patrick O'Neal, Darren McGavin, Nick Persoff, Martin Balsam, Dennis Weaver, Gene Saks, Richard Boone, Al Pacino, Bruce Dern, Steve McQueen, George Peppard, Martin Landau, Burgess Meredith, Carroll O'Connor, Robert de Niro, and Dustin Hoffman. Among the women were Joanne Woodward, Jane Fonda, Kim Stanley, Geraldine Page, Estelle Parsons, Shelley Winters, Anne Bancroft, Madeline Sherwood, Barbara Baxley, Kim Hunter, Jo Van Fleet, Eva Marie Saint, Carol Baker, Barbara Harris, Lois Nettleton, Lee Grant, Bea Arthur, Susan Strasberg. Ellen Burstyn, and Diana Sands.

32. Crawford, 220.

33. Crawford, 226.

34. *Cheryl Crawford Speaking on the Past Fifty Years in the American Theatre*, NYPL.

35. Crawford, 227.

36. Crawford, 227.

37. Crawford, 228.

38. Crawford, 227.

10. Four by Tenn

1. Crawford, 183–84.

2. Crawford, 184.

3. Crawford, 185.

4. Crawford, 185. Also Letter from Cheryl Crawford to Tennessee Williams, March 9, 1950, Cheryl Crawford Collection, Special Collections, UOHL.

5. See *The Selected Letters of Tennessee Williams 1945–1957*, vol. 2, ed. Albert J. Devlin and Nancy M. Tischler (New York: A New Directions Book, 2004), 306–8.

6. Letter from Tennessee Williams to Audrey Wood, April 11, 1950. By Tennessee Williams, from *The Selected Letters of Tennessee Williams*, vol. 2: 1945–1957, 306–7, copyright 2002 by the University of the South. Rpt. by permission of New Directions Publishing Corp.

7. *New York Times*, November 15, 1950.

8. Letter from Cheryl Crawford to Tennessee Williams, March 9, 1950, Cheryl Crawford Collection, Special Collections, UOHL. Also *Selected Letters of Tennessee Williams*, 306.

9. Spoto, 166.

10. Crawford, 185; also Spoto, 168.

11. Crawford, 186.

12. Crawford, 186.

13. *Chicago Sunday Tribune*, December 31, 1950.

14. Crawford, 187–88.

15. Quoted in Audrey Wood with Max Wilk, *Represented by Audrey Wood* (Garden City, New York: Doubleday and Company, Inc, 1981), 159.

16. Robert Coleman, *New York Daily Mirror*, February 5, 1951.

17. Crawford, 188.

18. Crawford, 188. Also Richard Watts, Jr., *New York Post*, February 5, 1951.

19. Quoted in Crawford, 187.
20. Crawford, 188.
21. Brooks Atkinson, *New York Times*, February 11, 1951.
22. "*The Rose Tattoo* Is—The Meaning of *The Rose Tattoo*," *Vogue* 117 (March 15, 1951): 56. Also see Spoto's discussion of the rose symbolism, 170–71.
23. Crawford, 189.
24. Letter from Tennessee Williams to Cheryl Crawford, March 3, 1951, Billy Rose Theatre Collection, NYPL. Also see *Selected Letters of Tennessee Williams*, 373–74.
25. Letter from Cheryl Crawford to Elia Kazan, June 20, 1951, Cheryl Crawford Collection, Special Collections, UHOL. Also see Crawford, 189.
26. Donald Spoto interview with Cheryl Crawford, January 18, 1984; quoted in, Spoto, 173.
27. Letter from Tennessee Williams to Cheryl Crawford, September 8, 1951, Billy Rose Theatre Collection, NYPL. Also see *Selected Letters of Tennessee Williams*, 402.
28. Letter from Tennessee Williams to Cheryl Crawford, February 10, 1952, Billy Rose Theatre Collection, NYPL. Also *Selected Letters of Tennessee Williams*, 419.
29. Crawford, 189–90.
30. Flanner, 34–35. Also "Miss Crawford: A Success in a Tough Career," *Philadelphia Inquirer*, March 2, 1947, 16, 18, in unmarked clippings file, 1940–1949, Cheryl Crawford Papers, Billy Rose Theatre Collection, NYPL.
31. Letter from Cheryl Crawford to Elia Kazan, June 11, 1958, Cheryl Crawford Collection, Special Collections, UOHL.
32. Letter from Tennessee Williams to Elia Kazan, October 21, 1952, Wesleyan University Cinema Archives, Middletown, Conn.. Also *Selected Letters of Tennessee Williams*, 459. Also quoted in *Five O'Clock Angel: Letters of Tennessee Williams to Maria St. Just, 1948–1982*, ed. Maria St. Just (New York: Alfred A. Knopf, 1990), 65.
33. Letter from Elia Kazan to Cheryl Crawford, undated, Cheryl Crawford Papers, Billy Rose Theatre Collection, NYPL.
34. Letter from Tennessee Williams to Cheryl Crawford, June 29, 1952, Cheryl Crawford Papers, Billy Rose Theatre Collection, NYPL. Also see *Selected Letters of Tennessee Williams*, 436–37.
35. Crawford, 190.
36. Quoted in Crawford, 190.
37. Tennessee Williams, *Camino Real*, in *The Theatre of Tennessee Williams*, vol. 2 (New York: New Directions Publishing Corp., 1971), 587, 589. Rpt. with permission.
38. Crawford, 190.
39. Kazan, 495.
40. Garfield lists the large contingent of Studio people in the cast. They were Joseph Anthony, Martin Balsam, Aza Bard, Barbara Baxley, Michael V. Gazzo, Mary Grey, Salem Ludwig, Vivian Nathan, Lucille Patton, Nehemiah Persoff, Fred Sadoff, Henry Silva, Frank Silvera, David J. Stewart, Jo Van Fleet, and Eli Wallach. See *A Player's Place*, 85.
41. Crawford, 191.
42. Margaret Bradham Thornton's *Notebooks Tennessee Williams*, 554. The letter from Tennessee Williams to Jo Mielziner, September 1952, is in the Billy Rose

Theatre Collection, NYPL. The playwright had originally approached Mielziner to design *Camino Real* but his concept (a bear pit or labyrinth) was rejected by the playwright.

43. Kazan, 497.

44. *New York Times*, March 20, 1953.

45. Richard Watts Jr., *New York Post*, March 20, 1953; John Chapman, *New York Daily News*, March 20, 1953; Brooks Atkinson, *New York Times*, March 20, 1953.

46. Crawford, 191.

47. Wood, 162.

48. Quoted in St. Just, 75.

49. Letter from Cheryl Crawford to Tennessee Williams, April 3, 1953, Cheryl Crawford Collection, Special Collections, UOHL. Also *Selected Letters of Tennessee Williams*, 467.

50. Letter from Tennessee Williams to Cheryl Crawford, March 31, 1953, Cheryl Crawford Papers, Billy Rose Theatre Collection, NYPL. Also rpt. in *Selected Letters of Tennessee Williams*, 466.

51. Crawford, 191. *Camino Real* closed in New York on May 9, 1953 with a loss of $115,000.

52. Letter from Tennessee Williams to Cheryl Crawford, undated, Cheryl Crawford Papers, Billy Rose Theatre Collection, NYPL.

53. Letter from Tennessee Williams to Cheryl Crawford, undated, Cheryl Crawford Papers, Billy Rose Theatre Collection, NYPL.

54. Letter from Cheryl Crawford to Tennessee Williams, November 8, 1954, Cheryl Crawford Collection, Special Collections, UHOL.

55. Walter Kerr, "Camino Real," *New York Herald Tribune*, March 20, 1953. Also Letter from Cheryl Crawford to Tennessee Williams, November 10, 1954, Cheryl Crawford Collection, Courtesy of Special Collections, UHOL.

56. Letter from Cheryl Crawford to Tennessee Williams, November 8, 1954, Cheryl Crawford Collection, Special Collections, UHOL.

57. Crawford, 192.

58. Telegram from Tennessee Williams to Cheryl Crawford, February 27, 1956, Cheryl Crawford Papers, Billy Rose Theatre Collection, NYPL. Also rpt. in *Selected Letters of Tennessee Williams*, 601.

59. Quoted in Crawford, 192–93.

60. *New York Daily Mirror*, December 18, 1953.

61. Letter from Tennessee Williams to Cheryl Crawford, December 1956, in *Selected Letters of Tennessee Williams*, 640.

62. Crawford, 194.

63. Crawford, 194.

64. Letter from Cheryl Crawford to Tennessee Williams, August 5, 1958, Cheryl Crawford Collection, Special Collections, UOHL.

65. Richard Watts, Jr., *New York Post*, March 11, 1959; Brooks Atkinson, *New York Times*, March 11 and 22, 1959; Walter Kerr, *New York Herald Tribune*, March 11, 1959; Robert Coleman, *New York Daily Mirror*, March 11, 1959; John McClain, *New York Journal-American*, March 11, 1959.

66. Robert Brustein, *Encounter* 12 (June 1959): 59–60; John Chapman, *New York Daily News*, March 11, 1959, 65.

67. Crawford, 196.
68. In the *Notebooks* Williams described *Period of Adjustment* as "kinder" and more "upbeat" than *Sweet Bird of Youth*, 729.
69. Crawford, 196.
70. Letter from Tennessee Williams to Cheryl Crawford, undated, in the University of the South, Archives and Special Collections, Jessie Ball DuPont Library, Sewanee, Tenn.
71. Donald Spoto interview with Cheryl Crawford on January 18, 1984. See Spoto, 243.
72. Letter from Cheryl Crawford to Tennessee Williams, February 17, 1961, Cheryl Crawford Collection, Special Collections, UOHL.
73. Wood, 172.
74. Letter from Cheryl Crawford to Tennessee Williams, August 30, 1960, Cheryl Crawford Collection, Special Collections, UOHL. Robert H. Hethmon listed the Actors Studio project of *The Night of the Iguana* in the 1959–1960 season. See *Strasberg at the Actors Studio*, ed. Robert H. Hethmon (New York: The Viking Press, 1968), 408.
75. Letter from Cheryl Crawford to Tennessee Williams, August 30, 1960, Cheryl Crawford, Special Collections, UOHL.
76. Letter from Cheryl Crawford to Tennessee Williams, undated, rpt. in Crawford, 198–99.
77. Quoted in Wood, 200. Also see Spoto, 196–97.
78. Wood, 179. See also Lewis Funke and John E. Booth, "Williams on Williams," *Theatre Arts* 46 (January 1962): 16–19, 72–73. Also rpt. in *Conversations with Tennessee Williams*, ed. Albert J. Devlin (Jackson: University Press of Mississippi, 1986), 97–106.
79. Letter from Tennessee Williams to Cheryl Crawford, January 8, 1961; rpt. in Crawford, 199.
80. Crawford, 200.
81. Tennessee Williams, *Sweet Bird of Youth* in *The Theatre of Tennessee Williams*, vol. 4 (New York: New Directions, 1972), 124. Rpt. with permission.

11. Who's Minding the Store?

1. Hirsch, *Method to Their Madness*, 248.
2. Crawford, 228. See also Hethmon, 397–400.
3. Hirsch, *Method to Their Madness*, 12.
4. Letter from Elia Kazan to John D. Rockefeller III, March 14, 1957, Cheryl Crawford Collection, Courtesy of Special Collections, UOHL.
5. Crawford, 228–29.
6. Schickel. 386.
7. Crawford, 228.
8. Telegram from Elia Kazan to members of the Actors Studio, undated; rpt. in Kazan, 632.
9. Crawford, 175.
10. Crawford, 175.
11. Quoted in Crawford, 176.
12. Brooks Atkinson, *New York Times* November 13, 1951; Walter Kerr, *New York Herald Tribune*, November 13, 1951.

13. Letter from Cheryl Crawford to Alan Jay Lerner, November 30, 1961, Cheryl Crawford Collection, Courtesy of Special Collections, UOHL

14. Crawford, 178.

15. Crawford, 229.

16. See Walter Kerr, *New York Herald Tribune*, December 12, 1958; and Brooks Atkinson, *New York Times*, December 12, 1958.

17. Crawford, 229–30.

18. Walter Kerr, *New York Herald Tribune*, November 21, 1958. Also see Garfield's discussion of the Actors Studio production of *The Shadow of a Gunman*, 129–33.

19. Crawford, 231.

20. Crawford, 231.

21. Author conversation with Martha Coigney, April 21, 2005.

22. Gussow, *Edward Albee*, 166–67.

23. Quoted in Hirsch, *Method to Their Madness*, 271.

24. Howard Taubman, *New York Times*, March 12, 1963.

25. Crawford, 233.

26. See Garfield, 223–24.

27. See description of the performance in Garfield, 224–25.

28. *New York Times*, December 23, 1963.

29. Quoted in Hirsch, *Method to Their Madness*, 277.

30. Crawford, 235.

31. Howard Taubman, *New York Times*, March 16, 1964.

32. Letter from Cheryl Crawford to Joanne Woodward and Paul Newman, May 9, 1960, Cheryl Crawford Collection, Courtesy of Special Collections, UOHL.

33. *New York Daily News*, April 20, 1964; *New York Herald Tribune*, April 20, 1964; *New York Journal-American*, April 20, 1964.

34. Crawford, 235.

35. Crawford, 235.

36. Kazan, 702–03.

37. Crawford, 236.

38. *Cheryl Crawford Speaking on the Past Fifty Years in the American Theatre*, NYPL.

39. Crawford, 236.

40. Crawford, 236. Having heard the "top of the ladder" story from James Baldwin several years later, Elia Kazan repeated it in his autobiography, 704–05.

41. Howard Taubman, *New York Times*, April 24, 1964.

42. Crawford, 236.

43. Telegram from James Baldwin to Cheryl Crawford and Arthur Waxman, September 12, 1964, Cheryl Crawford Collection, Courtesy of Special Collections, UOHL.

44. Crawford, 237.

45. Crawford, 237.

46. Crawford, 237.

47. Hirsch, *Method to Their Madness*, 284.

48. Howard Taubman, *New York Times*, June 23, 1964; *New York Herald Tribune*, June 23, 1964; *New York Daily News*, June 23, 1964.

49. Jerry Tallmer, *New York Post*, June 23, 1964.

50. Hirsch, *Method to Their Madness*, 286.

51. Cited in Kazan, 709.

52. Hirsch, *Method to Their Madness*, 269.

53. Crawford, 240.

54. Adams, 299.

55. Kazan, 710–11.

56. Quoted in James Feron, "'Charlie' Scorned by London Critics," *New York Times*, May 5, 1965.

57. Quoted in Daubeny, 324.

58. Daubeny, 321.

59. Quoted in Hirsch, *Method to Their Madness*, 289.

60. Quoted in Daubeny, 325. Also Hirsch, *Method to Their Madness*, 287.

61. Crawford, 241.

62. Daubeny, 325. Also Crawford, 238.

63. Crawford, 238.

64. Crawford, 239.

65. Crawford, 239.

66. Crawford, 241.

67. Kazan, 712.

68. Author conversation with Paul Bogart, January 17, 2007.

69. Letter from Cheryl Crawford to Paul Bogart, undated, in Mr. Bogart's personal collection.

70. Crawford, 242.

12. Dreams Deferred

1. Crawford, 106.

2. Flanner, 35.

3. Quoted in "Cheryl Crawford, Who Would Want to See a Play about an Unhappy Salesman?" *New York Times*, March 20, 1977, D-5.

4. Quoted in Crawford, 213.

5. Crawford, 213.

6. *New York Times*, March 20, 1977.

7. Letter from Cheryl Crawford to Carson McCullers, November 13, 1952, Cheryl Crawford Collection, Special Collections, UOHL.

8. Crawford, 204.

9. Laurents, 327–28.

10. Roger L. Stevens enlisted producers (Robert E. Griffith and Harold S. Prince) and *West Side Story* opened in September of 1957 for a record 734 performances.

11. Christopher Roche, "What Happened to the *New York Times?*" *The Sign*, November 1951: 34–37, 78.

12. Crawford, 255.

13. Kazan, 121.

14. Letter from Paul Green to Cheryl Crawford, April 22, 1975, PG-SHC.

15. Laurents, 325.

16. Crawford, 255. The critical U.S. Supreme Court decision, possibly affecting Crawford, was the ruling to limit the power of congressional committees whose purpose was to write new laws without prying into the personal affairs of witnesses. See Ted Morgan, *Reds: McCarthyism in Twentieth-Century America* (New York: Random House, 2003), 544–46.

17. Letter from Cheryl Crawford to Thornton Wilder, June 11, 1958, and, Letter from Cheryl Crawford to Thornton Wilder, January 11, 1955. Cheryl Crawford Collection, Special Collections, UOHL.
18. Letter from Cheryl Crawford to Paul Green, June 10, 1978; letter from Paul Green to Cheryl Crawford, June 16, 1978, PG-SHC.
19. Crawford, 256.
20. Memorandum from Harvey Schmidt to Author, dated January 15, 2009.
21. Memorandum from Tom Jones to Author, dated January 19, 2009.
22. Elinor Jones, unpublished journal, dated August 1978.
23. Crawford, 254.
24. Howard Taubman, *New York Times*, February 10, 1963, and April 1, 1963.
25. Crawford, 257.
26. Crawford, 257.
27. Kim Marra, "A Lesbian Marriage of Cultural Consequence: Elisabeth Marbury and Elsie de Wolfe 1886–1933," *Passing Performances: Queer Readings of Leading Players in American Theater History*, ed. Robert A. Schanke and Kim Marra (Ann Arbor: University of Michigan Press, 1998), 104–28.
28. Gussow, *American Theatre*, 27.
29. Crawford, 258.
30. Crawford, 258.
31. Author conversation with costume designer Willa Kim, November 21, 2007. Also see *Cheryl Crawford Speaking on the Past Fifty Years in the American Theatre*, NYPL.
32. Crawford, 258.
33. The *New York Post*, November 3, 1967, carried the story of Jean Arthur's "exhaustion"; Crawford's telegram was reprinted in the *New York Times*, November 4, 1967.
34. *New York Times*, November 26, 1967.
35. Crawford, 259.
36. Author telephone conversation with Harvey Schmidt, July 2, 2007.
37. Author telephone conversation with Harvey Schmidt, July 2, 2007.
38. Crawford, 259.
39. Crawford, 259.
40. Crawford, 260.
41. Crawford, 260. See also letter from Richard Chandler to composer Lehman Engel, November 22, 1965. Cheryl Crawford Collection, Special Collections, UOHL.
42. Crawford, 262.
43. Author conversation with playwright Elinor Jones, March 15, 2005.
44. Crawford, 110.
45. Elinor Jones, unpublished journal, entry dated August 10, 1978. Also author conversation with Elinor Jones, March 15, 2005.
46. Crawford, 263.
47. Author conversation with Elinor Jones, March 15, 2005.
48. Author telephone conversation with Gerald Freedman, November 2, 2007. Also Crawford, 263.
49. Crawford, 264. Crawford reopened *Colette* in October with Fenella Fielding as Colette, but the magic had gone out of the show along with the original piano player and cast.
50. Letter from Cheryl Crawford to Mary Martin and Richard Halliday on reading Marianne Moore's poetry, September 20, 1955, Cheryl Crawford Collection,

Special Collections, UOHL. Also Marianne Moore, "New York," in *The Complete Poems of Marianne Moore* (New York: Macmillan Publishing Company, Inc./ Penguins Books, 1994), 54. Rpt. by permission of Faber and Faber, Ltd.

51. Letter from Romulus Linney to the Author, dated October 26, 2007.
52. Clive Barnes, *New York Times*, March 20, 1972.
53. Author telephone conversation with Peter Wexler, January 18, 2007.
54. Author telephone conversation with Dolores Sutton, August 23 and November 8, 2007.
55. Author conversation with Vera Mowry Roberts (chairman of Hunter's theater department in 1974 when the session took place), November 12, 2007.
56. From Elinor Jones, unpublished journal, entry dated March 14, 1983.
57. Crawford, 264.
58. See the discussion of the Chelsea Theater Center production in Davi Napoleon, *Chelsea on the Edge: The Adventures of an American Theater* (Ames: Iowa State University Press, 1991), 151–61.
59. Quoted in Napoleon, 157 .
60. Napoleon, 158.
61. Author conversation with Carrie F. Robbins, June 28, 2007. Also Robbins faxed notes on the design solution to the author, July 8 and July 14, 2007, and on March 18, 2009.
62. Author telephone conversation with Carrie F. Robbins, July 2, 2007.
63. Crawford, 266.
64. Christopher Lehmann-Haupt, "Books of the Times: Autobiographical Stages," *New York Times*, April 26, 1977, 37. Ruth Norman's death was reported in the *New York Times*, December 28, 1977.
65. Author telephone conversation with composer Mira J. Spektor, January 10, 2009.
66. John Corry, "Cheryl Crawford Up in Lights," *New York Times*, December 15, 1980, C13.
67. See "A Tribute to Cheryl Crawford," *Chelsea Theater Center Playbill*, dated December 15, 1980, Cheryl Crawford Papers, Billy Rose Theatre Collection, NYPL.
68. Quoted in Hirsch, *American Theatre*, 13.
69. Hirsch, *American Theatre*, 13.
70. Author conversation with Ray Dooley, June 13, 2005. Also author conversation with Kent Stephens, June 16, 2005.
71. Frank Rich, *New York Times*, April 4, 1986.
72. Author telephone conversation with Sandra Deer, May 23, 2005; and e-mail from Sandra Deer to author, dated May 12, 2005.
73. Quoted in Elinor Jones, unpublished journal, entry dated August 1978.
74. Handwritten letter from Thornton Wilder to Cheryl Crawford, September 17, 1975, in Cheryl Crawford Collection, Special Collections, UOHL. Rpt. by permission of the Wilder Family, LLC c/o the Barbara Hogenson Agency, Inc.
75. Crawford, ix.
76. Crawford, ix.

Postscript

1. Judy Michaelson, "Our Town's Leading Business Women 2: Cheryl Crawford," *New York Post*, September 1, 1964, 25, in Clippings File, Cheryl Crawford Papers, Billy Rose Theatre Collection, NYPL.

2. Crawford, 270.

3. *New York Post*, September 1, 1964, 25.

4. *New York Daily News*, February 10, 1980.

5. Author Interview with Foster Hirsch, February 23, 2009; and Hirsch, *American Theatre*, 13.

6. Elinor Jones, unpublished journal, entry dated November 1978.

7. Lee Strasberg died on February 17, 1982 in New York City. Also see Schickel, 442–43; Crawford quoted in, *New York Times*, February 25, 1983.

8. Elinor Jones, unpublished journal, entry dated, August 10, 1978. Also see Hirsch, *American Theatre*, 15.

9. Hirsch, *American Theatre*, 14.

10. Crawford, 267.

11. *Women's Wear Daily*, May 11, 1977, 10, in Clippings File, Cheryl Crawford Papers, Billy Rose Theatre Collection, NYPL.

12. Crawford, 265.

13. *New York Times*, October 8, 1986; and *Variety*, October 15, 1986.

14. *New York Post*, September 1, 1964, 25. Crawford's statement was reprinted from her remarks upon receiving the Creative Arts Award at Brandeis University in 1964.

15. Hirsch, *American Theatre*, 14.

16. Leslie Bennetts, "Cheryl Crawford, Theatrical Producer," *New York Times*, October 8, 1986.

17. *New York Post*, September 1, 1964, 25.

18. *New York Times*, October 8, 1986.

19. Flanner, 35.

20. *New York Post*, September 1, 1964, 25.

21. *New York Post*, September 1, 1964, 25.

22. *Morning Telegraph*, May 30, 1941, in Clippings File, Cheryl Crawford Papers, Billy Rose Theatre Collection, NYPL.

23. *New York World Telegram*, n.d., in Clippings File, Cheryl Crawford Papers, Billy Rose Theatre Collection, NYPL.

24. *New York Post*, September 1, 1964, 25.

SELECTED BIBLIOGRAPHY

Adams, Cindy Heller. *Lee Strasberg, the Imperfect Genius of the Actors Studio.* Garden City, N.Y.: Doubleday, 1980.

Atkinson, Brooks. *Broadway.* Rev. ed. New York: Macmillan, 1974; rpt., New York: Limelight, 1990.

———. *The Lively Years: 1920–1973.* New York: Association Press, 1973.

Avery, Laurence G., ed. *A Southern Life: Letters of Paul Green 1916–1981.* Chapel Hill: University of North Carolina Press, 1994.

Barranger, Milly S. *Margaret Webster: A Bio-Bibliography.* Westport, Conn.: Greenwood Publishing Group, 1994.

———. *Margaret Webster: A Life in the Theater.* Ann Arbor: University of Michigan Press, 2004.

Beckerman, Bernard, and Howard Siegman, eds. *On Stage: Selected Theatre Reviews from "The New York Times," 1920–1970.* New York: New York Times Publisher, 1970.

Bentley, Eric. *In Search of Theatre.* New York: Vintage Books, 1953.

———. *What Is Theatre? Incorporating the Dramatic Event, and Other Reviews, 1944–1967.* New York: Atheneum, 1968.

Black, Cheryl. *The Women of Provincetown 1915–1922.* Tuscaloosa: University of Alabama Press, 2002.

Bloom, Ken. *Broadway: Its History, People, and Places: An Encyclopedia.* 2d ed. New York: Routledge, 2004.

Bordman, Gerald. *American Musical Theatre: A Chronicle.* New York: Oxford University Press, 1986.

Brantley, Ben, ed. *The New York Times Book of Broadway: On the Aisle for the Unforgettable Plays of the Last Century.* New York: St. Martin's Press, 2001.

Broadway Dreamers: The Legacy of the Group Theatre. PBS American Masters documentary, produced by Joan Kramer, David Heeley, and Joanne Woodward, 1989.

Brown, Jared. *The Fabulous Lunts: A Biography of Alfred Lunt and Lynn Fontanne.* New York: Atheneum, 1986.

Brown, John Mason. *Seeing More Things.* New York: McGraw-Hill Publishers, 1948.

Brustein, Robert. *Seasons of Discontents: Dramatic Opinions, 1959–1965.* New York : Simon and Schuster, 1965.

Caldwell, Carolyn E. *Cheryl Crawford: Her Contributions to the Development of Twentieth-Century American Theatre.* Ph.D. diss. University of Michigan, 1982. Ann Arbor: UMI Research Press, 1982.

Carr, Virginia Spencer. *The Lonely Hunter: A Biography of Carson McCullers.* New York: Doubleday, 1975.

"Cheryl Crawford," *Celebrity Register; an Irreverent Compendium of American Quotable Quotes.* New York: Harper and Row Publishers, 1963.

"Cheryl Crawford." *Current Biography 1945.* New York: H. W. Wilson Company, 1945.

Cheryl Crawford Speaking on the Past Fifty Years of the American Theatre. Produced by Humanities Institute, Brooklyn College, New York, 1980–1981, 145 min., 3 videocassettes, in Theatre on Film and Tape Archive, New York Public Library for the Performing Arts.

Chinoy, Helen Krich. "REUNION: A Self Portrait of the Group Theatre." Rpt. *Educational Theatre Journal* 28.4 (December 1976): 445–552.

Chinoy, Helen Krich, and Linda Walsh Jenkins. *Women in American Theatre.* Rev. ed. New York: Theatre Communications Group, 2006.

Ciment, Michel. *Kazan on Kazan.* New York: Viking Press, 1974.

Clurman, Harold. *All People Are Famous.* New York: Harcourt, Brace, Jovanovich, 1974.

———. *The Collected Works of Harold Clurman: Six Decades of Commentary on Theatre, Dance, Music, Film, Arts, and Letters.* Ed. Marjorie Loggia and Glenn Young. New York: Applause Theatre Books, 1994.

———. *The Fervent Years: The Group Theatre and the Thirties.* Rpt. New York: Da Capo Press, 1983.

———. Introduction. *Famous American Plays of the 1930s.* New York: Dell Publishing Company, Inc., 1968.

Conversations with Tennessee Williams. Ed. Albert J. Devlin. Jackson, Miss.: University Press of Mississippi, 1986.

"Crawford, Cheryl." *Celebrity Register.* New York: Simon and Schuster Publishers, 1963.

"Crawford, Cheryl." *Earl Blackwell's Celebrity Register.* Towson, Md: Times Publishing Group, 1986.

"Crawford, Cheryl." *International Celebrity Register.* New York: Celebrity Register, Ltd., 1959.

Crawford, Cheryl. "Chicken or the Egg?" *Theatre Arts* 32 (August–September 1948): 65.

———. "On Repertory and Money: Immediate Objectives." *The Flying Grouse,* February 1936, 3–8.

———. *One Naked Individual: My Fifty Years in the Theatre.* Indianapolis: Bobbs-Merrill, 1977.

———. "A Note on Casting." *Producing the Play.* Ed. John Gassner. Rev. ed. New York: Henry Holt, 1953.

Crawford, Cheryl, Margaret Webster, and Eva Le Gallienne. "We Believe . . ." *Theatre Arts* 30 (March 1946): 176–78.

Cronyn, Hume. *A Terrible Liar: A Memoir.* New York: William Morrow and Company, 1991.

Curtin, Kaier. *We Can Always Call Them Bulgarians.* Boston: Alyson, 1987.

Dalrymple, Jean. *From the Last Row.* Clifton, N.J.: James T. White, 1975.

Daubeny, Peter. *My World of Theatre.* London: Jonathan Cape, Ltd., 1971.

Eaton, Walter Prichard. *The Theatre Guild: The First Ten Years.* New York: Brentano's, 1919; rpt. St. Clair Shores, Mich.: Scholarly Press, 1971.

Engel, Lehman. *The American Musical Theater.* Rev. ed. New York: Macmillan, 1975.

Faderman, Lillian. *Odd Girls and Twilight Lovers: A History of Lesbian Life in Twentieth-Century America.* New York: Columbia University Press, 1991.

Five O'Clock Angel: Letters of Tennessee Williams to Maria St. Just, 1948–1982. Ed. Maria St. Just. New York: Alfred A. Knopf, 1990.

Flanner, Janet. *Janet Flanners' World: Uncollected Writings, 1932–1975.* Ed. Irving Drutman. New York: Harcourt, 1979.

———. "Profiles: A Woman in the House." *New Yorker* 24 (May 8, 1948): 34–49.

Garfield, David. *A Players Place: The Story of the Actors Studio.* New York: Macmillan, 1980. Rpt. New York: Collier Books, 1984.

The Gay and Lesbian Theatrical Legacy: A Biographical Dictionary of Major Figures in American Stage History in the Pre-Stonewall Era. Ed. Billy J. Harbin, Kim Marra, and Robert A. Schanke. Ann Arbor: University of Michigan Press, 2005.

Gelb, Arthur, and Barbara Gelb. *O'Neill.* New York: Harper and Brothers, 1962.

Gilder, Rosamond, ed. *Theatre Arts Anthology: A Record and a Prophecy.* New York: Theatre Arts Books, 1950.

Goldman, William. *The Season: A Candid Look at Broadway.* New York: Harcourt, Brace and World. 1969. Rpt. New York: Limelight Editions, 1984, 2000.

Gordon, Eric G. *Mark the Music: The Life and Work of Marc Blitzstein.* New York: St. Martin's Press, 1989.

Gottfried, Malcolm. *Broadway Musicals.* New York: Abrams, 1969.

Green, Paul. *Plough and Furrow: Some Essays and Papers on Life in the Theatre.* New York: Samuel French, Inc., 1963.

Grismer, Kay L. *Cheryl Crawford Presents: A History of Her Broadway Musical Productions, 1936–1949.* Ph.D. diss., Wayne State University, 1993. Ann Arbor: UMI Research Press, 1997.

Guernsey, Otis L., ed. *Curtain Times: The New York Theatre 1965–1987.* New York: Applause Theatre Books, 1987.

Gussow, Mel. *Edward Albee: A Singular Journey: A Biography.* New York: Simon and Schuster, 1999.

———. "First Things First: An Interview with Robert Lewis (1909–1997)." *American Theatre* 15 (January 1998): 27.

———. "She Did 'Bird,' Not 'Cat.'" *New York Times Book Review,* May 1, 1977, 9.

Helburn, Theresa. *A Wayward Quest: The Autobiography.* Boston: Little, Brown and Company, 1960.

Henderson, Mary C. *Theater in America: Two Hundred Years of Plays, Players, and Productions.* New York: Harry N. Abrams, 1986.

Herrmann, Dorothy. *S. J. Perelman: A Life.* New York: Simon and Schuster, 1986.

Hethmon, Robert H., ed. *Strasberg at the Actors Studio: Tape-Recorded Sessions.* New York: Viking Press, 1968.

Hewitt, Barnard. *Theatre U. S. A., 1688 to 1957.* New York: McGraw-Hill, 1959.

Hidden from History: Reclaiming the Gay and Lesbian Past. Ed. Martin Duberman, Martha Vicinus, and George Chauncey, Jr. New York: New American Library, 1989.

Himelstein, Morgan Y. *Drama Was a Weapon—The Left-Wing Theatre in New York.* New Brunswick, N.J.: Rutgers University Press, 1963.

Hirsch, Foster. *The Boys from Syracuse: The Shuberts' Theatrical Empire.* Carbondale: Southern Illinois University Press, 1998.

———. *Kurt Weill on Stage: From Berlin to Broadway.* New York: Alfred A. Knopf, 2002.

———. *A Method to Their Madness: A History of the Actors Studio.* New York: W. W. Norton, 1984.

———. "Still Savvy after All These Years." *American Theatre* 3 (March 1986): 12–15.

Houghton, Norris. *Entrances and Exits: A Life In and Out of the Theatre*. New York: Limelight Editions, 1991.

Jablonski, Edward. *Alan Jay Lerner: A Biography*. New York: Henry Holt and Company, 1996.

Jones, Tom. *The Fantasticks and Celebration: 2 Musicals by Tom Jones and Harvey Schmidt*. New York: Drama Books, 1969.

Jowitt, Deborah. *Jerome Robbins: His Life, His Theatre, His Dance*. New York: Simon and Schuster, 2004.

Kazan, Elia. *A Life*. New York: Alfred A. Knopf, 1988.

Kazin, Alfred. *Starting Out in the Thirties*. Boston: Little, Brown, and Company, 1965.

Kenton, Edna. *The Provincetown Players and the Playwright's Theatre, 1915–1922*. Ed. Travis Bogard and Jack R. Bryer. Jefferson, N. Car.: McFarland and Company, 2004.

Kirkwood, James. *Diary of a Mad Playwright*. New York: E. P. Dutton, 1989.

Lambert, Gavin. *Nazimova: A Biography*. New York: Alfred A. Knopf, 1997.

Langner, Lawrence. *The Magic Curtain: The Story of a Life in Two Fields, Theatre and Invention*. New York: E. P. Dutton, 1951.

Laurents, Arthur. *Original Story By: A Memoir of Broadway and Hollywood*. New York: Applause Theatre Books, 2000.

Lees, Gene. *Inventing Champagne: The Worlds of Lerner and Loewe*. New York: St. Martin's Press, 1990.

Le Gallienne, Eva. *At 33*. New York: Longmans, Green, and Company, 1934.

———. *With a Quiet Heart*. New York: Viking Press, 1953.

Lehmann-Haupt, Christopher. "Books of the Times." *New York Times,* April 26, 1977, 37.

Leiter, Samuel L., ed. *Encyclopedia of the New York Stage: 1930–1940*. New York: Greenwood Publishing Group, 1989.

Lerner, Alan Jay. *The Street Where I Live*. New York: Norton, 1978.

Leverich, Lyle. *Tom: The Unknown Tennessee Williams*. New York: Crown Publishers, 1995.

Lewis, Robert. *Slings and Arrows: Theater in my Life*. New York: Stein and Day Publishers, 1984.

Little, Stuart W. *Off-Broadway: The Prophetic Theater*. New York: Coward, McCann and Geoghegan, Inc., 1972.

Little, Stuart W., and Arthur Cantor. *The Playmakers*. New York: Norton, 1965.

Mandelbaum, Ken. *Not Since Carrie: Forty Years of Broadway Flops*. New York: St. Martin's Press, 1991.

Martin, Mary. *My Heart Belongs*. New York: William Morrow and Company, 1976. Rpt. New York: Quill, 1984.

McCarthy, Mary T. *Mary McCarthy's Theatre Chronicles, 1937–1962*. New York: Farrar, Straus Publishers, 1963.

Mordden, Ethan. *All That Glitters: The Golden Age of Drama on Broadway 1919–1959*. New York: St. Martin's Press, 2007.

Napoleon, Davi. *Chelsea on the Edge: The Adventures of an American Theatre*. Ames: Iowa State University Press, 1991.

Nathan, George Jean. *Encyclopaedia of the Theatre*. New York: Alfred A. Knopf, 1940.

———. *A George Jean Nathan Reader*. Ed. A. L. Lazarus. Toronto: Associated University Presses, 1990.

———. *Theatre Book of the Year, 1946–1947.* New York: Alfred A. Knopf, 1947.

———. *Theatre Book of the Year, 1947–1948.* New York: Alfred A. Knopf, 1948.

Newton, Esther. *Cherry Grove, Fire Island: Sixty Years in America's First Gay and Lesbian Town.* Boston: Beacon Press, 1993.

Notable Women in the American Theatre: A Biographical Dictionary. Ed. Alice M. Robinson, Vera M. Roberts, and Milly S. Barranger. Westport, Conn.: Greenwood Publishing Group, 1989.

Notebooks: Tennessee Williams. Ed. Margaret Bradham Thornton. New Haven, Conn.: Yale University Press, 2006.

Novick, Julius. *Beyond Broadway.* New York: Hill and Wang, 1968.

Peters, Margo. *Design for Living: Alfred Lunt and Lynn Fontanne: A Biography.* New York: Alfred A. Knopf, 2003.

Prince, Hal. *Contradictions: Notes on Twenty-Six Years in the Theatre.* New York: Dodd, 1974.

Red Channels: The Report of Communist Influence in Radio and Television. New York: American Business Consultants, Inc., 1950.

Roper, John Herbert. *Paul Green: Playwright of the Real South.* Athens: University of Georgia Press, 2003.

Rudisill, Amanda Sue. "Contributions of Eva Le Gallienne, Margaret Webster, Margo Jones, and Joan Littlewood to the Establishment of Repertory Theatre in the United States and Great Britain." Ph.D. diss., Northwestern University, 1973.

Savigneau, Josyane. *Carson McCullers: A Life.* Trans. Joan E. Howard. Boston: Houghton Mifflin, 2001.

Schanke, Robert A. *Eva Le Gallienne: A Bio-Bibliography.* Westport, Conn.: Greenwood Publishing Group, 1989.

———. *Shattered Applause: The Lives of Eva Le Gallienne.* Carbondale: Southern Illinois University Press, 1992.

Schanke, Robert, A., and Kim Marra, eds. *Passing Performances: Queer Readings of Leading Players in American Theater History.* Ann Arbor: University of Michigan Press, 1998.

Schickel, Richard. *Elia Kazan: A Biography.* New York: HarperCollins Publishers, 2005.

Schneider, Alan. *Entrances: An American Director's Journey.* New York: Viking Penguin, Inc. 1986. Rpt. New York: Limelight Editions, 1987.

Selznick, Irene Mayer. *A Private View.* New York: Alfred A. Knopf, 1983.

Sheehy, Helen. *Eva Le Gallienne: A Biography.* New York: Alfred A. Knopf, 1996.

———. *Margo Jones: The Life and Theatre of Margo Jones.* Dallas: Southern Methodist University Press, 1989.

Smith, Wendy. *Real Life Drama: The Group Theatre and America, 1931–1940.* New York: Alfred A. Knopf, 1990.

Spoto, Donald. *The Kindness of Strangers: The Life of Tennessee Williams.* Boston: Little, Brown and Company, 1985.

———. *Lenya: A Life.* Boston: Little, Brown and Company, 1989.

Stasio, Marilyn. *Broadway's Beautiful Losers: The Strange History of Five Neglected Plays.* New York: Delacorte, 1972.

Suskin, Steven. *Opening Night on Broadway.* Toronto: Schirmer, 1990.

Symonette, Lys, and Kim H. Kowalke, eds. *Speak Low (When You Speak Love): The Letters of Kurt Weill and Lotte Lenya.* Berkeley: University of California Press, 1996.

Taubman, Howard. *The Making of the American Theatre.* Rev. ed. New York: Coward-McCann, 1967.

Tennessee Williams' Letters to Donald Windham, 1940–1965. Ed. Donald Windham. New York: Holt Rinehart and Winston, 1977.

Theatre Guild Magazine (1928–1932). Retitled *The Stage* (May issue 1932). New York: John Hanrahan Publishing Company, 1928–1932.

Waldau, Roy S. *Vintage Years of the Theatre Guild 1928–1939.* Cleveland: Press of Case Western Reserve University, 1972.

Wallach, Eli. *The Good, the Bad, and Me: In My Anecdotage.* New York: Harcourt, Inc., 2005.

Webster, Margaret. *Don't Put Your Daughter on the Stage.* New York: Alfred A. Knopf, 1972.

Webster, Margaret, Eva Le Gallienne, and Cheryl Crawford. "Plans for the American Repertory Theatre, Inc." Margaret Webster Collection, Manuscript Division, Library of Congress, Washington, D. C.

Who Was Who in the Theatre, 1912–1976: A Biographical Dictionary of Actors, Actresses, Directors, Playwrights, and Producers of the English-Speaking Theatre. Detroit: Gale Research Co., 1978.

Wilder, Thornton. *Thornton Wilder: Collected Plays and Writings on Theater.* Ed. J. D. McClatchy. New York: Library of America, 2007.

Williams, Tennessee. *Memoirs.* New York: Doubleday and Company, 1975.

———. *The Selected Letters of Tennessee Williams 1945–1957.* Vol. 2. Ed. Albert J. Devlin and Nancy M. Tischler. New York: New Directions Publishing, 2004. Rpt. New York: New Directions. 2007.

———. *Where I Live: Selected Essays.* Ed. Christine R. Day and Bob Woods. New York: New Directions, 1978.

Wilson, John. *The Dorothy Patten Story: From Chattanooga to Broadway.* Chattanooga: Chattanooga News-Free Press, 1986.

Wood, Audrey, with Max Wilk. *Represented by Audrey Wood.* New York: Doubleday, 1981.

Wright, William. *Lillian Hellman: The Image, the Woman.* New York: Simon and Schuster, 1986.

Young, Stark. *Immortal Shadows: A Book of Dramatic Criticism.* New York: Charles Scribner's Sons, 1948.

INDEX

Actors Equity Association, 71, 94, 160
Actors Studio, 103, 108, 116, 117–29, 133,
138, 144, 151–54, 156–69, 179, 186, 189,
195, 197; beginnings, 117–20; codirectors of, 119; financing of, 119, 126,
129, 164, 169; permanent home for,
121; resignation of Crawford, 169;
resignation of Kazan, 152; resignation
of Lewis, 122; Strasberg as artistic
director, 123; television broadcast of,
126, 168–69
Actors Studio Theatre (A.S.T.), 151–52,
157–69, 170, 195; administration of,
151–52, 157–58; end of, 164–67
Adler, Luther, 34, 41, 163
Albee, Edward, 124, 125–26, 158
Albert, Eddie, 142
Albright, Hardie, 60
Aldis, Mary, 16, 17, 18, 19
Aldwych Theatre (London), 164, 165, 166
Alice in Wonderland (Carroll), 92, 94,
98–99, 101, 118
Alliance Theatre (Atlanta), 189
All in the Family (television), 169
All My Sons (Miller), 93, 117, 118, 120
All the Living (Albright), 60
Ambassador Theatre (Broadway), 181
American Blues (Williams), 130
American Communist Party (also,
Communist Party—USA), 47
American Federation of Musicians
(AFM), 86, 87, 94
American National Theatre and Acad-
emy (ANTA), 97–98, 114–16, 117, 160,
162, 197
American Repertory Theatre (A.R.T.),
83–102, 106, 107, 108, 115, 116, 118, 128,
151, 169, 197; acting company, 91–92;
brochure for, 90, 95, 96; budget for,
89–91; coproducers for, 88–89; Craw-
ford's resignation, 55, 99–100, 101;

failure of, 96, 98; issues of gender and
sexuality, 90, 94, 95, 101; reviews of,
96–97; union demands, 94
American Tragedy, An (Dreiser), 51
Anderson, Judith, 61, 62, 64, 115, 142
Anderson, Maxwell, 51
Anderson, Robert, 140
Andorra (Frisch), 168, 177
Androcles and the Lion (Shaw), 94, 97
Annie Get Your Gun (musical), 799, 109,
110
Another Sun (Thompson), 64–65
Antoinette Perry ("Tony") Award, 135,
160
Any Wednesday (Muriel Resnik), 124
Aronson, Boris, 110, 133, 135
Antonio, Lou, 125
Arthur, Jean, 78, 180, 194
As You Desire Me (Pirandello), 61
As You Like It (Shakespeare), 24, 93
Atkinson, Brooks, 53, 60, 64, 78, 98, 110,
135, 139, 155
Auden, Wystan ("W. H."), 84, 104
Avera, Tom, 119
Awake and Sing (Odets), 44, 46, 47, 48
Ayres, Lemuel, 138

Baby Doll (Williams), 184
Baby Want a Kiss (Costigan), 221, 159,
160, 161
Baker, Carroll, 129
Baker, Kenny, 74, 78, 80
Balanchine, George, 72
Baldwin, James, 124, 159, 161–63
Ballard, Lucinda, 110, 111
Balsam, Martin, 121
Bancroft, Anne, 127, 158
Bankhead, Tallulah, 66, 73, 109, 113, 137
Barber, Philip, 35
Barker, Margaret, 44
Barnes, Howard, 96

Milly S. Barranger is distinguished professor emerita at the University of North Carolina, Chapel Hill, where she served as chairman of the Department of Dramatic Art and producing director of PlayMakers Repertory Company. She is author of *Margaret Webster: A Life in the Theater*; *Theatre: A Way of Seeing*; *Understanding Plays*; *Theatre: Past and Present*; and *Unfriendly Witnesses: Gender, Theater, and Film in the McCarthy Era*. She is also coeditor of *Notable Women in the American Theatre: A Biographical Dictionary*.

Theater in the Americas

The goal of the series is to publish a wide range of scholarship on theater and performance, defining theater in its broadest terms and including subjects that encompass all of the Americas.

The series focuses on the performance and production of theater and theater artists and practitioners but welcomes studies of dramatic literature as well. Meant to be inclusive, the series invites studies of traditional, experimental, and ethnic forms of theater; celebrations, festivals, and rituals that perform culture; and acts of civil disobedience that are performative in nature. We publish studies of theater and performance activities of all cultural groups within the Americas, including biographies of individuals, histories of theater companies, studies of cultural traditions, and collections of plays.

Other Books in the Theater in the Americas Series

Shadowed Cocktails: The Plays of Philip Barry from Paris Bound *to* The Philadelphia Story
Donald R. Anderson

A Gambler's Instinct: The Story of Broadway Producer Cheryl Crawford
Milly S. Barranger

Unfriendly Witnesses: Gender, Theater, and Film in the McCarthy Era
Milly S. Barranger

The Theatre of Sabina Berman: The Agony of Ecstasy *and Other Plays*
Translated by Adam Versényi
With an Essay by Jacqueline E. Bixler

Messiah of the New Technique: John Howard Lawson, Communism, and American Theatre, 1923–1937
Jonathan L. Chambers

Composing Ourselves: The Little Theatre Movement and the American Audience
Dorothy Chansky

Ghost Light: An Introductory Handbook for Dramaturgy
Michael Mark Chemers

The Hanlon Brothers: From Daredevil Acrobatics to Spectacle Pantomime, 1833–1931
Mark Cosdon

Women in Turmoil: Six Plays by Mercedes de Acosta
Edited and with an Introduction by Robert A. Schanke

Rediscovering Mordecai Gorelik: Scene Design and the American Theatre
Anne Fletcher

A Spectacle of Suffering: Clara Morris on the American Stage
Barbara Wallace Grossman

American Political Plays after 9/11
Edited by Allan Havis

Performing Loss: Rebuilding Community through Theater and Writing
Jodi Kanter

Unfinished Show Business: Broadway Musicals as Works-in-Process
Bruce Kirle

Staging America: Cornerstone and Community-Based Theater
Sonja Kuftinec

Words at Play: Creative Writing and Dramaturgy
Felicia Hardison Londré

Entertaining the Nation: American Drama in the Eighteenth and Nineteenth Centuries
Tice L. Miller

Stage, Page, Scandals, and Vandals: William E. Burton and Nineteenth-Century American Theatre
David L. Rinear

Contemporary Latina/o Theater: Wrighting Ethnicity
Jon D. Rossini

Angels in the American Theater: Patrons, Patronage, and Philanthropy
Edited and with an Introduction by Robert A. Schanke

"That Furious Lesbian": The Story of Mercedes de Acosta
Robert A. Schanke

*Caffe Cino: The Birthplace of Off-Off-
     Broadway*
Wendell C. Stone

Teaching Performance Studies
Edited by Nathan Stucky and Cynthia
     Wimmer
With a Foreword by Richard Schechner

*Broadway's Bravest Woman: Selected
     Writings of Sophie Treadwell*
Edited and with Introductions by
     Jerry Dickey and Miriam López-
     Rodríguez

*The Humana Festival: The History of
     New Plays at Actors Theatre of
     Louisville*
Jeffrey Ullom

*Our Land Is Made of Courage and
     Glory: Nationalist Performance of
     Nicaragua and Guatemala*
E. J. Westlake